SOULS OF TERROR

Anthony P. Norse

Mary,

Write... Write... Write,
Right?!

Best,

"AP. Norse"

This book is a work of fiction. With the exception of historic facts, places and people, names, characters, businesses, organizations, places, events and incidents are either from the author's imagination or are used fictitiously. Any resemblance to actual persons, either living or deceased, or actual events is entirely coincidental. Any opinions expressed are those of the characters and should not be mistaken for those of the author.

Published by Northern Edge Books

ISBN 978-0-9866458-0-8

Cover by Steffanovitch Designs

For Michael and family . . . wherever you are. May you always think critically and work and play in freedom.

Acknowledgments

This novel stems from the support and contributions of many thoughtful individuals around the globe. In no particular order, deep appreciation goes to Mark Elwood, Vijay Cuddeford, Margaret Sachs, Helen Hughes, B.P. Coits and Diana Winters.

Thanks also to Dan Dugan and Debra Snell (of People for Legal and Non-sectarian Schools), Frank Albo (author, The Hermetic Code), Peter Staudenmaier (for explaining the inexplicable), and the fine folks at the International Cultic Studies Association and the Canadian Coalition for Nuclear Responsibility.

I also extend sincere appreciation to many people for sharing personal cultish experiences. In recognizing and discussing the depths of our dilemmas, we are often better able to navigate a healthy future.

I'd be remiss if I did not acknowledge Anthroposophists and other esotericists in North America and Europe for offering information and for their willingness to discuss controversial topics. Yes, I understand the need of some people to request anonymity.

Finally, to a wonderful family for patience and support (and an elderly cat who grudgingly shared my lap with a cordless keyboard on more than a few cold winter nights) . . . thank you.

Prologue

Ithaca, New York

Greg Matheson did not notice the missing light bulb in the bathroom. After another long day of books and papers and Internet research, the caffeine buzz had only just let go of his mind. He was exhausted and his only thoughts now were of a quick shower and plenty of sleep. He flicked the light switch a few times and cursed twice. The bathroom door slammed shut behind him. Darkness. He heard a deep, guttural voice.

"Can you see?"

Greg felt stunned and suddenly wide-awake. He spun toward the voice and spoke quickly: "What the hell—who is this?"

"Your words are empty."

Greg searched his memory for a hint, but the voice was unfamiliar. "This is not funny," he said. He felt uneasy in the dark bathroom. *An old buddy from back home, perhaps?* "How'd you get in here?"

"Talk to me now," the low raspy voice continued. "Tell me about light. Tell me about the dark. Speak to me of history and morality and . . . mortality."

Greg shivered at the creepy tone. It contained a slight German accent.

The man continued, clearly angry now. "The *materialist*, the spreader of lies, has nothing to say?"

Greg found the doorknob and pulled. A stream of light from the hall entered the bathroom, just enough for Greg to see a gloved hand slamming the door shut. A sharp pain bit into his neck. He felt dizzy and tried to scream but there was barely a sound from his lips. He grabbed for the doorknob again but suddenly felt tired. Very tired. His arms went limp and he fell to the floor. *Am I dreaming? Am I dying?*

The voice: "Listen carefully. I want to know where you are going. Who will you meet? I want names. What do you know about the Group of Forty-Eight?"

Greg gasped for breath and tried again to scream but his voice was nothing more than a whisper. "You mean my trip to Europe?" His body could not move but his mind was racing. *What on earth was this man talking about?* "I don't know about any groups."

"Do not take me for a fool." The man was breathing hard. "Evolution has no place for fools. I want places and names."

Greg's mind was a mess of tangled thoughts. His trip to Europe was simply for research—for part of his thesis. Perhaps this man had mistaken him for someone else?

Suddenly, bright light filled the bathroom. A strong halogen lamp blinded Greg as he lay motionless on the floor. He smelled something medicinal. He shut his eyes and tried to move, tried to get up and run from this nightmare. *How did he get into my apartment? How did he bring this light into my bathroom?*

"Please," Greg said, "I don't understand." Strong fingers pried his eyes open. The halogen bulb sent pain deep into his brain. The fleshy face of the intruder hovered inches away and Greg could see sweaty pores on the man's nose. Bushy gray eyebrows and dark eyes behind thick glasses stared down at him.

The stranger grunted and sighed. "Tell me what you know of the Christ Impulse at this time in our evolution. What do you know of our work?"

Greg fought the light and tried to find an answer that would make the pain disappear. "The Christ Impulse," he said in a shaky whisper, "is often used in the esoteric movement known as Anthroposophy to describe—"

"Empty words!" Spittle hit Greg's chin. "Any knowledge you might have of our work will end now."

The fingers left his eyelids and Greg immediately squeezed them shut. He felt something cold slice into his neck. He needed to scream but was somehow unable to open his mouth. Panic ripped at his mind as he felt blood, like warm molasses, oozing over his neck and shoulders. A horrible burning pain in his head forced every instinct he had ever known to react. Scream. Run. Fight. His brain was on fire, but he was unable to move.

The menacing voice again: "Not so clever now, are you?"

Greg felt a strange pulling sensation on his throat, from the inside out.

With every beat of his heart, he could feel something being sucked out through a slit in his neck. Unbearable pain. Moments later, the lights dimmed and there was only darkness.

Day One

1

Ithaca, New York

Detective Mark Julian crouched and stared at the corpse. The shirt was ripped and the pants were down around the ankles. Blood was everywhere. The detective combed his thick black hair with leathery fingers. "God damn," he said. "What a mess."

Although the university had its own police force, the more experienced Ithaca Police Department would be in charge here. Experience was called for and that meant this would be Mark Julian's murder investigation.

A young campus cop stood beside him and stared at the body. "Ever seen something like this? I mean, this twisted?"

Mark Julian shook his head, stood and looked around the bathroom. He approached the medical examiner and pointed to the ceiling. "What the hell is that?"

The elderly man looked up. A bloody, gooey something appeared to be nailed there. "I can tell you what it is, but damned if I know what it's doing there."

The detective stared at the thing on the ceiling. "So, what is it?"

"It's the poor fellow's larynx. Surgically removed. Your killer knew what he was doing. If the patient were not dead on the bathroom floor, I'd say this was a pretty decent laryngectomy."

Mark stood and stared up at the dripping larynx. "So why does someone nail the guy's larynx up there?"

"No idea."

Mark gazed at the body on the floor, pools of blood still surrounding what was left of the neck. One side of the head was a mess of raw flesh. "Where's his ear?"

"You really want to know?" the medical examiner asked.

"I need to know."

"I'll confirm it later but after a quick look, I'm pretty sure his ear was stuffed into his rectum."

"God damn. What's the point?"

"You're the detective. Sorry, Mark, this is a mystery."

A young policewoman arrived. She looked visibly shaken. "Got an ID, detective. Greg Matheson, age twenty-four, no priors. Student here at the university. Guy down the hall says he's a workaholic, no enemies. Real bright. No hint of trouble." She paused. "Nobody heard anything last night."

Detective Julian looked up. "So what the hell is his larynx doing on the ceiling and why is his ear up his ass?" He walked to the window, opened it and took a deep breath of fresh air.

2

Pinedale, Oregon

Mike stood in line beside the rows of pretty pink and purple flowers. Before it was finally his turn, he took a deep breath and prepared himself for the daily ritual. The teacher was tall, thin, had long wavy ash-blond hair and always wore a plain, long cotton dress and sandals. Always. Her voice was calm and melodic, but loud.

"Good morning, Mik-eye-ell." She extended a thin, bony hand. She always pronounced his name *Mik-eye-ell*, which would be fine if that were his name, but his name was Michael. He preferred to be called Mike. The teacher often seemed to hold his hand for a second longer than the other kids' hands and this morning was no exception. In fact, when her eyes gazed deeply into his and she smiled and squeezed his hand for what seemed like a very long time, Mike was tempted to pull back and run away. But he did not run. She was his teacher and he had been trained to respect her authority.

"Good morning Miss Meyer." After his hand was returned, he passed into the small cloakroom, hung his sweater on a hook and donned his slippers before walking slowly to his desk. He had been treated differently since the start of the school year and different is not usually good when you're ten years old.

The girl beside him tapped his shoulder and smiled. "Miss Meyer has a crush on you. Everyone knows it."

"No she doesn't." Mike looked at the floor.

"You're clueless—everybody knows she thinks you're special. She likes your blond, curly hair and baby blue eyes." The girl giggled and Mike felt his face flush. He had learned early in life that fair skin does not help in hiding emotions. He sat quietly and stared at the blackboard.

When Miss Meyer had finished greeting the children, she glanced at Mike and took her place at the front of the class.

"Please stand, children. Nice neat rows. Now, begin the morning verse all together with voices as clear as church bells or we'll do it again."

And as they had done every day for as long as each of them had attended the Loving Sun Waldorf School, the class dutifully chanted the morning verse:

The Sun with Loving Light makes bright for me each day
The Soul with Spirit Power gives strength unto my limbs
In sunlight shining clear I reverence, O God
The strength of humankind
Which thou so graciously
Hast planted in my soul
That I with all my might
May love to work and learn
From thee come light and strength
To thee stream love and thanks

Mike sat down and looked out the window. The kids were right. He was treated differently by the teacher. He could feel it. Miss Meyer was always looking at him, always smiling and touching his shoulders and hair. Even that day after school when she shook hands with each student in the class as they left, she used two hands to softly caress his little hand. Other kids giggled and he felt awkward. He could not tell his mother because Miss Meyer had become good friends with his mother lately. Maybe he could talk to his dad.

"Mik-eye-ell!" His mother waved and walked towards him after school. It was a sunny September day and his mom seemed to have a happy bounce in her step. She sighed slowly as she arrived. "What a lovely day." She glanced from Mike to Miss Meyer. "It's as if the whole universe is waking up and smiling."

Miss Meyer held out slender hands and the two women hugged. Mike watched and wondered when they had stopped using the usual handshake.

Miss Meyer stared at his mother and smiled. "Yes, Serena, the universe is waking up. At long last." His teacher continued to smile. "How's your German coming along?"

Mike's mother raised both eyebrows. "Nicht Gut. Ich habe . . ." She frowned. "I have a hard time with the verbs but the night school teacher is amazing!" She grinned.

The night school class included a few Waldorf parents at the school with Miss Sophia Meyer as their teacher.

"You must continue to practice every day, Serena," the teacher said. "Meditate on every syllable and open your mind to the impulse of the words." Miss Meyer was from Germany but had only a hint of a German accent. She looked down at Mike. "And you should be learning German, too. But first things first."

Mike felt his teacher's fingers pass through his hair, gently massaging his scalp. He noticed some kids looking at him as they were being picked up by their parents. They were grinning. He wanted to go home.

His mother spoke: "How were things today, Mik-eye-ell?" Recently, his mother had also begun pronouncing his name *Mik-eye-ell*, although it was not as exaggerated as Miss Meyer, who said it smoothly with a German accent.

Miss Meyer sighed. "Our Mik-eye-ell is doing very well. I've noticed such improvement in eurythmy class." She bent over and stared into his eyes. "You must have noticed the improvement, Mik-eye-ell," she said, in the familiar singsong voice he had come to dislike. "Your movements are straight from heaven!"

"Actually," Mike said, "I don't really—"

His mother took his hand. "We need to be on our way." As they hopped into their little green Audi, Mike turned to see Miss Meyer still watching them as she stood alone at the entrance to the school.

3

Pinedale, Oregon

Mike sat at the desk in his room, pretending to do homework but secretly reading a comic he'd borrowed from the local library. His big beeswax crayons lay on piles of half-finished *form drawings* his mother insisted he complete that week. *Form drawings are important*, his mother had said. He had heard Miss Meyer recently asking his mother how many hours each week were spent working on these maze-like drawings at home. Mike had never understood the point. In grade one, they were kind of fun but now they were just plain boring and besides, why weren't the other kids forced to do them at home?

He heard his father arrive from work. Seconds later, his bedroom door opened and Mike was pleased to see that his dad was wearing a big smile. Chris was not a big man but when Mike looked at his dad's neatly trimmed beard and blue eyes he always felt safe and happy.

"Hey Mike, what's up?" His dad sat on his bed.

"Hi dad. I was just gonna do my homework."

"Ah yes, the dreaded homework," his father said, smiling. "Still working on those form drawings for Miss Meyer?" He looked at the papers on Mike's desk.

"Yeah, still doing form drawings." Mike took a breath. "Dad, I just don't get it. I mean, what's the point? I keep doing these things over and over again."

The smile left his dad's face. "Hey buddy, it's part of your education. I can't claim to understand all the reasons for everything in Waldorf, but your mom tells me that Miss Meyer thinks you're very good at lots of things."

Mike looked out the window. He wondered if he should tell his dad how strange things were at school these days—how the kids teased him about being the "teacher's pet."

His mother arrived in the doorway. "Dinner's almost ready," she said.

Mike noticed uncomfortable glances between his mom and dad—not the first time he'd seen that happen recently. During dinner that night both his parents were polite with each other but Mike knew something was wrong. When he was in bed he heard them arguing. Again.

"You just do not understand," his mother was saying, almost yelling. "You don't even want to understand!"

"What I understand is that you have become someone I no longer know," his father said.

Mike pulled the pillow over his ears, but he could still hear his parents. He remembered the days when he never heard them arguing. He remembered them doing fun stuff together as a family. Sometimes, the three of them would take a picnic to the park or decide on the spur of the moment to go ice-skating together or make popcorn and watch the Three Stooges on a rainy Sunday afternoon. It seemed like so long ago.

"I don't know if this school is good for Mike," his dad said.

Mike waited for his mom's response. He'd heard it before:

"You just don't get it, Christopher. It's not like those other awful schools. Waldorf is much gentler and the teachers care so much about the children. Sophia Meyer is—"

"Oh come on, Serena. If Sophia Meyer cares so much, why can she not see that Mike is not happy? He should be laughing once in a while, having fun with other kids—not always guided through the weird Waldorf stuff every day. Why does he need to do form drawings all the time? Did you know he hates doing eurythmy? Kids in other schools get to do real artwork. Mike is sick and tired of painting those weird Waldorf blobs. And why does Sophia Meyer always sidestep questions? She never did tell us why the kids are not allowed to have black crayons. And what about her forcing the left-handed kids to be right-handed? What is that all about?"

"You just don't get it." His mother sounded calm now. "Wet on wet painting and eurythmy can connect children with the spirit world. Rudolf Steiner gave us plenty of indications for—"

"When we looked into Waldorf years ago," his dad interrupted, "they told us eurythmy was a form of dance and all the art was simply that—art." He paused. "Something is wrong and you don't see it."

Mike knew his mom would be smiling now and that would make his dad even angrier. He was right.

"Damn it, Serena, what has happened to you?"

"Keep your voice down, Christopher."

Mike heard footsteps coming up the stairs. He closed his eyes, pretending to be asleep. The door opened for a moment and then quietly closed.

4

Ithaca, New York

Professor Paul Sung was born in San Francisco's Chinatown during a time when having Chinese heritage was not considered a quality by most Americans. His father was second generation Chinese and his mother's side was Polish-Jewish. At nineteen, Paul's mother had left Krakow for the United States, two years before Germany invaded Poland. Most of her relatives did not survive the war. She met Paul's father in San Francisco in 1946 and after a fairy tale wedding, the young couple opened a small gift shop which they ran for many years in the city's famous Chinatown.

As a boy, Paul had always been curious why busybodies would stare and ask if his heritage was Asian or Polynesian or perhaps Native American or . . .

"My dad's family is from China and my mom is Jewish—from Poland."

"You're a Chinese Jew!" they would say. "That's weird."

He found this preoccupation with religion and race interesting, but sometimes disturbing. During his teenage years, Paul discovered the least problematic response to such questions: "I'm American."

He had been considered "gifted" as a child. Although his parents were far from wealthy, they had made sure Paul received the best education they could afford. After high school, six academic scholarships had come in handy. He grew up speaking English, Mandarin and some Polish. By the age of twenty-five, he was fluent in German and spoke some Italian. He studied at three American and two prestigious European universities before accepting teaching positions at Yale and now Cornell. His fascination with religion and racial politics eventually turned into a long academic career.

Paul had just shaved and was thinking about Corn Flakes and coffee when he got the phone call. He was shocked at the horrible news. He had known Greg Matheson for a few years as a very bright, hard-working graduate student. Greg had excelled at Paul's Comparative Religion and Philosophy courses.

Although he had not been taking any of his classes this year, Greg was known on campus as Professor Sung's protégé.

Paul hung up the phone in disbelief. Who could have wanted Greg dead? Paul agreed to meet with the police in an hour but had no idea what help he could offer. Greg was a bright young man who had been fascinated with the history of occultism in Europe. To the best of Paul's knowledge, Greg had no enemies, very little money and probably no time for a girlfriend. He had been addicted to research, certainly not drugs, and there should be no reason for anyone to kill him.

Paul parked a block away from Greg's apartment on campus and noticed police cars and yellow tape securing the area. Police incidents at Cornell were rare. A group of people had gathered to see what was happening. He showed his ID to a uniformed cop who led him into the apartment building lobby and introduced him as "that professor guy you wanted to see" to Detective Mark Julian. After the standard questions, Paul felt compelled to apologize for not being able to offer any help. The murder was indeed a mystery.

"Thanks for coming," the detective said. "I hear you were pretty close to the victim."

"Not really," Paul said. "Not recently, anyway. He took some of my courses a couple of years ago."

"But I hear you were his mentor—almost a father figure?"

Paul had heard that line before and it made him feel uncomfortable. "I never felt like a father figure. Greg was always curious and worked hard." Paul cleared his throat. "I just cannot believe someone killed him."

"Sometimes," the detective said, "there is no reason for murder. It's as if something just snaps in a person and next thing you know someone is dead. No reason."

It was Paul's turn to ask some questions. At first he was reluctant to know the details, but he knew he'd regret it later if he left without at least some information.

"How did he die?"

The detective stared at him for a moment, as if trying to decide whether or not to confide in the professor. "You really want to know?" He undid one button on his black leather jacket, glanced around the lobby and looked again at Paul. "You understand this is confidential."

"Sure," Paul agreed.

"He was attacked in his apartment, drugged and murdered." The detective paused, as if waiting for a response. Paul said nothing. "Maybe you can make sense of this next bit. The killer went to great lengths to surgically remove his larynx and nail it to the ceiling." He then shared the news of where they found Greg's ear.

Paul felt stunned.

The detective studied his face. "Any idea, Professor, why someone would do this to one of your students at the university?"

Paul shook his head. "I have no idea. It makes no sense. I already told you Greg was a quiet, private individual—no enemies, no reason anyone would want to hurt him." He paused. "And like this . . ."

"Beats me, Professor. I thought you might know. The medical examiner is up there now. Says the murderer knew what he was doing. Ask me, I'd say the killer is insane and unfortunately, crazy killers are rarely satisfied with only one victim."

"Was anything stolen?"

"Hard to know right now. His apartment was trashed. The killer might have taken some cash from his wallet. We found it beside the body but the credit cards were still there. They always take the credit cards. Weird."

Paul took a deep breath. "Any finger prints?" He immediately regretted the question—he sounded a little too curious, as if he'd seen too many police shows on television. He had not.

Detective Julian seemed to be studying him again. "You sure you can't help us, Professor?"

5

Dornach, Switzerland

The tiny attic office was cold and dark. Karl Heisman struck a match, lit two tall beeswax candles and sat at his massive old roll-top desk. Like everything else in the room, the desk had been in the family for generations. Karl turned the key and rolled up the big wooden cover that hid many years of family secrets. Thirty old leather-bound books lined the back of the huge desk. Karl sighed and pulled out one of his grandfather's diaries. The pages were yellow and brittle with age. He had read them all many times since the passing of his father some ten years ago.

Karl opened the diary and as he had done often over the years, he read about his grandfather's life. Despite the occasional ink smudge, the handwriting was perfect and a joy to read. Karl easily found the bookmarked pages he knew so well:

(translated from the original German)

> January 4, 1913 Berlin - Herr Steiner spoke privately to a few of us after tonight's lecture. His presence is life affirming, as was the topic tonight—words cannot describe the joy of knowing that death is not the end of the soul!

Karl flipped pages:

> May 18, 1913 Berlin - We have been learning about the archangels recently. Herr Steiner has blessed me with special knowledge and with time I will grow to live within the Stream of the Archangel Michael.

Karl gently closed and returned the book to its place at the back of the desk and pulled out another diary and another old leather bookmark:

December 3, 1922 Stuttgart - We've been discussing the Germanic
Folk Soul recently. Since Herr Steiner's return from London, there
has been much work happening in order to form the foundation for
the religious renewal movement. Herr Doktor explained in detail
how the spirit works through human skin. Why is it so difficult for
some people to understand the reality of evolution? We have much
to learn from Rudolf Steiner. These Negros and Asians are not at
fault. It is simply their destiny to step aside. Indeed, the white race
is the race of the future!

Karl continued to flip through diaries. He felt relaxed and strong and convinced that his present incarnation would be remembered by humanity
forever.

6

Ithaca, New York

Paul Sung had a difficult time concentrating on his work. Grisly murders simply did not happen at Cornell. Until now. Images of Greg flashed through his mind all day—images of a clean-cut, eager young academic with plenty of potential and a passion for history.

Paul was looking at PhD theses from the previous year but could not concentrate on anything except for the young man whose larynx had been removed and nailed to his ceiling. Feelings of sadness played havoc with Paul's mind. He was also curious. Why remove Greg's larynx?

Paul wondered about Greg's latest research. What, if anything, had the young man been up to that might have contributed to his murder? Paul grabbed his laptop, left his office and wandered down the hall to his favorite café near the library. The smell of cinnamon buns and java was a welcome reprieve from the troubles of that sad September morning.

He sat with a steaming cup of soy latte, popped open his laptop and searched a few databases for information about the academic world of Greg Matheson.

Paul already knew that Greg had been fascinated with occultism in Europe and the birth of the New Age movement. As he sipped on his latte, a familiar *ping* informed him that an email had arrived. He learned that a webpage had already been created in memory of Greg Matheson. News travels fast and university students are always eager to share good, bad and ugly news. Someone had created a Face Book "mourning message wall" and it already had at least a dozen notes:

> Greg—you were such an inspiration. Miss you already.
> Greg—I'm stunned. You deserved more and better.
> Grego—You were the best. Now you won't be taking that special
> trip after all.

Paul considered adding a comment but decided to leave that task for the young man's closer friends. *What special trip was Greg going to take?* He pulled his cell phone from a shirt pocket and punched in the number of a fellow faculty member.

"Hello—Bob Richardson here."

"Bob, it's Paul Sung."

"Hey Paul, how are you? Did you hear about Greg Matheson?"

"I did. So sad. The police talked to me already."

"I can't believe it. Such a bright kid, too."

"Bob, he was taking one of your courses, wasn't he?"

"Yeah, and he talked me into supporting his research in Europe. He got a nice grant for the trip. He was not only a gifted academic, but a damn good arm twister, as well." Bob sighed. "Not that it matters now that he's dead."

A second of silence and then Paul asked the question. "Why was he going to Europe?"

"His thesis," Bob said. "European mystics at the turn of the century—Blavatsky, Besant, Steiner and others. Birth of the New Age movement. Right up your alley. He sure admired you, Paul. He'd done all he could here—even learned German—and was going to spend some time in Germany, Switzerland and maybe Italy. He wanted to connect some interesting dots—that's what he told me. The guy was obsessed, Paul. Tons of research. Someone told me he rarely sleeps." He paused and corrected his mistake. "Rarely slept. I can't believe he's dead."

"Thanks, Bob. Let's keep in touch." Paul hung up and recalled Greg's obsession with cults and new religious movements. He remembered his own sleepless nights as a passionate young academic.

He refreshed the laptop connection and noticed many more *mourning message wall* references to Greg's trip to Europe. Apparently, the young man had been very excited about the trip—the trip that would never happen.

Day Two

1

Ithaca, New York

Detective Mark Julian thought he had seen it all during his twenty-three years on the force. Twenty years in New York City had shown him the most disgusting elements of the human condition, and the past three years in Ithaca, while certainly more peaceful, had not been without a few violent incidents. Like many cops, he'd seen enough rape and murder and irrational, cruel human behavior to make most people give up completely on the human race.

He had been punched, elbowed, knifed once, and had been used as target practice during a drive-by shooting in the Bronx. He had also caught his fair share of bad guys and was secretly proud of the fact that he had never yet needed to shoot a human being. But if necessary, he was trained to shoot to kill. He had nothing against guns and had always scored high at New York rapid-fire pistol events. It's just that he figured his bulk and verbal skills were deterrent enough. He was a big man and in pretty good physical shape for a guy of forty-six.

Mark wanted to avoid his telephone. He had a sinking feeling he'd be getting another call announcing the next gruesome surgical murder. That's what they called it—the surgical murder. But the crazed killer had yet to strike again. Mark had spent time interviewing Greg's family and friends, each person confirming what he had already learned: the deceased had been a hard-working young academic with no enemies or problems. By all accounts, the most trouble he got himself into—ever—was trying to break up a fight one night at a local pub. The guy was as clean as clean can be.

Mark went over Greg's medical history, looking for a connection with any doctors who might have held a grudge. The medical examiner suggested the removal of his larynx had been done by an expert. Greg's health had been fine, no medical problems whatsoever, no reason for anyone to want to see him dead and his larynx stuck to his ceiling.

Mark sat at his desk, staring at photos of a separate crime scene. Some-one had robbed a local liquor store, beat the crap out of an old man (died later) and stolen one hundred and thirty seven dollars and two bottles of cheap scotch. Mark pulled his eyes from the photos and found the window across the room. Maybe it was time for an early lunch. Maybe it was time to retire . . .

His phone rang. "Homicide. Detective Julian."

"Hello, this is Paul Sung. We met yesterday regarding the murder . . . ?"

"Yes, Professor, how are you?"

"Good. Listen, you said to call if I had any further information."

Mark grabbed a notepad. "What have you got?"

"It's probably nothing."

"What have you got?" the detective repeated.

"Actually, are you able to stop by my office sometime? We could discuss it in person—if you have the time?"

Mark had time. "I can be there in an hour."

2

Ithaca, New York

Professor Paul Sung was sixty-two years old, divorced with no children. His receding hairline annoyed him and the fact that he was only slightly overweight was no consolation. He knew that within a few short years he would resemble the vast majority of retired profs who chuckled publicly about old age and "love handles" but fretted in private while dealing with mortality. Years ago he had worked hard for his PhD in philosophy and for the past many years his life had been simple, neat . . . and usually unfulfilling. He had tenure but very little excitement or joy in his life.

His wife had left him ten years ago for a Wall Street lawyer with a big house and a place in Palm Springs. It hurt for a while but he had recovered. At least, that's what he told himself.

From time to time Paul would flirt with mature graduate students, fantasize for a week or two, feel silly and guilty and then forget all about it. His life was limited to teaching at Cornell, speaking at conferences, reading philosophy—mainly esoteric and atheist—and watching old films on television. He was a closet Bogart fan.

Paul's work schedule kept him busy but his social life was nonexistent. The only family he had was a brother in California; his best friends these days were books by writers like James Joyce, Richard Dawkins and Karl Popper.

It wasn't that he did not enjoy the company of others; it was that the energy needed to discover and nurture relationships was more than he was willing to expend. Maybe that was simply the burden of one who deals with esoteric studies. Or perhaps it was the reality of being an academic atheist living in the United States. *Reality is what one makes of it*, he would teach his students. Paul's was often a separate reality.

Professor Paul Sung was considered a leading authority on the history of what is commonly known as the "New Age Movement." It was a fascinating topic but what really interested Paul was guiding the rare, dedicated student who wanted to dig beneath the surface of a university course. Greg Matheson had been one such student. It was perhaps Greg's death that contributed to Paul's deeper-than-usual melancholy. He was also painfully aware that he felt a little guilty. After all, Paul Sung had been largely responsible for guiding Greg's academic interests.

He sat in his little office, shuffling papers and thinking of Greg. The young man had been so bright and full of passion, with such a serious thirst for knowledge. A rare quality in students these days. And now Greg was gone.

Paul's cell phone beeped. "Paul Sung."

"Hey Paul, it's Bob Richardson. Got a second?"

"Sure Bob, what's up?"

"I thought I'd let you know, or have you already heard?"

"Heard what—which means I guess I haven't heard."

"Someone trashed my office last night."

"I didn't hear that, Bob. Sorry to hear it now. Any idea who or why—anything missing?"

"That's what's weird, Paul. I have a couple of expensive paintings and three very valuable artifacts in a glass case. Easy to steal but they are still there."

"Just a vandal, I guess," Paul said, hoping to reassure his colleague.

"I'm not sure about that. The campus cops asked if anything is missing. When I saw that the expensive stuff and my computer were still there, I figured it was simple vandalism. No need to file a report. I was going through some work files later and guess what's missing?"

"Enlighten me, Bob."

"Everything relating to Greg Matheson. Someone went through my computer and my filing cabinets."

Paul said nothing for a moment. He needed to digest this news. "Maybe an insensitive student looking to copy Greg's work for better grades . . ."

"Not likely." Bob paused. "Pretty strange, don't you think? I mean creepy strange."

3

Ithaca, New York

Detective Mark Julian arrived at Paul Sung's office just before noon. They decided to meet over a quick lunch at the little café by the library.

After a minute of small talk, Mark spooned pea soup into his mouth, waiting for the professor to share what was on his mind. He watched the older man bite into his sandwich, and then he glanced out the large windows to the courtyard below. Students stood and sat in little groups chatting and laughing, some eating bagged lunches, others sipping from bottles or paper cups. Mark thought of Greg Matheson, an innocent young man whose life had been snuffed out by a deranged killer.

Paul Sung wiped his mouth with a napkin and stared across the little table. "It might not be anything, but after you left yesterday I learned that Greg was about to take a trip to Europe as part of a research project." He sipped from a glass of water. "Nobody here has any idea who would have wanted Greg dead, so I wondered—and I don't really know why I thought this—but I wondered if for some reason, maybe somebody did not want him to go to Europe."

Mark finished his soup. "What was he going to do in Europe?"

"He was researching certain individuals—occultists from turn-of-the-century Europe. Greg was a perfectionist." The professor took a bite of his sandwich. "He was a very bright guy."

"So I keep hearing. You think someone connected to one of these occultists didn't want him poking around Europe? Maybe some kinky old family secrets over there?"

"I'm not sure." Paul paused and glanced around the café. "There's something else. And again, I'm not sure if this means anything either but . . ." He sighed and shook his head. "I sound like a half-baked sleuth from a TV police show."

"I can use any leads." Mark pulled a notepad from his jacket pocket. "Go on, Professor—please."

"Just after I phoned you this morning, I got a call from a colleague—"

"Name?"

"Bob Richardson—he teaches here at Cornell. He told me his office was trashed and he's missing some files pertaining to Greg Matheson. Nothing else was stolen. Maybe you heard about it?"

Mark scribbled in his notepad, expressionless. "No."

A young, pony-tailed brunette stopped at the table. "Excuse me Professor Sung," she said, a smile forming on pale pink lips. "I was hoping to finish my paper by today but I'm wondering if it's OK to get it to you by tomorrow?" She paused. "It's so sad about Greg Matheson."

"Very sad," Paul said. "Sure, get it to me by tomorrow."

Mark watched her walk away and then looked at Paul. "So, how much do you know about Greg's research?"

"Quite a bit, actually. I looked at some old notes yesterday and remembered that I suggested to Greg that he consider following up on some areas of my research."

"Really?" Mark scribbled again in his notepad.

"Ten years ago I wrote a book about a particular branch of esotericism as it relates to the birth of what we now call the New Age movement."

"Can I get a copy of the book?"

"It's pretty dry stuff. If profs don't publish something once in a while, our academic futures are often gloomy. My book was published by the university press—mainly aimed at students and academics. I don't mean you can't read it, detective. Just that it's not easy unless you have some familiarity or context with the subject."

Mark smiled. He had little interest in the New Age movement but if the book would help with his murder investigation, he might as well have a look. "That's fine," he said. "I didn't think you were calling my intelligence into question. Still, I'd appreciate a copy."

"No problem."

They made their way back to Paul's little office where he cleared some papers from a chair for Mark and then rummaged through boxes in a closet. Within a couple of minutes, Mark was holding a copy of *The Esoteric Impulse of a New Age,* by Dr. Paul Sung. The book was thick.

Mark thumbed through the pages, stopping occasionally to look at drawings and black and white photographs. "Tell me, Dr. Sung—"

"Please, call me Paul."

"Tell me what you think happened to Greg Matheson. I get the feeling you have some ideas. You phoned me for a reason. Why is he dead?"

Paul drummed his fingers on the messy desk. "I don't really know but it could—and please let me emphasize the word *could*—have something to do with his research."

"And you say this because . . ."

"Greg was fascinated by the occult. He was a serious student, but not everyone shares the belief that it is a good idea or even possible to study the occult academically."

Mark stopped writing in his notepad. "Meaning?"

"Meaning some people are not fond of university students or professors or journalists poking noses into their spirit world." He paused. "It's probably similar to your line of work. I can't imagine people wanting you to poke into their lives, habits, and so on."

"So you're saying these occultists are doing something illegal?"

"Not necessarily, but maybe some of them are doing things they would rather not share with outsiders. Many esotericists resent that academics study them and their beliefs. It feels intrusive, disrespectful."

"Any suggestions as to who we might be looking for?"

Paul continued to tap on his desk.

Mark studied the professor. The man seemed nervous. "I get the feeling you might feel responsible for Greg's death—I mean, you suggested he dig deeper into the occult. Am I right?"

"I don't know," Paul said. "Maybe." He stopped tapping the desk.

"Then help me find his killer," Mark said. He smiled. "That's all we can do now."

Paul sighed. "I'll try to help."

"Who are we looking for, Paul?"

"I've been thinking about Greg Matheson, his research and the way he was killed. Something rang a bell but I could not put my finger on it. I checked with Bob—Bob Richardson—to see exactly what Greg was up to lately. A few questions came to mind, disjointed thoughts at first because it's been a few years since I studied this particular topic in depth, and then I did what anyone with Internet access does many times each day." He paused. "I Googled a few European mystics—folks Greg would be studying—along with the words *larynx* and *ear*."

"And?"

"Have you ever heard of Rudolf Steiner?"

"No."

"Anthroposophy?"

"No."

"Waldorf education?"

Mark shifted in his chair. "Vaguely. My ex-wife's sister sent her daughter to a Waldorf school. The woman was a flake—a burnt-out hippy type. I heard enough about the school to help me think it was as flaky as she was."

Paul smiled. "Waldorf schools have a lot to offer but are based on a philosophy—or some say a religion—called *Anthroposophy*, a spiritual movement founded by Rudolf Steiner. He was a prominent occultist in Europe a hundred years ago."

"OK," said Mark. "So what did this Steiner guy have to say about the larynx and the ear?"

"He had lots to say," Paul answered. "But it might sound hard to believe."

The detective managed a smile. "Try me."

4

Pinedale, Oregon

It was a surprisingly cool September afternoon and Mike stood alone outside after school. The other kids had all gone home and his mother was in the building, meeting again with Miss Meyer. Mike watched the clouds and was thinking about his problems.

The teasing had been constant at recess and lunch that day. More than a few kids had chanted "teacher's-pet-teacher's-pet" over and over and over and a couple of girls went farther with comments and silly songs about Mike and Miss Meyer "sitting in a tree, k-i-s-s-i-n-g." Of course, that was ridiculous. But it was very embarrassing.

Life at home was slightly better than life at school, but being an only child meant he felt very alone when his parents argued. While Mike had no doubt that his mom and dad had plenty of love to send his way, they certainly had not been getting along with each other lately. Within ten minutes of him being in bed he would hear them arguing—every night. For the past few nights the arguments had become louder and angrier and although Mike was not always able to hear exactly what they were saying, he could make out most of the heated discussions. They usually involved him and his school and how his life should or should not be at home.

One argument involved TV. Mike's dad had tried to change some of his mother's strict rules—especially the one about *no TV until summer vacation*. Kids in Waldorf schools are not supposed to watch TV. His dad had suggested that on occasion he and Mike should be allowed to watch a sporting event on the tube, but Mike's mom had become really upset and insisted that the television be banned altogether. She said if they got rid of the television there would be no more arguing. It seemed to Mike that the more his dad tried to find a compromise, the more his mom pushed harder for her position.

She often used Miss Meyer to back up her arguments, while using Mike's education as a weapon against his dad. No junk food. No television. No listening to recorded music or even the radio. She would get angry with his dad for not supporting Mike's education.

Sometimes he would hear his dad getting angry too; he'd yell at his mom to *lighten up!* He'd tell her that kids needed to have some fun in life and then she'd tell him that he does not understand—he is not able to know that *Michael is special.* When the arguing got really loud, Mike would close his eyes, wrap his head in his pillow and imagine his favorite hockey players hoisting the Stanley Cup after a hard fought series. Mike would imagine himself listening to the roar of the crowd instead of the angry voices of his parents.

As his mind returned to the present, he wondered why his mom was taking so long to talk with Miss Meyer inside his classroom. School was over for the day and he wanted to go home. Everyone else had left long ago.

To his surprise and delight, he saw a raccoon wandering through some tall grass beside the building. A moment later three smaller raccoons appeared and followed their mother or father through the parking lot. Mike had only ever seen raccoons once before and he needed to share this exciting news with someone. He tried to get into the school to tell his mom, but the door was locked. The raccoons were still there, two of the younger ones wrestling in the grass, as if they had not a care in the world.

Mike grinned and pushed through the bushes beside his classroom window. He peered in through a gap in the curtain. He was about to knock on the window and announce the wonderful raccoon sighting to his mother and Miss Meyer, but his knuckles stopped before they found the glass. He squinted and looked again but there was no mistake.

He would never forget this strange sight. His mother and Miss Meyer stood up against the blackboard, bodies pressed together, and to Mike's astonishment, they were kissing. Not the short, quick little nice-to-see-you type kisses but the long, sexy type kisses between men and women that Mike had seen on TV once when his mom was not home.

He stood and watched for a moment, surprised to see them pushing their bodies together, surprised to see them nibbling each other's lips as they kissed, surprised to see Miss Meyer's hands reaching up to touch his mother's breasts under her sweater.

Mike turned and ran and stood like a statue beside their car, promising himself he would never *ever* tell anyone what had just happened.

5

Pinedale, Oregon

When Chris pulled into the driveway after work, he knew something was wrong. The curtains were closed—not only in the living room but in both bedrooms upstairs, as well. His wife never closed the curtains during the day. Within a minute he had run through the entire house. He called out constantly as he ran.

"Serena! Mike! Anyone home?"

Horror stories popped into his head. Too much late night television news, he thought. The house was tidy, no sign of a struggle. It was simply empty. Chris searched his mind for something he must be missing. Had Serena said something to him that morning? Had she told him she was going somewhere with Mike and would be back later—after dinner maybe? Perhaps she was visiting her mother—only an hour's drive away but why would she close the curtains? Maybe her sister had picked her up . . . but she had not spoken with her sister for almost a year. Strange, he could not remember the reason for their sibling squabble.

He sat at the kitchen table and phoned two of her friends, her mother and then her sister. Nobody had any idea where Serena and Mike might be. Then Chris tried phoning Mike's Waldorf School. Maybe there was a school play or event he had forgotten about? A recorded message made no mention of anything happening that night.

Slowly, methodically, he walked through the house again, looking for clues. Finally, upstairs in his bedroom, on his pillow he found a note:

> Dear Christopher,
> I'm very sorry but some things are best left unsaid to those without the Will to understand. Please don't worry. Karma has a way of explaining everything in time. Blessings, Serena.

Chris read the note three times, and then collapsed on the bed. His stomach was already in knots and his head began throbbing. Suddenly, anger pulsed through his body like wildfire. He bounced off the bed and ran downstairs.

"You're with Miss Meyer," he said to himself. "You're with that nutty Waldorf teacher!"

He grabbed the school phone list from the kitchen counter and glanced at the names. To his dismay, the list was comprised of parents' phone numbers only. No teachers.

"Where do you live, Miss Meyer?" he said to nobody.

He picked up the phone and called the first parent on the list from Mike's class. The woman had no idea how to contact Miss Meyer and knew nothing about his wife or son. He phoned the second parent and got the same response. He scanned the list, looking for a name he might recognize—someone with whom he could actually talk. Suddenly, Chris felt very much like spilling his feelings; he wanted to talk about the emptiness in the pit of his stomach.

The Feldmans. He remembered talking football with Steve Feldman at one of the school events. Nice guy—he seemed like a normal dad. He punched in the phone number and learned that neither Steve Feldman nor his wife knew where Miss Meyer lived. Mrs. Feldman said she doubted whether Miss Meyer even had a phone as she had sworn off electronics when she became a Waldorf teacher—*smart woman, eh?*

It was dinnertime but Chris was not hungry. He sat at the kitchen table, his mind a storm of disjointed thoughts. Phone the police? No, nothing illegal had happened. Serena didn't have a cell phone. Who could he talk to? He stood and paced the kitchen. The sense of helplessness was overwhelming.

He grabbed a beer from the fridge and made himself a sandwich. Tomorrow was another day, he decided. Serena was probably staying with her new best friend, the teacher. She would take Mike to school the next day. He would be there, waiting. He would talk to her then. He would fix everything tomorrow.

6

Ithaca, New York

Maybe it was only a dream. Bob Richardson opened his eyes, blinked twice and tried to collect his foggy thoughts. He knew he was home, sitting up in his bed it seemed, and he knew his wife was there beside him. No, something was not right. He must be dreaming. Curiously, the dream involved pain. If he were dreaming and if he were conscious of the dream—a so-called lucid dream—he should be able to toss the pain out like an old tissue. But try as he might, the pain in his neck refused to leave. Within a few seconds, Bob decided he was not dreaming; he was very much awake.

Now, what's with this pain?

He lifted a hand to touch his neck. His hand, however, would barely move. His arm would not move. He opened his eyes wide, hoping to distinguish fantasy from reality. He tried to move his feet. They would not cooperate. Bob began breathing hard, panic flooding his mind. He realized then that he was partially paralyzed. *A stroke!* He needed to wake up his wife and get her to call 911. He needed to . . .

He heard a muffled cry from somewhere in the bedroom. Suddenly, he saw a dim light; someone had lit a candle. Then another candle was lit, and another. He smelled beeswax. His eyes were able to focus now and the image hit him hard. He felt sick.

Sitting in a chair against the far wall of the bedroom, tied up with rope, mouth gagged with cloth, was his wife. When their eyes met, Bob felt his blood turn to ice. He jumped out of bed and ran to her side, or at least he saw himself jumping out of bed. He could not move. He screamed, or at least he imagined himself screaming. The strange, garbled noise that came from his mouth was not what he had hoped for. He had no voice. Bob was inexplicably, incredibly, unable to move. He was not dreaming.

7

Ithaca, New York

Mark Julian sat in his old brown Lazy Boy. It was too big for the living room in his small apartment but he had owned the chair since college and it had history. He held a bottle of Becks in one hand and Dr. Paul Sung's book, *The Esoteric Impulse of a New Age*, in the other.

He had been sitting there for over an hour, trying to make sense of the book. Mark was certainly not a stupid man, but Paul's warning about it being written for an academic audience kept ringing in his ears. It was not an easy read.

So far, he had learned that the occultist, Rudolf Steiner, was born in what is now Croatia in 1861, spent most of his life in Austria and Germany and died in 1925. As a young man, Steiner found employment editing the works of Johann Wolfgang Von Goethe and earned a PhD in philosophy from the University of Rostock in 1891. Steiner's interest in philosophy swung to the esoteric and he eventually found his calling as a prominent occultist in Europe—mainly in Germany. Steiner founded the first Waldorf School in Stuttgart, Germany in 1919 in response to a request by Emil Molt, the owner of the Waldorf-Astoria cigarette factory. Herr Molt was interested in Steiner's occultism and wanted a school for the children of his employees at the factory.

From time to time Mark would pull the book away from his face and ponder certain confusing passages. Particularly perplexing were repeated references to the *akasha* and the *etheric body* and *astral worlds*.

Mark pulled another beer from the fridge and kicked back in the Lazy Boy. He picked up the book again and looked at the cover. His concentration faded and the deep, personal questions arrived as they always did—through the back door of his mind.

Why did his life always need to revolve around his work? Why not leave it at the office once in a while? What on earth, for example, was he doing at this minute? Sitting alone in his apartment on his own time and reading about mystics and oddballs from another century. He looked at his watch. Not too late—he should be watching the World Series on TV. The Yankees were long gone but still—it's the World Series.

But Mark's mind was hooked on the surgical murder. Why is the university kid dead? Mark both loved and hated work-related mysteries; he knew he should learn to be less obsessive when it came to his job.

During his years in the Bronx, he'd been forced to talk to a woman in HR about what they called his "obsession with justice." They told him he worked too much. So what? He never put in for much overtime. Imagine that—they were concerned that a cop was obsessed with helping to protect the innocent and catch the bad guys. Too many criminals walked away free. Too much bullshit plugged up the system with red tape and lame excuses. Someone needed to care. Was he really obsessive or was it that not enough people cared about justice?

He dropped the book on the floor and glanced around his living room. His eyes stopped on an eight-by-ten framed photograph above the couch. He should have put that print into storage with all the other memories years ago. He took a deep breath and a long swig of beer. The picture shouldn't be there. But he could not let it go. Not yet.

On the good days, the marriage had been perfect. He stared at the photograph. She was beautiful, not drop-dead gorgeous, but beautiful. Short, dark-brown hair and hazelnut eyes that would melt his heart when she smiled. She was petite and she smiled a lot . . . at least during the first few years.

She beamed at him now from the photograph. He was beside her in the picture. Smiling. Mark had used the self-timer, balancing the camera on a rock and hoping he could run back into the frame in time. They were backpacking in the Adirondacks—a four day trip with no phones and lots of time to soak in the scenery and each other.

They had been lovers since high school. Nobody thought they would get married and nobody thought she would drink herself into AA and a divorce. She worked in advertizing and he was a cop. Thirteen years.

"What time will you be home tonight, Mark?"

"Not too late." He knew it was a lie. It always was. Maybe he worked too much. Justice . . .

Mark picked up Paul Sung's book. It was not going to be an easy read. One beer led to another and after four Becks, he looked at the clock and decided it was time for bed.

8

Ithaca, New York

Bob Richardson lay on his bed, propped up by pillows and staring at the terrified face of his wife across the room. A dozen candles cast dark shadows on the walls. He tried to move his head, hoping to catch a glimpse of whoever had done this to them. He was still paralyzed. Maybe the man had left—robbed them and gone away. Maybe . . .

"Why is it so difficult," said a low, raspy voice, "for some people to mind their own business?"

Bob had never known fear like this. The voice was beside him on the bed. A man was lying where his wife should have been. Bob felt the mattress move as the man shifted his considerable weight, but he was still unable to turn to see who was speaking.

"Look at her now, Professor Richardson," the man said calmly. "Your lovely wife seems upset, frightened, and do you know why?"

Bob tried to say something but his voice was barely audible. He knew now that the pain in his neck had been from a needle. Beneath the fog and sleep and confusion and fear, he knew this was no stroke. He had been drugged. He was forced to stare at his wife as she sat terrified, bound and gagged on the chair.

"She is upset because of you," the voice continued. "Because of you and your support of ill-advised curiosity." The tone was angry now.

The mattress shifted again and Bob could feel the man's breath on his ear. *Who is this? How did he get into the house? What does he want?*

Suddenly, he thought of his children, asleep in their rooms down the hall. *Please just stay in your rooms until this is over.*

The stranger spoke again. "My guess is you will start to have some feeling in your extremities now. I'll bet your voice has almost decided to come out of hibernation."

Bob forced his hand to move an inch. He grunted and managed to whisper one word: "Why?"

"Why?" the man repeated. "Why?" He laughed a low rumbling sound that sent a shiver through Bob's body; the effects of the drug had indeed begun to subside. "Because you have something that does not belong to you. And I want it."

Bob continued to stare at this wife. Her eyes were wide, terrified, panic written all over her face as if to say, *For God's sake, give him what he wants!*

Slowly, Bob's sluggish mind pulled itself from the fog. The man was looking for something. Greg Matheson did not have it, so Bob's office was then turned upside down. This man now assumed that Bob was in possession of that certain something. Unfortunately, the man was dreadfully misinformed.

Bob tried his voice again. He was able to turn his head slightly towards the stranger beside him on the bed. "I don't know," he began, his voice scratchy, barely audible, "what you want." He felt something strike the side of his head. His wife gasped and cried uncontrollably. "I don't know," he said again. He felt dizzy and without warning, the contents of his stomach exploded from his mouth, covering himself and the blankets with vomit.

"You disgusting pig," the man said, getting out of bed and standing between Bob and his wife. The intruder looked at the frightened woman. "And you live with this pig?"

Bob's head was spinning. More vomit escaped. He spat the last of it onto the bed and looked up at the man. He was big—well over six feet tall—and he must have weighed over two hundred and fifty pounds. He appeared to be in his mid-sixties, but in good physical condition. He wore thick black-rimmed glasses. A full head of graying hair, bushy eyebrows and a large nose gave him a somber Groucho Marx appearance. Unlike Groucho, however, this fellow was deadly serious.

The man removed his glasses and rubbed both eyes with huge fingers. He was breathing hard, obviously upset at Bob's inability to control his stomach muscles.

He pulled a long, thin knife from beneath his khaki trench coat and then crouched beside Bob's wife, holding the blade to her throat. She breathed in frightened little gasps.

"I don't have time for this," the stranger said.

Bob tried to clear his throat. His voice was no more than a loud whisper. "Take anything you want," he said, "but please leave us alone."

The man's face suddenly changed from anger to surprise. "Of course, you are concerned about your children."

Bob felt a horrible, deep sadness course through his veins. It quickly turned to anger and with tremendous effort he moved his body slightly on the bed. The stench of his vomit made him want to puke again. He wanted nothing more than to attack this man. He not only wanted him out of the house—he wanted to hurt him.

He tried to clear his throat again and force the words to escape. "Don't do anything to my . . ."

The man smiled, pushing his glasses back up to the bridge of his fleshy nose. "But I already *have* done something," he said playfully. "One must always consider hazards or interruptions in any line of work. Perfection is required and children have a tendency to get in the way—especially those that have not yet fully incarnated. One of your children woke up and struggled before I could sedate her. It seems her karma needed a knife and not a needle."

Bob tried to lunge at the intruder but only managed to roll off the bed and onto the thick carpet. Rage was burning every fiber of his body but he was helpless to act. He managed to prop himself up against the bed. He had no energy and little control of his body. He could see his wife but that was all he could do. Watch.

The big man smiled at Bob and then stared into his wife's terrified eyes from less than an inch away, the knife still pressed up against her throat. She trembled, her entire body shaking with fear. The stranger's eyes moved down to study the tip of the knife against her flesh, and then suddenly, his other hand ripped off her cotton pajama top, exposing both breasts. Tears flowed from her closed eyes.

"No!" Bob tried to scream. His voice was still nothing more than a loud whisper. "Tell me what you want."

The man stood tall and gazed down at Bob. "I want information. If you do not give me what I want I will kill the other child. Then I will kill your wife and then I will kill you." He smiled again. "Your souls might not be of much value. It's up to you now. Karma really is that simple."

Bob tried to think quickly, tried to clear the clouds from his mind. "I still don't know," he said. "I will give you anything but please—"

"Professor Richardson," the man said. "Only one chance now so let us discover if you are able to fill your empty words with substance."

Bob detected a slight German accent. If he could engage the man in conversation—try to reach some semblance of humanity, reach him at a different level. If only he could . . .

"Why was Greg Matheson going to Europe?" The big man paused and took another deep breath. "You helped to arrange his trip. You know the answer to the question." His eyes turned to steel and he stared hard at Bob. "Tell me what you know about the Group of Forty-Eight and the Christ Impulse and our work. Speak from the I. Our collective karma and your destiny are deeply connected to your answer."

Bob was stunned.

Karma. Destiny. The Christ Impulse. This man sounded like an Anthroposophist. Bob knew Anthroposophy as a quasi-religious movement ostensibly aimed at guiding people into the spirit world. He had known a few Anthroposophists over the years. They were somewhat quirky but friendly and certainly not insane. The man in his bedroom, however, was deranged. Could he be an Anthroposophist? Why does he want information about Greg's trip? Greg is dead . . .

Bob tried to find his voice. "Greg was studying the history of occultism," he croaked. "People like Alice Bailey and Aleister Crowley—but he was fascinated by Blavatsky, Besant, Leadbeater and a few others. His main interest was Rudolf Steiner and Anthroposophy. He was going to Europe to further his research." Bob took a breath and suppressed another urge to vomit. The intruder was staring at him closely now, studying him, taking in every word.

"What do you *Materialists* know of our plans?" the man yelled. He was suddenly furious; his big face was beet red, his eyes wide and crazy. "Tell me about your connections to Doctor Paul Sung. What do you know of our work?"

What work? Bob knew his response would need to sound convincing but he was afraid that confusion and uncertainty might already show on his face. He had no idea what this monster was talking about. He tried desperately to find an answer that would sound convincing.

Bob started to speak. "Greg knew nothing of your work and I will not interfere with your destiny. I respect the Christ Impulse and have no quarrel with you."

The giant crouched again beside Bob's terrified wife. The tip of his thin blade pressed against her neck. She trembled with fear, her eyes wide again and glued to her husband, praying for Bob to make this horrible man go away.

"You are lying," the stranger said. "The Christ Impulse is the most real impulse in our evolution! It is that which directs a handful of men during these *materialist* times! You try to destroy the spirit but the Christ Impulse flows through me now! The Group of Forty-Eight will accomplish that which is destined and your dark soul will no longer interfere."

He spun quickly on his heels and left the room, knife in hand. Bob could hear him walking down the hall. Ten seconds later he returned, wiping blood from the knife with a child's T-shirt. He stood again beside Bob's wife.

Bob screamed a whispering, scratchy scream. He tried to jump to his feet but could only crawl towards his wife. The room spun crazily and he was unable to stop another stream of vomit from escaping. Tears welled in his eyes as he dragged himself to his wife, the mother of his beautiful children.

Our beautiful children . . .

The man's eyes and voice were cold as he spoke:

> "It is essential that the forces which manifest as evil, if they appear
> at the wrong place, must be taken in hand by human endeavor in
> the fifth post-Atlantean period, in such a way that humanity can
> achieve something with these forces of evil that will be beneficial
> for the future of the whole of world evolution."

Bob suspected those words belonged to the founder of Anthroposophy, Rudolf Steiner. But why not choose one of the more peaceful Steiner quotes, where he spoke of love and social renewal? Bob remembered something his colleague Paul Sung had once said—something some of his students had decided to print on T-shirts and sell at an atheist conference last year at Cornell. Paul had not been pleased with the personal publicity, especially as the students had superimposed a photo of his face over his quote: *Was religion invented as an excuse to justify irrational human behavior?*

Through the pain and tears, Bob could see the blurred image of twisted wooden legs attached to the old Chamberlain chair where his wife now sat, terrified. Suddenly, strangely, he remembered buying that chair. He dragged himself across the carpet towards it now. Fond memories floated, dream-like, through his clouded mind. He and his wife had stopped at a little roadside antique shop on their way home from Boston a few years ago.

"We must have that chair," she had said, her bright eyes glowing after a romantic weekend away. "Oh please, Bob, can we buy it? It will be perfect in our bedroom . . ."

Bob grabbed the wooden chair leg and tried to pull himself up. More than anything in the world he wanted to hold his wife close to him now. He wanted to tell her how much he loved her. He wanted to explain his confusion—that he had no idea who this madman was or why he was in their home. He felt dizzy and exhausted but needed to at least try to plead for their lives.

He heard more muffled cries from his wife and then he felt her body twitch. He wanted to believe the lunatic had not just calmly killed his children—and his wife. He wanted to believe it was all a mistake and *can't we just take a moment to remember our humanity?* He wanted to believe . . . but as he used every aching muscle in his body to pull himself up to be with his wife, warm blood began flowing down from the chair, dripping onto his hands and arms and forming a burgundy puddle on the thick, white carpet. His wife stopped twitching.

Bob tried to scream but he felt something cold and hard brush quickly against his neck. He noticed more blood streaming down—this time from just below his chin. It flowed over his chest and joined the warm, soggy pools on the carpet. He suddenly felt very cold and extremely tired. He slumped to the floor and lay at the feet of his wife. There was a brief ringing in his ears and then there was only darkness.

Day Three

1

Pinedale, Oregon

On the morning after his wife and son had left, Chris Thompson did not go to work. He told of an urgent family matter that needed his attention and he would need a few days off. The credit union could survive without him.

He stood alone outside the Loving Sun Waldorf School before anyone else had arrived. He had not slept much and had rehearsed the scene a dozen times already. He would greet his wife and Miss Meyer politely and ask to speak with Mike for a moment. His wife would not dare make a scene at the school. When he knew Mike was fine, he would suggest to his wife that they see a marriage counselor or a therapist.

When the first car pulled into the little parking lot, Chris tried not to appear upset. *Stay calm, be pleasant, relax . . .*

"Excuse me," he said to an elderly, white-haired woman as she unlocked the front door to the school.

"Good morning," the woman said, smiling. She wore a wool sweater, red scarf, long gray cotton skirt and brown loafers. She introduced herself as Deirdre Summers.

Chris knew he sounded nervous. "I'm wondering what time Miss Meyer usually arrives? My son is in her class and his mother will be dropping him off this morning and I—"

The woman appeared confused. "Miss Meyer? Sophia Meyer has taken a leave of absence and will not be back for some time. She left yesterday." Ms. Summers motioned for Chris to follow her into the school. She flicked light switches on as they walked down a hall towards the main office as she spoke:

"I'm surprised you did not know. A note went home to all parents." She looked at Chris as though he were one of those *I'm too busy with work to know about my child's education* type dads. "We're lucky to have such a deeply insightful replacement. He just arrived from Europe." She looked at her watch. "He should be here in about twenty minutes if you'd care to wait." The old woman smiled again. "And who is your son?"

"Michael Thompson."

Her smile disappeared for a second and returned so fast, Chris knew it lacked sincerity.

"Oh, he's a wonderful boy," she said. She turned and looked at papers on her desk.

Something is wrong. The woman is distressed, as if wanting to tell me something . . .

Chris felt his pulse jump. "I'm sorry, but you appeared surprised when I mentioned my son's name."

"Did I?" Deirdre Summers hesitated before looking up again. "Sometimes it is not for us to ask questions, but only to allow our karmic paths to unfold." With a new sense of confidence, her eyes met his in an eerie game of chicken.

Chris needed answers. "What are you talking about?"

A man in his mid-forties and a younger woman arrived and were chatting behind her in the little office. The young woman looked up and Chris saw something in her eyes. Concern, perhaps? She was listening to the conversation.

"You are Michael's father?" Ms. Summers asked.

"Yes, I am Michael's father." He was beginning to feel annoyed with this batty old bird.

"Michael's mother has taken him out of the school for the time being."

"What!" The word came out stronger than he had intended. Ms. Summers' colleagues looked up. "Sorry," Chris said to all three of them. Then, to the old woman: "What do you mean—his mother has taken him out?"

"That is what I mean."

"But I'm his father." Chris heard the panic in his voice. "She cannot just—"

"I'm sorry but your marriage problems are really none of my business." She shuffled papers on her desk and turned to her colleagues.

"Excuse me," Chris said again. Confusion and anger bubbled inside.

The woman ignored him for a moment. She turned, still wearing a plastic smile. "Mr. Thompson," she said, "I'm afraid there really is nothing we can do under the circumstances. I'm sure you understand."

"What circumstances?" He could feel his heart pounding hard.

The woman's eyes widened and the smile disappeared completely. For a moment she appeared to be angry. The smile returned and she spoke softly, as if to a toddler before naptime. "There is nothing I can do. Have a nice day."

"This is ridiculous!"

The man behind Ms. Summers stepped forward. He was big, overweight, wearing a suit and tie. He glared at Chris and folded his arms. "This is a school, sir, and we do not appreciate parents yelling at our staff."

"I'm sorry," Chris said. He felt cold sweat trickle down from his armpits. "It's just that I don't understand what's going on."

Ms. Summers leaned forward. Suddenly, she seemed more sympathetic. "I would not worry about it, Mr. Thompson. Things always have a way of working themselves out." The stupid smile returned to her face and Chris knew it was time to leave.

As he approached his car, he saw parents arriving with their children. Just another day. Then he heard someone call his name.

"Mr. Thompson!" It was the younger woman from the office. She hustled over and stood beside him in the gravel parking lot, looking perplexed. "I . . . heard some of what you were saying in there." She motioned to the school.

Chris knew she was carefully searching for something to say and he decided to help. "Please, just tell me what you know."

The woman sighed. "We do good work here at the school. I hope you know that."

"I don't know what to think," Chris said. "Mike has disappeared with my wife—and perhaps his teacher."

The woman bit her bottom lip and studied him carefully. "I should not really say this but—"

"Please," Chris interrupted. "If you know where my son is, I deserve to know."

"It's just that . . . some of us have never been fond of Sophia Meyer."

"Really? And why is that?"

"As we work with Anthroposophy in our lives as Waldorf teachers, some of us think Sophia has . . . well, misinterpreted much of what that actually means."

"But I thought she was an experienced teacher—respected by younger teachers?"

"Please, Mr. Thompson, I don't want to be seen as criticizing her but I think you deserve to know that some of us think Sophia is, well a little . . . unbalanced."

Chris stared at the young woman. "Mentally unbalanced?" He felt his muscles tensing as he spoke. "Where is she now? Where is my son?"

"I'm so sorry. I really don't know. I wish I could help."

The young woman seemed truly troubled by his dilemma. As if sensing his next question, she shook her head. "I really am sorry," she said. "If I hear any news I will phone you immediately." She smiled and frowned awkwardly. "I'm sure things will work out just fine." She turned and joined a group of children as they made their way into the school.

Chris watched her for a moment, and then got into his car and pulled onto the street. His son and wife had left and were with a mentally disturbed teacher. *What the hell was happening?*

2

Ithaca, New York

Detective Mark Julian sat at his desk, sipping his first coffee of the day and talking to a woman on the phone. She was upset that nothing had happened since her husband was killed six weeks ago in a parking lot and "nobody is doing a damn thing to avenge his death!"

Mark would usually let people vent for a minute before explaining staff shortages, work schedules, etc., and then he would launch his missile: "Lots of work has gone into this case but we cannot seem to collect enough evidence. Are you sure there is not something else you can tell us?" *Put the ball back in her court.* "After all, we're on the same team here." And then he would politely say good-bye and get back to work. Fact was, Mark had spent many unpaid overtime hours on that very case. Another senseless murder and not enough resources to find the killer.

He noticed a phone line blinking as he tossed the ball back into the woman's court and ended the conversation. He took the new call.

"Detective Julian—homicide."

"Hey Mark, how ya doing?" It was a cop he had worked with last year.

"What's up?" Mark asked.

"You will not believe what I'm looking at right now."

"Try me."

"Dead people. You gotta see this, Mark. Holy shit. You gotta see this."

Twenty-five minutes later Mark Julian stood in the middle of the horrific crime scene. He looked up to see something bloody nailed to the far corner of the ceiling. Then he looked at the body at his feet. Professor Richardson's body was missing a left ear. Two cops stood by the bed and were looking at the ceiling. The medical examiner was already there, bending over the bodies and shaking his head. Mark made his way down the hall and stepped into another bedroom.

He saw a young female forensic photographer. She held a tissue to her nose and her eyes apologized for breaking the cardinal rule—the one that dealt with keeping emotions in check while at a crime scene. She steadied her camera over the body of a teenage girl on the floor. There was lots of blood. The girl's once pretty young head rested at a weird angle from her neck. Her larynx was intact and both ears still belonged to the bloodied head. Some consolation.

"The bastard strikes again," Mark said.

The photographer looked at him. "Identical scene in the next bedroom," she said. "They were sisters. One year apart in age, I was told." She took a deep breath, trying to steady her frayed nerves for the photographs. *Click. Click. Click.*

3

Pinedale, Oregon

As he was driving home from the Waldorf School, Chris felt small and alone. He noticed that his knuckles were white on the steering wheel. Guilt overwhelmed his senses and caused a flood of questions to flow through his tired mind.

Why did I not see this coming? What happened to my marriage—to my family?

Sitting with his laptop and a notepad at his kitchen table, Chris sipped on a hot café latte. He stared pensively at the frothy drink. It was two years ago at Christmas that his wife had given him a fancy coffee machine, along with a warm hug and a Christmas kiss. They had been together for fifteen years. Now she had disappeared with his son. It felt like a bad dream. At least the coffee smelled and tasted good; he appreciated the caffeine buzz after a nearly sleepless night.

He wanted to find someone to listen to him scream at the injustice of what had happened, but he knew his priority needed to be finding his wife and son. Still, a friend would be helpful. For the past many years, however, his work and family had replaced his old friends. He tried to think of someone to contact, someone who might understand, someone to offer advice . . . or at least a shoulder to cry on.

He came up blank.

The only face that finally came to mind was that of his sister, Kate. But they barely spoke these days. It would be an understatement to suggest that Kate and his wife did not get along. The two women despised each other. Although she lived not far away in Portland, Kate never came to visit. She thought the world of Mike and would always send gifts on birthdays. But shortly after Mike started at the Waldorf School, Serena had insisted that Chris's sister stay out of the family's life.

Chris had pleaded with her and tried to get his sister to be more polite. But when Serena called Kate a boorish tomboy and Kate responded by calling Serena a spoiled New Age flake, things fell apart completely. That was during Christmas dinner four years ago. Kate was outspoken and extremely honest—to the point of finding fault with almost every facet of Serena's life. Not that those faults were not present, but Kate did not understand the concept of "tact." The two women were polar opposites and the real victim of their rivalry was Mike.

Chris remembered pre-Waldorf days when Kate would take Mike to the park and chase him around the playground. Kate-the-Grizzly-Bear and Mike the helpless little camper fleeing for his life and laughing until he cried when she caught him. Kate always found those special "tickle spots" under his arms.

Chris smiled at the memory and found himself tapping his sister's number into his phone. He desperately needed to talk and Kate seemed to be his best bet. He left a brief message on her answering machine and then thought of how he could spend his time wisely.

He was sure Serena and Mike were with Sophia Meyer. He knew that Miss Meyer was a dedicated Waldorf teacher and he also knew that his wife had become enamored with everything Waldorf. The founding philosophy of Waldorf was called *Anthroposophy*. He'd been told that word simply meant *Wisdom of Man*.

He stared at the Google homepage on his laptop. Snippets of conversations slowly made their way to the forefront of his mind—parent meetings at the school, things his wife had told him about Miss Meyer, words that were used to describe Mike's school work.

He knew that both women believed in the need for Mike to excel at all Waldorf disciplines. Chris thought he should try to learn more about what his son had been doing at the school. He typed into his computer's search engine: "eurythmy and form drawings and Waldorf education." The search yielded over two thousand results. He also knew that Mike had been doing wet-on-wet paintings for years at Waldorf—a watercolor technique involving special paints and paper. Google came up with more than eight thousand results. Clearly, he would need to refine his search. He finished his coffee and tried a few more searches—with similar results. He clicked on a few links but soon realized the futility of the exercise.

He thought again of his son. Where had they taken him? On a frustrated whim, Chris went back to the Google homepage and typed, "Problem with Waldorf." He scanned the first few results until he came to a link that piqued his interest. He read:

> Does your child's Waldorf School seem more like a religious seminary? Concerned about your child's Waldorf education? What is Anthroposophy? Has Waldorf affected your marriage? You are not alone. Visit one of the Waldorf Critical websites and discover what lies beneath the surface of Waldorf education.

This sounded interesting—alarmist perhaps, but certainly worth a look. He clicked around a few different websites. Two hours later Chris sat back in his chair and felt like the shocked and bitterly disappointed child who has just discovered that there really is no Santa Claus.

He felt stunned at his ignorance. Chris knew the many wonderful qualities of Waldorf education—and there were many—but he had been unaware of the deeply esoteric foundation of his child's school. He learned that many people described Waldorf and its founding philosophy as "cult-like."

In two short hours, Chris discovered that many Waldorf teachers are devout Anthroposophists who truly believe in their karmic mission to work with the souls and spirits of children as they incarnate. They accomplish this task by connecting spiritually with children, who they are convinced, have chosen them as spiritual guides from a pre-earthly existence. Waldorf teacher training, he learned, is full of lessons dealing with *soul* and *karma* and *destiny* and *reincarnation*. Teachers believe they have a special karmic connection with the souls of children in their care.

Although Waldorf schools supply parents with plenty of wonderful quotes by and about Rudolf Steiner, the founder of Waldorf education, Chris now discovered more pronouncements Steiner had made to the first Waldorf teachers under his tutelage—quotes still taken as gospel truth by Waldorf teachers today:

> We can accomplish our work only if we do not see it as simply a matter of intellect or feeling, but in the highest sense, as a moral spiritual task. Therefore, you will understand why, as we begin this work today, we first reflect on the connection we wish to create from the very beginning between our activity and the spiritual worlds. Thus, we wish to begin our preparation by first reflecting upon how we connect with the spiritual powers in whose service and in whose name each one of us must work.

Among the faculty, we must certainly carry within us the knowledge that we are not here for our own sakes, but to carry out the
divine cosmic plan. We should always remember that when we do
something, we are actually carrying out the intentions of the gods,
that we are, in a certain sense, the means by which that streaming
down from above will go out into the world.

You will have to take over children for their education and instruc-
tion—children who will have received already (as you must remember) the education, or mis-education given them by their
parents.

Chris learned that although the schools referred to Rudolf Steiner as a
"philosopher," or a "scientist," he was more deeply connected to occultism
than philosophy or science. The man had never been a parent, had no formal
teacher training and had spent very little time with children. Surprisingly,
however, Chris discovered that Waldorf teacher training is based almost
entirely on the beliefs of this self-professed clairvoyant. Waldorf teachers in
training had to read Steiner—lots of Steiner. Required reading included
books like *Knowledge of the Higher Worlds and Its Attainment, Occult Science,
Reincarnation and Karma, Manifestations of Karma, and The Spiritual Hierarchies.*

Chris warmed up leftover soup and sat back at his kitchen table, staring at
the laptop. He had known there was a spiritual element to Waldorf education, but he'd been given very innocent explanations about what that en-
tailed. Nobody had said anything about reincarnation or spiritual hierarchies.
He realized now that he had always felt uncomfortable with the lack of
books—especially textbooks in the school. He remembered his concerns
about reading and writing being discouraged for younger children. Just what
had his son been learning and why had Serena taken him away?

When Mike was a toddler and Chris and Serena began to think about his
education, the young couple had been excited to discover the gentle Waldorf
Island in the turbulent sea of pop culture, junk food vending machines and
cookie-cutter academics of conventional education. They were told Waldorf
was an arts-based school with lots of wooden toys and crafts and outdoor
playtime for children. They had wanted Mike to learn slowly, naturally, and
Waldorf had seemed like the perfect fit. And in some ways it was a good fit.

Chris finished his soup and stared through the kitchen window at the line of poplar trees that bordered his property, watching them sway in the cool September wind. Had he been duped? Had his wife fallen into some sort of weird cult? Is that why she had left him and taken their son? He remembered various comments and concerns of other Waldorf parents over the years. Many families had pulled their children from the school out of frustration and unanswered questions. But there were always new families arriving.

Chris recalled the excitement of Mike's first day in grade one. He remembered meeting Miss Meyer, thinking it odd that Waldorf teachers stay with the same group of students for eight years, but also feeling grateful that the woman seemed kind, always shaking hands and smiling and speaking quietly to the children as they ran and jumped and played in the woods beside the school.

He remembered betting his wife that Miss Meyer must have lived in a hippy commune in the seventies or eighties, with her long cotton dresses and bulky plain blouses, wool socks and sandals. Serena had laughed at the suggestion and they ordered pizza for dinner that night and ate Haagen Dazs for dessert and watched hockey on TV. Even Serena had cheered when the Portland Winter Hawks scored the winning goal in overtime.

Those days had long since passed. He could not remember the last time they had eaten pizza for dinner, let alone watched anything on TV. Dinners were good but always very healthy—including certain grains that needed to be served on certain days of the week, as per "Steiner's indications." Chris had not understood Serena's strange explanation but he knew it had something to do with Anthroposophy.

Chris looked down at his laptop. There was an email address on one of the info-packed Waldorf critical websites, where people could send questions to volunteers with expertise in Anthroposophy and other "cult-like" organizations. Questions could be submitted anonymously and would be kept confidential.

Almost unconsciously, Chris began writing his question, oblivious to the fact that he was actually spilling his guts in an email to a total stranger. His anonymous "question" included his feelings of guilt and stupidity for allowing this situation to happen. He told of the distance between himself and his wife since she had drifted deeper into Waldorf and Anthroposophy, how frustrated he had been for a couple of years now and how unable (or unwilling?) he was to communicate with his wife. He went so far as to write about the complete lack of intimacy between them for more than a year. Before he could change his mind he signed it, "Sad Dad" and pushed *send*.

He sat for twenty minutes, lost in thought, staring at the trees in the wind until the ping of his laptop told of an email received:

> Hi Sad Dad,
>
> I'm sorry to hear of your current dilemma. Although your case is extreme, we've seen many relationship problems where one spouse falls hard for the spiritual movement and the other feels confused, angry, and hurt. Unfortunately, Waldorf promoters often neglect to inform parents of the esoteric foundation of the "philosophy" and you are certainly not the first parent to feel duped or confused. The movement's PR can feel disingenuous and misleading after the fact and it often takes time for parents to realize the fit for their families might not be right. Some schools have excellent teachers, however, and are less Anthroposophic and/or more open than others.
>
> There is tremendous potential for Waldorf education but parents are often concerned when their children seem to drift away from reality. This is not what they signed up and paid for. If the movement is to truly "move" in a positive direction, the leadership will need to clearly explain the esoteric foundation to parents and learn to resolve the obvious problems associated with spiritual and racial hierarchies. I'll attach a list of reading material and websites that might help you understand the foundation of Anthroposophy and Waldorf education. Best of luck.

Chris opened the attachment and counted references to seventeen books and twenty-three websites. *Spiritual and racial hierarchies?* He walked to the living room and stretched out on the couch. He could not remember the last time he'd cried. It was probably years ago when his parents had died. The car crash had happened when his wife was pregnant with Mike.

He thought again of his son. Tears flowed. The pent-up frustration and resentment from the past couple of years exploded with every heavy heartbeat. He felt sad, alone and completely helpless.

4

Dornach, Switzerland

Karl Heisman was in his element. As a child, his family had moved back and forth between Austria, Germany and Switzerland. As an adult, he called the little town of Dornach home. His favorite place in Dornach was the attic of a small house on the hill overlooking the valley. The house had been in his family for generations. He had accomplished great things in that attic—things most people would never begin to understand.

A cool wind swept down from the Jura Mountains as Karl lit two candles and read favorite selections from his grandfather's diaries (translated from the original German):

> November 13, 1937 Tübingen – Difficult times and although we have sympathizers within the Party, trust issues continue to plague the Anthroposophical Movement. Good news is the young Gotthold Hegele continues to have influence as the head of the Office of Political Education of the National Socialist Student League. I have no doubt that Gotthold will be a fine physician in the near future.

> December 22, 1941 Berlin – It is increasingly difficult to accomplish our spiritual work these days. There was good news, however, from Franz Lippert. He was granted his wish to work in Herr Himmler's biodynamic plantation at Dachau.

> April 3, 1944 Berlin – I heard from my friend, Georg Halbe today. It seems his work with the Party has moved him from the Nazi journal, Odal, to the Ministry for the Occupied Eastern Territories to now working with Herr Goebbels and the Propaganda Ministry.

As was his routine, Karl continued to read from the treasured memories of his grandfather in the comfort of the special little office in the attic. When he was finished, he blew out the candles and sat alone in the dark, breathing slowly and listening to the gusting wind outside. *Soon*, he thought. *Everything is unfolding.* Karl smiled. *Soon.*

5

Leaving Pinedale, Oregon

Mike felt frustrated as he spoke to his mother. "I still don't get it," he said. "Why did we sleep at Miss Meyer's apartment last night and why can't dad come with us now? He never even said good-bye. Why not? Why is Miss Meyer coming with us and why—?"

"So many questions," his mother said. "Why do you ask so many questions?" She smiled and held his hand.

Mike's mom had developed the annoying habit lately of answering questions with questions, which meant his questions were never answered. This same technique was used by his teacher, Miss Meyer, and it made all the kids at school angry. Of course they would never tell anyone they were angry. They had learned to respect the authority of their teacher.

Although Mike felt confused, he had to admit it was pretty cool to be sitting in an airplane, zipping through the clouds and seeing tiny buildings below from time to time through the window. He'd never been in a plane before and this was certainly more exciting than going to school. Luckily, he got to sit by the window. His mother sat beside him and beside her was Miss Meyer.

His teacher sat quietly reading a book. Mike looked at his mother. She was holding a book but she was not reading. He looked at the book cover—something about *reincarnation*. Whatever that meant. His mother was smiling, occasionally leaning across him to look out the window, squeezing his hand gently from time to time. And she sighed a lot.

As time passed, the novelty wore off and boredom set in. The flight attendant asked Mike if he'd like something to read—a comic book or a MAD magazine perhaps? His eyes lit up until his mother answered for him, thanking the woman but insisting that Mike was just fine. Mike began to protest but knew it would not further his chances of getting some comics.

His mother reached into her canvas bag and pulled out some thick blank paper and beeswax crayons. "Why don't you do some form drawings, Mik-eye-ell? It will help to pass the time."

"No thanks." He turned his head, peered at the clouds, and blinked away the tears that wanted to escape from tired eyes.

Mike's mom told him a few times that he was so lucky to be going on a surprise holiday to Europe and that he really should thank his lucky stars because he was the *chosen one* from the whole school, the whole city, state and even country. It seems there had been some sort of secret contest he didn't know about, and he was selected to accompany his mother and Miss Meyer on a free holiday.

Mike stared again out the window. Another hour passed and lunch was served. His vegetarian omelet looked better than it tasted. After lunch, Mike used the tiny washroom, returned to his seat and continued to stare aimlessly out the window. He felt very much like the teacher's pet. He hoped his dad would join them soon.

6

Ithaca, New York

Professor Paul Sung sat at his office desk and picked up his phone. "Paul Sung."

"Professor, this is Detective Julian—Mark Julian."

"Hello detective. How goes the investigation?"

"I'm afraid I have bad news. Your colleague Bob Richardson has been killed."

Paul was stunned. "Killed as in murdered?" He could hear the angst in his own voice.

"I'm afraid so. I'm sorry to have to tell you." Deep breath. "His wife and children were also murdered."

Paul felt his stomach turn. He closed his eyes and pictured Bob's wife in his mind. He'd only met her once at a party. He'd never met the kids but he knew they were a close family. The sick feeling swelled in his gut. *Bob and his family—dead?* "How? When?"

"Last night."

Paul suddenly thought of Greg Matheson. "Please don't tell me it was the same guy as . . . ?"

"I can't say much right now. I'm phoning to give you the news and I have a suggestion for you, as well."

"What's that?" Paul's voice was shaky.

"Is there somewhere else you can stay? I think it would be safer for you not to live at home for the next little while. Just a precaution, you understand."

"You think I could be next?"

"It's always best to err on the side of caution."

Paul thanked the detective and hung up the phone. His knees felt weak. He tried to push the image of Bob's dead body from his mind. His next thoughts were of the detective's warning.

He stood by the window. Rain pounded the courtyard below. The occasional student scurried across the stone path between flowerbeds, holding a book or a bag overhead as a makeshift umbrella. Paul was supposed to teach a class that afternoon but he was in no mood to discuss the work of Goethe and Schilling. He would need some time to think, time to mourn and consider what Detective Julian had just told him:

Is there somewhere else you can stay?

Should he check into a hotel? He could stay at the Statler on campus; he'd spent a night there once after drinking too much at a faculty party. Not cheap but very comfortable—and probably safe. Should he ask to stay at a colleague's house? A few names flipped through his head until he realized he might be putting their lives in danger by simply being with them.

Hi, a madman might be trying to kill me and nail my larynx to the ceiling—can I stay with you for a while?

Fifteen minutes later, Paul was pulling into the driveway of his neat little house just outside the university district. He had lived alone in that house for over ten years and was proud he had managed to keep it looking good after his wife left. He had decided to pick up a few things from home and check into the Statler. Better to err on the side of caution, Mark Julian had said.

Not unlike other university towns, Ithaca had a reputation of being a great place to live and work. In fact, it had recently won accolades for *quality of life* from a prestigious magazine. Ithaca, it seemed, was home to an enlightened citizenry. How journalists decided such things was a mystery to Paul but there was no denying the fact that Ithaca *was* a good place to live. The thought of a madman wandering the streets at night, planning and committing horrible murders, was hard to digest.

Paul sat in his car in the driveway. He looked up and down the tree-lined street and saw perfect little houses with nice little gardens readying themselves for fall and then the cold of winter. Three doors down, a man raked leaves into piles as a small dog danced at his feet. It *was* a good place to live.

He glanced at the front door to his house and felt his blood turn to ice. The door was open. His immediate reaction was to get the hell out of his car and run away fast, but his rational mind compelled him to start the engine and back out of the driveway. He would use his cell phone to call Detective Julian and then drive to the police station where he would be protected. Maybe the police would trap the murderer in Paul's house. Maybe—

"Paul!"

He recognized the voice and stopped his car. He saw Detective Mark Julian standing by the door of his house. The detective walked towards him.

"Paul," he said again. "Sorry, it looks like I scared the hell out of you."

Paul stepped out of his car. "You did." His heart was slowly returning to its normal beat. He looked again at the front door of the house. "Mind telling me what you're doing here?"

The man up the street with the rake and the dog was staring at them.

"Let's go inside," the detective said.

As they entered the house, the detective continued speaking. "After I spoke with you on the phone I wondered if the killer might be brave enough to pay you a visit in broad daylight. So I had one of my guys stop by and sure enough, your front door was open. I came right over. We had a look inside but nobody is here."

"But he *was* here?" Paul asked. "You're sure it was him?" His heart zipped back up to high speed. He noticed the holster and handgun under the detective's black leather jacket.

"I think so," Mark said. They were in the living room now, Paul's eyes surveying the mess. A bookshelf was on the floor, books and papers scattered everywhere. "He must have spent quite some time in here going through your stuff." They walked into Paul's little office just off the kitchen. "Notice anything missing?"

"I don't know," Paul said. "What a mess." The room looked as if a tornado had attacked; desk drawers had been removed and emptied, compact discs were everywhere, even a couple of his favorite Native American prints lay on the floor, shards of glass surrounding the cracked frames. He looked at the detective. "I don't know what this guy wants."

"Let's try to figure it out," Mark said.

Paul thought about his dead colleague. Bob and his family had been murdered by someone who was now looking for him. It seemed surreal, like something from a nightmare.

"I'd really appreciate it if you could try to identify anything that is missing," Mark said. "I doubt the killer will return soon. But just in case, we have an unmarked car in the lane and another vehicle up the street. We're safe."

Paul slumped into his old office chair. This was his home and he felt terribly violated, not to mention frightened. The image of his larynx nailed to the ceiling entered his mind, despite the reassuring words from the detective. Sure, his life had not been fulfilling lately, but this was not the sort of excitement he had been looking for.

7

Ithaca, New York

Mark Julian watched the professor shuffling through papers on his desk. "I appreciate your help," he said. "Can you check your computer to see if anyone was in there?"

Paul discovered that twenty-three files had been accessed since he left that morning. "That's strange," he said. He drummed fingers on his old oak desk, and then opened a few of the files, scanning their contents.

Mark stood behind him and looked over his shoulder. "What have you got?"

Paul continued to open and close recently viewed files. "I have not looked at these for years." *Click*. "Most of them are research notes for my book."

"Yeah, I've been reading your book," Mark said, neglecting to add that he had needed beer to help motivate his interest in the tome.

As if reading his mind, Paul said, "It's pretty dry academia and full of obscure occult references. Why the hell would anyone be interested in my old research papers? It's basically notes to myself from a long time ago, but someone has spent time going through all this old material on my computer. Why not just buy the book? Or get it from a university library?"

Mark opened a foldout chair and sat beside Paul, trying to see which files were appearing on the screen. "Tell me," he said, "is there anything there that has to do with Greg Matheson or his trip to Europe? You see where I'm going?"

"A connection," Paul answered. "I know Greg read my book years ago because he was in my class. He would always ask questions about my research. So, where is the connection?"

More files opened as both men watched the monitor. "He was looking for something," Mark said. "We know that. Let's assume the guy has already read your book, but he wants something more and he thinks Greg has it.

Then he moves on to Greg's current teacher, Bob Richardson, and still comes up empty. Then he comes to you—at least to your home." He paused. "There must be a connection here somewhere, Paul. What is this guy willing to kill for?"

Mark noticed a frown on the professor's face as he studied a document on his monitor. "Important?" he asked.

"These notes are from over eleven years ago. This particular document deals with Anthroposophy and Rudolf Steiner's connection to Freemasonry. I used it in a course I prepared for graduate students. It was a onetime course, discarded into the trash bin of academia due to its obscure subject."

"But someone broke into your house and read it today. Why?"

"I don't know. I was disappointed that the course was dropped. It was a good topic for serious students of esoteric movements."

"Like Greg Matheson?"

"That's right. In fact, I tried to incorporate the material into a chapter in my book, but the publisher already thought the book was too long and that chapter was killed prior to publication."

Mark was reading over Paul's shoulder. He was about to ask a question when the professor spoke.

"Maybe . . ."

"Maybe what?"

A moment of silence as Paul read from the monitor. "Sorry," he said. "It's been a while since I've looked at this." He cleared his throat. "I spent a few years researching material for my book, knowing it would only be read by a handful or two of graduate students and a few hundred historians, at best. As you might have come to realize, my book is not exactly an easy read."

Mark refrained from agreeing. "So, why is this important to our killer?"

Paul continued: "The birth of what we commonly call the New Age movement is generally accepted to have happened during the time of Helena Blavatsky and her Theosophy movement in the 1870s. At that time—as is still the case today—there was a yearning in the West for something other than conventional religion. There were many different esoteric groups in Europe and some made their way to North America, all ostensibly seeking the same thing. They were often at odds with each other and their beliefs were certainly counter to those of conventional religions.

"Blavatsky was labeled a charlatan by some and a gifted mystic by others. Her claim to fame was her magnum opus, called *The Secret Doctrine*, basically her version of the meaning of life. *The Secret Doctrine* is still held in high esteem by Theosophists today."

"And what does this have to do with our killer?"

"Occultists speak in symbols. I suspect the removal of larynxes and ears is symbolic."

"Meaning?" Mark asked.

"The murderer might believe he is working with what he sees as the essence or what they call the *impulse* of Anthroposophy. I don't know the ultimate goal, but by removing the victim's larynx, our suspect is accomplishing two symbolic tasks. One, the missing larynx means the person can no longer speak. Perhaps someone was afraid Greg and Bob had said—or were about to say—too much."

"But the victims are already dead," Mark said. "Who cares if the larynx is removed?"

"Symbology," Paul said. "It's very important. Life and death of the body are not as important as the symbology connected to the life and death. And secondly, without the larynx the victim will not be able to—symbolically—reproduce in the future."

"I'm lost, Professor."

"Steiner believed the larynx will be the organ of reproduction in the future." He paused. "Occultists work with symbols and with opposites—light and dark and good and evil, and so on. Anthroposophists believe in two such spirits, for example: the influence of Ahriman represents darkness while Lucifer is the light."

"Lucifer?" Mark said. "As in the devil?"

"No. Same name but different version, so to speak. This is not the same Lucifer Christians often mistake for the devil." Paul pushed his chair back from the desk and stretched his legs. "Symbology might be the clue to solving the murders. The larynx is an internal organ so it is taken out—after death the internal organ appears outside of the body. The ears—external organs—are pushed back inside the body and as ears deal not only with hearing but with morality—according to Anthroposophy—our murderer places the ear into what would be considered an immoral place. Thus, the immoral victim can no longer hear. Hear no evil, speak no evil."

Mark tried to understand this nonsense. He shook his head and sighed. "So, this Steiner character was mentally unbalanced?"

Paul smiled. "No. He was an occultist. When one studies or is immersed in esoteric disciplines, it becomes easier to appreciate them. In some ways,

Steiner was a genius. He would never have supported murder. This killer is a madman."

Mark raised an eyebrow, wondering how the professor could be interested in making a career of studying and teaching gibberish. "So you think we're looking for someone who admires Steiner and Anthroposophy?"

"I would not be surprised." Paul pulled his chair up to face the monitor. "But he would be despised by his peers if they were to discover his actions. Anthroposophy has nothing to do with killing people."

Paul stared into his computer monitor. "But I'm missing something and I think it has to do with the future. Perhaps this is the angle Greg was taking in his research." He opened another file and read quickly. "I'll need to see that unpublished chapter again. Rudolf Steiner became the head of the German Theosophical Society in 1902 and he also developed an interest in Freemasonry around that time. Anthroposophists are often uncomfortable with that part of their movement's history."

"And you think Greg Matheson might have asked a few too many questions and got himself killed?"

"Maybe. I remember Greg asking me about Steiner's connection with Freemasonry when he took my course years ago. He was fascinated with Steiner's views on the future of humanity. I shared some of my research with him—including the chapter that never made it into the book."

"Do you have a copy of that chapter?" Mark asked.

"Probably," Paul said. "It's not in this computer but I remember emailing the file to Greg last year after he kept bugging me about it. It should be at my university office." He looked outside as rain began spattering the windows. "I don't know what is in that unpublished chapter that someone might kill for."

Mark folded his chair and leaned it against a wall. "Let's go and find out," he said. "But you cannot come back here for a while. I hope you realize that."

"I'll check into the Statler Hotel on campus."

"Good. I'll place someone there to keep an eye on you."

Mark waited for the professor to fill a suitcase. They stopped briefly by the front door on their way out of the house. Mark noticed Paul looking at the broken lock.

"A locksmith will be here shortly," Mark said. "And we'll continue to watch the house in case he returns." He motioned to a parked van half a block up the street. "They'll take care of your house. And they'll be delighted if this guy returns. What he did to those people—the kids and all." He paused. "My guys would just love to meet him."

8

Ithaca, New York

Officer Stan Noles was bored. What kind of an assignment was this, anyway? Sure, he'd only been with the Ithaca police force for eighteen months but sitting in a professor's office at Cornell for an entire shift was not what he had signed up for. Why not let the campus cops do this job? He pulled back the curtains and looked outside, hoping to see something more interesting than the four walls of the office.

Stan was supposed to be watching for possible intruders. He'd been told it had something to do with the surgical murders but he knew those murders had happened late at night. What could happen at a busy university building in the middle of the day?

Just my luck, he thought, it's raining outside and no lovely young women to watch in the courtyard. He considered turning the computer on and playing a game of backgammon online, but he knew that would not go over well with Detective Julian, if his boss arrived early.

He walked to the door and looked up and down the hallway. A few people strolled in and out of offices and he could hear chatter and the occasional chuckle. Suddenly, the smell of fresh coffee wafted up the hall from the little café near the library. Maybe he could dash out for a coffee. His orders had been specific: Stay in the office and phone Detective Julian to report anything unusual. Still, the café was not far and he could be back in less than a minute.

As he stood in the hall outside Paul Sung's office, Stan Noles' silent prayers were answered. A young campus police officer was walking towards him.

"Hey buddy, how's it going?" Stan asked.

The young man looked up and smiled. He appeared to be in his early twenties, short, thin and he wore thick glasses. His uniform was too big. "Doing good, how are you?"

"Listen," Stan said, "can you do me a favor and stay here for one minute while I grab a cup of coffee?"

The young man frowned and then smiled. "I guess so," he said. "What are you doing here?"

"Just make sure no crazies get into the office until the prof gets back."

"Not many crazies around here," the young cop said.

"So you don't mind? I'll just be a minute—hey, can I get you something?"

"No, I'm fine thanks." The younger man smiled. "You go ahead. I'll take care of things here."

"Thanks." Stan walked down the hall, looking forward to his first sip of coffee.

The young man stepped into Paul's office and walked to the window. It was raining hard outside and fat raindrops splattered on the glass. He looked down at the courtyard and barely heard the office door close behind him. He turned to see a large man with bushy eyebrows and black-rimmed glasses staring at him. The man was wearing a khaki trench coat.

"Who are you?" the guard asked.

"I work here," the strange man answered. "What are you doing in my office? Please leave now." The voice was deep with a slight German accent.

The young guard had seen Professor Sung a few times around campus and this man was not him. "I'm afraid you've got the wrong office," he said.

It happened with incredible speed. The intruder produced a knife and within a split second had thrown it with such force that it all but disappeared into the young officer's neck. His glasses fell to the floor and his eyes blinked wildly as a shaking hand reached for his cell phone. The hand missed its mark. A gurgling sound came from his mouth and his jaw opened, then closed. Two seconds later he fell and lay beside a pool of his blood on the tile floor.

Officer Stan Noles was surprised to see the door closed when he returned to the office. He had decided to eat a donut in the café while chatting with the cute young brunette behind the counter. He had another donut in one hand and a steaming cup of coffee in the other.

I didn't tell the guy to close himself inside the office.

He balanced the donut on the Styrofoam cup and reached for the door-knob. The door was locked.

This campus cop takes his job seriously. He locked himself in the office.

On a lark, Officer Noles knocked harder and yelled: "Open up, it's the police!" He smiled, thinking the young man might appreciate the joke. There was no response. Then he heard movement inside the office. "Come on, hurry up."

As he heard the door unlock, Stan Noles pushed it with a foot and stepped inside. "Finally," he said, passing his hot coffee from one hand to the other and walking to the desk. He looked around the room but could not see the young officer. The curtains were closed and the office was a mess; book and papers were scattered all over the desk and floor.

"What the hell?" Stan put his coffee on the desk. That's when he noticed the puddle of blood and the body on the floor. The door slammed shut.

He turned and reached for his gun. Too late. A giant man was on him. Stan caught a glimpse of a black glove and a knife. A second later the blade quickly sliced deep into Stan's neck. He fell in a bloody heap and lay beside the other body on the floor.

9

Ithaca, New York

The two men walked from the parking lot into White Hall, Cornell's home of Religious Studies. "I've learned to hate the rain," Paul said. They both shook water from soaked jackets. "When I was younger it didn't bother me much but these days I regret turning down a job offer at the U of Hawaii a few years back."

"Doesn't bother me," Mark said. "At least, not as much as the heat. Unless I'm in the stands with a beer in hand and watching the Yankees, New York summers are too damn humid."

Paul was surprised to find that he enjoyed the detective's company. Perhaps it had to do with feeling safe being with a cop during these troubled times or maybe Mark Julian's life just seemed more exciting than his own? There was something solid about the man. He seemed sincere—genuine. Paul liked that.

As they made their way into the hallway leading to his office, Paul noticed a large man wearing a khaki trench coat walking quickly in the opposite direction. A few students could be seen strolling and talking and the man's presence there would not have seemed out of place if not for his size. He was huge.

"Where the hell is my officer?" Mark pulled at the door to Paul's office. He knocked and knocked again. His voice was sharp and cold. "Hey, open up!" He hammered on the door.

Paul fumbled for his key and slipped it into the lock. "I'm sure it's fine," he said. But he knew something was not right.

The detective pushed the door open. "Damn!" He motioned for Paul to step back. He then put a hand on the gun under his black leather jacket, and swung the door open quickly, drawing the weapon and bursting into the office.

Paul stayed outside, feeling confused. And frightened.

Within thirty minutes the entire building was shut off from the rest of the campus. Yellow police ribbon was everywhere, as were cops. Paul sat on a cushioned bench in the hall. He felt sick to his stomach for the second time that day.

Mark arrived and sat beside him. "How are you doing?"

"Stunned," Paul said.

"Listen, I shouldn't really ask you to check your office—it's a major crime scene and forensics won't be here for twenty minutes—but do you know where you kept that unpublished chapter, the one we were talking about?"

"It's in my desktop computer," Paul said. "It would take me a few minutes to find it."

"And I'll need to know if *he* found it," Mark said. "It's a real mess in there. Not a pretty sight." He looked at Paul, as if waiting for a response.

Paul took a deep breath. "I can check my computer, if you like. I won't disturb anything."

"You sure you're OK?" Mark asked. "I don't want to seem callous but if you puke in there, the forensic guys will be mad as hell at me for contaminating the scene."

Paul took another deep breath and let it out slowly. He'd known death before—once as a witness to a car accident and again at a few funerals—but he had never seen two young men lying in pools of blood. He stood. "I can do this. Let's go."

Five minutes later they emerged from the crime scene with the required file, freshly transferred from Paul's desktop to his BlackBerry. Paul's legs felt like rubber. He sat back down on the bench and tried to stop his heart from exploding through his sweat-drenched shirt.

Mark sat beside him. "So you're sure the guy did not find the chapter?"

"Pretty sure," Paul said. "It was not recently accessed and I doubt he was able to cover his tracks that fast. He didn't try to hide his search history on my home computer, either. My guess is he first looked for hard copies—or he was looking for something else and then started poking around inside my computer. If he didn't know where to look, it would have taken him a while to find it. He probably ran out of time."

"Well, that's the only good news we've had today," Mark said. His cell phone rang; he put it to his ear and scribbled a phone number. "I need to tell some parents that their sons have just been killed in the line of duty." He stood, phone still in hand, and wandered slowly down the hall.

Paul's knees had stopped shaking but he still felt sick. He looked at his BlackBerry and opened the unpublished chapter file, scanning it quickly for a clue to the murders. Not surprisingly, he found nothing of significance; of course, he knew his mind was currently not in the best shape to be searching for a clue to horrible murders. He closed the file and decided to check his email: one from a colleague wanting to borrow a book, another from a student wanting an extension on a term paper and another from someone in Pinedale, Oregon with subject line of: *Urgent - Please Help with Anthroposophy & Waldorf.* Curious, Paul opened that email:

> Dear Dr. Sung,
> Please accept my apology for bothering you but I have read some of your online articles and a few excerpts from your book, The Esoteric Impulse of a New Age, and I desperately need to speak with you. Your name comes up often as a leading authority on Anthroposophy and other esoteric movements. I discovered your email address at Cornell and I hope this finds you now.
>
> Briefly, I am convinced my wife has been brainwashed by at least one unbalanced Anthroposophist and I am very concerned about her and the safety of my son. I believe they are now somewhere in Europe. Although it might sound like a simple domestic dispute, I am convinced my wife is not of right mind and my child could be in danger. I know this all sounds farfetched but please contact me at your earliest convenience as I have a few questions.

Paul saved the man's phone number in his BlackBerry. He had received strange emails in the past—it came with the territory of dealing with occultists and deeply religious people, but this one was unique. And the timing was strange, almost eerie. Murders in Ithaca and a possible abduction in Oregon . . . with Anthroposophy as the common denominator? Until now, nobody had mentioned his book for years. Weird. Paul wished again that he had taken that teaching job in Hawaii.

He saw the detective walking back down the hall, his difficult phone call apparently completed.

"Did you read your file?" Mark asked.

"Quickly," Paul said. "Sorry. I just cannot find a connection between the unpublished chapter and the murders. The chapter, as I already told you, deals mainly with Steiner's interest in Freemasonry. He thought Freemasonry would play an important role in the future of humanity. I know some of that information is not readily available and I had to spend some time in Europe studying Steiner's lectures—" Paul stopped talking and stared at the detective. His face and mind were frozen.

"What is it?" Mark asked.

Paul was lost in thought. "Europe. I spent over a week in Berlin at the *Bundesarchiv*—the German Federal Archives, and a few days of research in Stuttgart, home of the first Waldorf School. Then I took a train to Switzerland—to Dornach, a town near Basel. I spent some time at the Goetheanum."

"The what?" Mark asked.

"The Goethe-a-num," Paul said, carefully pronouncing each syllable. "Based on the German literary giant, Johann Wolfgang von Goethe, it's the headquarters of the General Anthroposophical Society. It's a massive, cement structure with neighboring buildings. The Goetheanum is a fascinating place containing a wealth of information." He paused. "For those who are allowed to access the archives there."

"And you were not allowed access?"

"Yes and no. I have a friend who works there," Paul said. He wondered if *friend* was an accurate description. Benjamin Hirsch was a retired Waldorf teacher from New York who now lived in Dornach. Paul had met him a decade ago and was grateful for more than a few good discussions and debates between them over the years. Although Benjamin seemed to enjoy his company, their conversations often became animated and Paul wondered if theirs was truly a friendship. Benjamin had been a social activist in his youth and believed Anthroposophy had much to offer those seeking a more civil society.

Paul knew that Benjamin had trouble with Steiner's more controversial pronouncements; the foundation of the movement was often the topic of their long discussions. Benjamin seemed to want to cherry-pick Steiner's beliefs, endorsing some while conveniently ignoring others. At the end of their last discussion, Benjamin surprised Paul by admitting that he and other Anthroposophists were, in fact, willing to explore the controversial elements of their spiritual path. That, Paul knew, meant dealing with questions of race.

"Do you think," Paul had asked Benjamin some years ago, "that in exploring those controversial elements, Anthropsophists would also be helping

Waldorf education to move forward?" Benjamin was well aware of the controversy.

His friend said nothing for a moment and then answered thoughtfully: "We need to explain to parents the esoteric impulse of the education and yes, that means discussing everything. Opening up old wounds might drive some families away, but in order for wounds to heal, they must be addressed." Benjamin had said he hoped the healing would begin soon.

Paul thought of that discussion now and how it might relate to current events. "Anthroposophists," he said to the detective, "are generally good-natured—sometimes secretive, but usually quite pleasant. My friend was called away on business during my second day there and as soon as he left, some other Anthroposophists became upset and suggested I leave. Not just leave the library and archives area but leave the grounds, which are usually open to the public. There was a heated argument between various people and in the end I left. I was offered no explanation."

"You think someone was afraid you would discover something you were not supposed to know?"

"I'm not sure," Paul said. "I met my friend a few days later and he was very apologetic. I already knew there were serious divisions within the leadership of the Anthroposophic Society. Apparently, a small group felt that I was not welcome to carry out my research. That incident never occurred to me before now—before the killing started." He looked down at his Black-Berry. "And now I get a strange email from Oregon."

"Say again." Mark raised his eyebrows.

Paul told of the recent email and commented on the strange timing. "Strange indeed," Mark said. "I'll need to check it out. Can you forward me the email?"

Paul agreed. "This is all new to me," he added. "But I suppose I should learn to be a little paranoid."

"Learn to be cautious," Mark said. "What could this email have to do with murders in Ithaca?"

Paul was distant, his mind still mulling over the past few days. "When I read about the missing boy I was reminded of something I wrote in the unpublished chapter—something I had almost forgotten, but it's related to what I was researching at the Goetheanum years ago. It's about reincarnation and a boy—a young boy growing up in India . . ."

The detective's cell phone rang. "I gotta go," he said. "I'll assign a uniform to escort you to your hotel. He'll hang around for a while and we'll have a plainclothes cop nearby, as well. I'm afraid we'll need to close this area of the university tonight and tomorrow."

"OK," Paul said. He suddenly felt something he had not experienced since childhood. Fear.

"You all right?" Mark asked. "You don't look well."

"I'm fine," Paul said, not feeling at all fine. "There are pieces to this puzzle and I need to find them." He tried to push away the fear and force a smile. "I appreciate your help."

"Likewise. I'll be in touch tomorrow." Mark walked back into the crime scene while Dr. Paul Sung was led to a waiting police car that drove him to his new home away from home at the Statler Hotel.

Paul's stomach was queasy but his mind was alert. He would need to go over his notes again to satisfy his curiosity. The strange email from Oregon suddenly seemed very important.

10

Pinedale, Oregon

I t was the worst time of Chris Thompson's life. Although she was not fond of computers, Chris learned that his wife had definitely spent some time on their laptop, looking at various airline websites. Chris used the computer's cookies to discover that Serena had purchased three tickets to Zurich and billed them to a credit card he'd never heard of before.

Sophia Meyer's card, perhaps?

His sister sat across the kitchen table, staring at his laptop, reading quickly and biting into a peanut butter and banana sandwich. She swallowed, took a long swig from a bottle of guava juice, burped and looked at her brother.

"This is un-fucking believable," Kate said. "I knew Serena was a New Age nut but this . . ." She shook her head and continued to read. "I mean, who would have guessed that Waldorf schools are fronts for a wacko cult?"

"That's not entirely accurate," Chris said. It felt good to share his troubles with someone but he'd almost forgotten his sister's habit of over-simplifying things. He had not forgotten, however, her penchant for profanity.

She downed the last of her juice and looked at her brother. "Did you see the Waldorf teachers reading list? It has nothing to do with education, Chris. It's New Age bullshit. I'll bet most parents have no idea what goes on in those classrooms."

Chris pulled a glass from the cupboard and filled it with water. He was not thirsty but he didn't feel like meeting his sister's eyes. Now was not the time for him to espouse the virtues of Waldorf education. Mike had enjoyed many school activities—and he was not the type of kid who would thrive in a more conventional academic environment. Chris knew there were lots of positives, but there was no mistaking the hidden stuff he had learned about recently—the esoteric underpinnings of the school. He looked at his sister. Was she generalizing or was she partially correct with her brazen judgment? In either case, the guilt and swirling emotions that bubbled up in him now would appear as a weakness to his sister. She had never thought highly of weak people.

Kate was honest and blunt and rubbed most people the wrong way. She was also a survivor. Chris knew she had been sexually abused by their uncle when she was twelve years old. Sadly, the family secret was never really a "secret." He knew that she had confided in her parents and their stupid response had been to pretend the abuse was just a misunderstanding. Nobody ever spoke about it.

Kate had been rebellious as a teen; she quit high school, globetrotted with a backpack, returned to Oregon, got busted for smoking pot—probably because she swore at the cop and told him to "have a toke, tight ass." She was tall, slim, blond, a cute forty-three years old and in excellent shape. Despite hopping from job to job for most of her adult life, she had managed to excel at three or four martial arts. Chris could not remember which ones.

She finished her sandwich and pushed the laptop away. "So, you think they are in Switzerland, right?"

"Yes, and they must have flown there for a reason," Chris said. "That's where Anthroposophists have their world headquarters." He stared out the window, blinked away tears and cleared his throat. "But I guess they could be anywhere in Europe." He rubbed a hand across the back of his neck and stared at his sister.

"So let's go," Kate said.

"Let's go? As in let's go to Europe?"

"Damn right," Kate said. "Mike has been taken to Europe without your knowledge and I know you told me no law has been broken, but Mike is there and we gotta get him back." She tapped the table. "Seems to me it's that simple."

Chris was stunned. "Kate, I —" He paused, not wanting to sound weak *(god, this brought back memories)*. "I have not seen you for over a year and here you are willing to hop on a plane and look for Mike with me? What about work? What about your life? I don't even know what you're doing these days."

"Between jobs." She smiled. "Old habits die hard."

He turned and looked outside again. "I should have kept in touch better but —"

"But your nutty wife made it impossible. Hey—shit happens. I always hoped things would improve so I could see Mike once in a while. And you. Unfortunately, Serena was never squished by a bus and now she's totally flipped out and Mike is gone. You're my brother and Mike is my nephew. I say let's go bring him back."

Chris smiled and felt like giving Kate an appreciative hug but he decided against it. Before he could think of the logistics involved in taking off to Europe, he said, "Thanks Kate. I really appreciate your support."

Kate had no time to respond. The phone rang and Chris answered.

"This is Paul Sung from Cornell University. Is that Chris Thompson?"

Chris felt his pulse skyrocket. He glanced at his sister. "Yes, this is Chris. Thanks very much for getting back to me. Listen, I know this sounds crazy and I—"

"No, it does not sound crazy," Paul said. "Any word on your son?"

"No. Doctor Sung, I—"

"Please, call me Paul."

"Thanks. I have some questions if you have a few minutes." He grabbed a notepad. "I read something about Steiner's involvement with Theosophy. I was wondering about the incident with —"

"I'd better stop you there," Paul said. "I think I know where you're going with this and I am sure the conversation will be more useful in person."

"In person? But you're in New York and I'm in Oregon." Chris's mind was a hurricane of questions.

"Why don't you stop here on your way to Europe?"

Chris could not contain his surprise. "How on earth do you know my plans?"

"That's what I would do if I were you. In fact, I'd be booking a flight right now. I suggest you take a plane to Zurich with a brief stopover in New York. I'm at the Statler Hotel on the Cornell campus. You have call display?"

Chris was still confused but somehow he trusted the voice on the phone. It felt reassuring. "Yes."

"So you have my cell number. Call me when you know what time I can expect you. And it might be a good idea not to tell anyone where you're going."

"Dr Sung—Paul," Chris said, "I don't understand. I read some of your online articles but honestly, I never expected that you'd express such an interest in my problem. Don't get me wrong, I'm delighted to have your help, but—"

"Let's just say," Paul said, "we might be able to help each other. We'll talk later, OK?"

"OK. And thanks." He hung up and stared sheepishly at his sister. "Want to stop in New York before we go to Switzerland?"

Kate smiled, stretched both arms across the table and—surprisingly—took one of Chris's hands in hers. She squeezed. "Sure, and then let's go get Mike."

Day Four

1

En Route to Switzerland

Mike slept through the constant vibration of jet engines. The occasional rattling of his seat could not shake away the bad dream.

He was walking down the lane behind his house with his dad, both carrying hockey sticks on their way to win the Stanley Cup, despite the game only involving the two of them playing ball hockey on a cracked tennis court near the park. In the dream they were both wearing full hockey gear and, incredibly, they were also wearing ice skates and gliding over the gravel covering the lane. Suddenly, Mike's dad got stuck in a mud puddle and he began sinking, a strange, confused look appearing on his tired face. "Skate Mike— skate!" his dad yelled. "Go! Go! Go!"

Mike pivoted like a skilled defenseman and tried to skate back to his father. He needed to help him escape from the strange, oozing, sucking mud. "Grab my hockey stick, dad!" he cried. "I'll pull you out!" His dad had sunk up to his waist now and refused to take Mike's stick. His own stick had disappeared beneath the mud.

"Skate Mike—skate!" he yelled again. "Get out of here—now!"

Suddenly, Mike realized they were no longer in the lane behind their house; they were outside his classroom at school. Beside the bushes that covered the window. His dad was still sinking into the mud puddle. He looked in horror as his dad continued to descend, only his neck and head visible now. Mike peeked into the classroom and there they were again—his mom and Miss Meyer. Suddenly, he heard a chorus of voices and he knew it was a group of girls from his school. They were chanting: K-I-S-S-I-N-G!

His dad continued to scream: "Skate Mike—skate! Get away from this place!"

Mike looked back and forth between the classroom and his sinking dad. He was covered in sweat and began to tremble. He felt confused and afraid . . .

"Mik-eye-ell." It was his mother's singsong voice. "Wakey-wakey, sleepy one."

Mike's heart was racing as he opened his eyes. "What!" *It was only a dream.* He looked out the window and felt his pulse slowing down. *It was only a dream.*

Suddenly, Miss Meyer's face was in front of his. Her eyes were wide with excitement. "Welcome to Switzerland, Mik-eye-ell."

They collected their luggage and stood in the large foyer at the Zurich airport. The place looked brand new to Mike—very clean with lots of glass walls. He could hear a steady stream of announcements in a few different languages—including English. People hustled everywhere, some with baggage, most of the men wearing suits and ties.

A few minutes later a man in a gray suit arrived, gave Miss Meyer a polite hug and kissed her on both cheeks. Miss Meyer introduced the man to his mother and then she looked at Mike.

"And this is Mik-eye-ell," she said, still smiling proudly. "This is Mik-eye-ell," she repeated.

"It is such a pleasure to meet you," the man said. He was short, fat and almost bald. He bent down to shake Mike's hand. The man was sweating a lot and the top of his head and his pudgy nose were shining. His face was almost perfectly round and a little mustache twitched as he spoke. "We are so pleased to have you here as our guest. My name is Herr Ackermann." He was grinning from ear to ear. "You would say *Mr. Ackermann* in English but I prefer German." The man seemed really nervous.

Mike politely shook the sweaty hand, and then quickly wiped his hand on his pants. Herr Ackermann smelled like a hockey bag but Mike was glad to have his help loading their luggage into the van.

"It's less than an hour's drive," Herr Ackermann said with a German accent. "When were you last here, Sophia?"

That was the first time Mike had heard anyone address his teacher by her first name.

He looked out the window as they drove. Everything seemed so different. They were on a highway, and the man must have been ignoring the speed limit because they were zooming along at an incredible speed. Outside, he saw farms and small houses and cows grazing in fields, surrounded by huge mountains. Mike stared at those wonderful mountains, most covered in snow at the top, reaching up to touch the clouds. He had never seen such massive mountains. He wondered if they would be able to visit them up close. Maybe he could try to climb one? That would be fun.

Mike only half-listened to the grown-ups talking as they drove; sometimes his mom would practice speaking German and the man would say how good she was doing, but they all knew that his mother's German was not good. Grown-ups were strange that way, Mike thought. They often say things they know are not true.

They turned off the highway at a sign marked *Dornach* and the mountains were much smaller here, more like big rolling hills. They drove up a narrow road beside small brick houses with pretty little gardens. In the distance on a hill, Mike saw a strange-looking building, like a gigantic cement hockey helmet with windows. They made a few turns along the way and ended up driving straight towards the helmet.

Mike had questions about the building but knew they would not be answered. His questions never were. The helmet continued to grow and Mike pressed his face against the van window as they approached. The massive building was unlike anything Mike had seen before. It no longer resembled a hockey helmet—it was more like something from a distant planet in a far away galaxy from Star Wars. Eventually, their van drove to a small parking lot behind the building.

"Come, come, please come," Herr Ackermann said, motioning for the three of them to follow him to the south side entrance. "Your bags will be taken care of, no problem." He smiled and walked quickly, nervously.

"I can't believe we are finally here," Mike's mom said, staring in awe at the cement building as they walked. "It's incredible!" Her voice trembled as she spoke and she pulled a tissue from her purse and wiped her nose. "I'm sorry."

"Kein problem," Herr Ackermann said. "No problem. Under the circumstances, a little emotion is understandable."

Herr Ackermann looked at Mike as they arrived at the front steps. Mike stared up at the vaulted, gray-brown concrete structure with its sweeping arches and odd-shaped windows. Herr Ackermann sighed and smiled. "Mik-eye-ell," he said proudly, "I am so very pleased to welcome you back to the Goetheanum!"

Mike frowned but said nothing. *Welcome me back? I've never been here before.*

Serena finally looked away from the magnificent structure to the sur-rounding gardens. "Where is everyone? All the pictures I've seen showed visitors everywhere."

"Quite right," Herr Ackermann said. "But today is special and we are closed to the public." He bent down and looked closely at Mike. His eyes were wide and his breath smelled bad. "Tell me, Mik-eye-ell, how do you feel? You know this place, ya?"

Miss Meyer put a hand on Mike's shoulder, gently pulling him away from the pudgy little man. "It's been a long flight," she said. "Perhaps we can go inside?"

Serena, Sophia and Mike followed Herr Ackermann up the sculpted con-crete steps and into the building. Mike had no idea what this place was or why he was here. Some sort of holiday or school trip, he had been told. He asked his mother how long they would be visiting and she smiled and told him to be patient.

When they stepped through the front doors, Mike was surprised to see how much natural light flowed in through the windows. The walls were pastel peach and beige in color and there was a noticeable lack of corners—everything seemed rounded. It reminded him of a super-sized hobbit house from Lord of the Rings.

A winding stone staircase took them up to a hallway where they followed Herr Ackermann into a large room with a big, round wooden table and plenty of handcrafted wooden chairs. On the table were plates of fruit and vegeta-bles and freshly baked bread (such a wonderful smell!) and butter and pots of jam and different colored cheeses and pitchers of pressed apple juice and two bottles of wine.

Herr Ackermann told them to sit and enjoy the food. He left the room and Miss Meyer prepared a plate of food for Mike.

"I don't get it, mom," Mike said. "I just don't get it. I mean, does dad even know where this place is? Can we climb a mountain when dad gets here?"

Miss Meyer frowned at his mother. His mother smiled. "Remember," she said, I told you that dad *might* be able to come. In any case, we'll have a wonderful time here. The plane ride was exciting, wasn't it? And this building—this magnificent building—and this room with the wonderful food." She sighed. "We are so blessed to be here."

Miss Meyer handed Mike a plate of buttered bread, sliced cheese and grapes. Then they all held hands and Miss Meyer recited a grace before they all chorused, "blessings on the meal," to her beaming delight.

"I hope dad can come," Mike said, biting into the delicious whole grain bread and imagining him and his dad knee-deep in snow and standing on top of a mountain.

Suddenly, the door opened and six men entered the room. Five of them wore suits and ties and one wore a gray turtleneck sweater and a brown leather jacket. Herr Ackermann followed the men into the room and they all sat around the table. Not a word was spoken. All eyes were on Mike.

2

Ithaca, New York

Detective Mark Julian was the last to arrive. After learning that Paul had invited the visitors from Oregon, Mark had made a few phone calls to check their identities. When he felt confident that the brother and sister were legitimate, another thought entered Mark's mind: Why did Paul think there might be a connection between the surgical murders and a runaway wife and child from Oregon? The professor had suggested the meeting and as Mark had no other leads, he had agreed to attend. He told himself he would politely listen for a few minutes before getting back to work.

Introductions were made as they sat around a small glass table in Paul's hotel room. Sandwiches, a fruit and vegetable platter, soft drinks, juice and water were on the table.

Mark found his eyes drawn to the blond woman from Oregon. She was tall, athletic-looking and quite striking. She had soft blue eyes, naturally flushed high cheeks and wore a powder-blue Adidas sweat suit and new white runners. Although he was usually attracted to petite, feminine-type women, for some reason Mark found Kate very attractive.

Paul sat back in the rattan chair and looked at Mark. "I really appreciate your being here," he said. "It might be helpful for you to have some background information for your case." He smiled and glanced at each of them in turn. "And I'll apologize right now for the professorial tone of what I have to say. I've been teaching this for a couple of decades, so please feel free to pose questions at any time."

Chris sipped from a can of apple juice. "We've already learned about the so-called surgical murders," he said to Mark, "and something about an unpublished chapter from the book, but Paul has not filled us in on how it might relate to my wife and son." His eyes flitted from face to face. "I must tell you that this scares the hell out of me now. What the killer did, and especially to the two kids . . . it's unbelievable."

"If I'm correct," Paul said, "I would not worry too much about the safety of your son."

Mark's eyebrows shot up. "Because . . . ?"

"Because the boy might be extremely valuable to those he is currently with—far too precious to put in harm's way."

Kate sighed and tapped a finger on the table. "Listen," she said, "all I know is Mike is somewhere in Europe and my brother and I will be on a late night flight to Zurich, so anything you can tell us now will be very helpful." She raised a hand. "Please, let's get on with it."

Mark looked at Kate. "Straight to the point," he said.

Kate stared hard at Mark. "Damn right. Straight to the fucking point." She continued to stare, as if testing him with the f-bomb and a steely gaze.

Mark had no response. He peered into her eyes for a moment and wondered why he was attracted to this woman.

Paul pushed his chair back and stretched his legs. "I'll try to get to the point. The unpublished chapter from my book has to do with Rudolf Steiner and his connection to Freemasonry and . . ." He paused. "And it also touches on an event that led Steiner to abandon his ties with Theosophy."

"I'm sorry," Kate said, "but what does this have to do with my nephew and why did you just say he might be valuable to these Anthroposophist nuts?"

Paul sighed. "I am getting there. The spiritual movement known as Theosophy was founded by a woman named Helena Blavatsky in New York in 1875. Her movement gained momentum in North America and in Europe and attracted some prominent members of society on both continents. After failing to launch an academic career, Rudolf Steiner turned to Theosophy and was named the head of the German section of the Theosophical Society in 1902. By 1912 Steiner had had more than a few disagreements with the leaders of the Society, especially when his colleagues announced the reincarnation of Christ in a young, impoverished boy from India. They believed him to be the *World Teacher*."

Mark was hoping the professor would say something to justify him staying. He had a murder to solve and the clock was ticking.

"There are often internal disputes within esoteric groups," Paul said. "In this case, Steiner was not convinced that Christ would ever reincarnate and he was also unimpressed that anyone would choose what he called *the Hindu lad* as the new messiah. Steiner decided it was time for him to break away from Theosophy. He then formed the Anthroposophical Society."

"And the boy?" Chris asked.

"He was taken from his village and placed in a Theosophical seminary for a few years, where he was taught how to meditate, eat proper food, exercise, and so on. His teacher and mentor was a Theosophist named Charles Leadbeater, who among other things, decided to educate the boy in the ways of the West. The boy's name was Jiddu Krishnamurti. Perhaps you've heard of him?"

"Vaguely," Chris said. "I've done some reading over the past couple of days." He paused and looked at Paul. "Including some online excerpts from your book. It seems that some of Steiner's views were racist. Is that why he was opposed to Krishnamurti—because he was not white?"

"That is a contentious issue within the movement, even today," Paul said. "Anthroposophists have a difficult time coming to terms with Steiner's racial beliefs. Steiner believed in the superiority of what he called the *Germanic Folk Soul* and the *white race*. His cosmology stems, in part, from the Aryan Myth. It deals with the European construct of an Aryan Race based mainly on linguistic similarities. Of course, this is simply not true. Believers in Aryanism held that Nordic and German peoples were the purest members of this special race. In fact, the foundation of Anthroposophy is steeped in spiritual and racial hierarchies."

Paul stretched his neck. "During the past few years, a group of high-ranking Anthroposophists has been meeting to discuss these controversial topics. While committed to working with many of Steiner's spiritual concepts, they are trying to get the Anthroposophical Society to finally deal with Steiner's racist beliefs. And they have some support within the leadership group. These progressive Anthroposophists are hoping to reach a consensus within the Society to publicly distance their spiritual movement from any hint of racism and anti-Semitism. These issues cannot continually be ignored.

"For example, Steiner was concerned that Europeans will be overly influenced by Asians and Africans. It might make more sense if I read a few passages." Paul pulled some papers from a file folder and quoted Rudolf Steiner:

> "How could one fail to be struck by the profound differences in spiritual culture between, let us say, the peoples of Europe and Asia! How indeed could one not be struck by the differences connected with the color of the skin?"

"How can we fail to realize that the Asiatic peoples have retained certain cultural impulses of past earthly epochs, whereas the Euro-American peoples have advanced beyond them? Only a man without a sound soul life can be impressed with the Oriental mysticism which Eastern humanity has preserved from earlier times, when lower forces of seer-ship were general. Such unsound spiritual life, however, has frequently gripped Europe. People have thought that they must practice Asiatic yoga and similar things in order to find their way into the spiritual life. This tendency proves nothing except an unhealthy soul-life."

"Thus when we ask which race belongs to which part of the earth, we must say: the yellow race, the Mongols, the Mongolian race belongs to Asia, the white race or the Caucasian race belongs to Europe, and the black race or the Negro race belongs to Africa. The Negro race does not belong to Europe, and the fact that this race is now playing such a large role in Europe is of course nothing but a nuisance."

"What a load of crap," Kate said.

Chris looked at Paul. "You said Steiner was anti-Semitic, as well?"

"Steiner went through a few different stages in his life," Paul said. "From anti-Semitic to philo-Semitic and back again." He referred to another paper:

"Judaism as such has long outlived itself and no longer has a legitimate place in the modern life of peoples; the fact that it has nevertheless succeeded in maintaining itself is an aberration in world history, the consequences of which had to follow."

Mark was not surprised when nobody spoke. He looked at Paul and wondered why he would choose to study such hurtful nonsense.

Paul broke the awkward silence. "My father's side of the family is Chinese and my mother's is Jewish." He smiled. "I suppose that might be one reason I find this topic so intriguing."

"It must seem repulsive to you," Chris said.

"I find it more interesting than repulsive," Paul replied. "An Anthroposophic worldview does not stem from hatred. They do not hate non-whites or Jews—in fact, many Anthroposophists are not themselves white and there

are a number of Jewish Anthroposophists. There are even some Waldorf
schools in Israel. Although the philosophy is deeply esoteric, many non-
occultists find value in programs like Waldorf or Steiner education—at least
for a while."

"Until they start to understand it," Kate said. "How can anybody take this
racist evolution stuff seriously? Wasn't Darwin around at that time?"

Paul smiled. "Yes. Suffice to say Steiner did not think much of Darwin. In
fact . . ." he shuffled through more papers. "Steiner believed Darwin was
wrong." Paul quoted Steiner again:

> "Darwinism has made many errors in regard to the differentiation
> expressed by the races existing on earth. The higher races have not
> descended from the lower races; on the contrary, the latter repre-
> sent the degeneration of the higher races which have preceded
> them."

Paul poured juice into a glass and looked at his audience. "We know today that the division of people based on race or racial group is nothing more
than a social construct, yet it remains an important cornerstone of the
Anthroposophic movement. While the so-called white race is the race of the
future, other races are actually devolving. Some Anthroposophists refer to
evolutionary biology as *Darwinism*—usually as a pejorative label for what
they find wrong with scientific approaches to understanding life in general."

"I'm speechless," Chris said. "Is my wife buying into this stuff?"

"Again, there's more to Anthroposophy than racial hierarchy," Paul said.
"Your wife might not have learned of the racial elements. Or like many in
the movement, perhaps she chooses to ignore them. Steiner also preached
love and social harmony and overt racism is certainly not taught in the
schools. Although he often spoke of higher and lower races and predicted an
upcoming racial war, Steiner was not a violent or mean-spirited man."

"Racial war?" Chris asked.

"That's right," Paul said. "Steiner saw different races living together at
the same time as problematic. He spoke about what he called a *War of All
Against All* as a means to divide the good and evil races. This war will mark
the transition to the next era in cosmic and human evolution." Paul shuffled
through his notes and read aloud:

"After the great War of All Against All, there will be two kinds of human beings. Those who had previously tried to follow the call to the spiritual life, who cultivated the spiritualizing and ennobling of their inner spiritual life, will show this inward life on their faces and express it in their gestures and the movements of their hands. And those who have turned away from the spiritual life, represented by the community of Laodicea, who were lukewarm, neither warm nor cold, will pass into the following epoch as those who retard human evolution, who preserve the backward forces of evolution which have been left behind."

"They will show the evil passions, impulses, and instincts hostile to the spiritual in an ugly, unintelligent, evil-looking countenance. In their gestures and hand-movements, in everything they do, they will present an outer image of the ugliness in their soul. Just as humanity has separated into races and communities, in the future it will divide into two great streams: the good and the evil. And what is in their souls will be outwardly manifest; they will no longer be able to hide it."

Kate glanced around the table. "Anyone find that creepy?"

"Again," Paul said, "it's difficult to grasp Steiner's cosmology—especially during a short lesson while sitting in a hotel room. Perhaps this will help." He read aloud from another Steiner lecture:

"You might now be inclined to say: Is it not an extremely bitter thought that whole bodies of peoples remain immature and do not develop their capacities; that only a small group becomes capable of providing the germ for the next civilization? This thought will no longer disquiet you if you distinguish between race-development and individual soul-development, for no soul is condemned to remain in one particular race. The race may fall behind; the community of people may remain backward, but the souls progress beyond several races."

"I just cannot believe that Serena would buy into this stuff," Chris said.

"C'mon, Chris," Kate said. "Face facts—she's always had a few loose screws."

Mark looked at Chris. The poor man's wife and son had left him and this information must be difficult to fathom. Kate did not seem to be helping her brother in the least. Still, there was something about her that Mark found intriguing. *Wasn't I only going to stay for a few minutes . . . ?*

Chris looked up from his notes. "What finally happened to Krishnamurti?"

Paul cleared his throat. "Krishnamurti eventually ended up distancing himself from Theosophy and developed his own sort of philosophy, denouncing organized spirituality and guru worship."

Kate raised her glass of juice in a toast. "Smart guy. Here's to Krishnamurti."

Mark smiled.

"We're getting there," Paul said. "Christ also plays a central role in Steiner's Anthroposophy but it's not the same as the Christian Jesus Christ. In fact, Steiner believed there were two Jesuses. Long story, but for now let's just say there are various forces or impulses or spirits at work. There is a thin line between darkness and light. Sometimes one appears as the other." He paused and stared blankly at the wall, as if trying to find the best words for this audience. "It's not an easy concept to understand—these dualities, these forces that guide the esotericist. Can one really claim to know the light in the spirit without first experiencing the shadows?" He looked at each of them in turn.

"You're sounding a little spooky, Professor," Kate said.

Paul smiled. "So, we know that Anthroposophy draws heavily from Theosophy and relies also on Steiner's own occult cosmology and contains some elements of Christianity. The three esoteric heavyweights in Anthroposophy are Ahriman and Lucifer and Christ—or as they say: the *Christ Impulse.*"

"Lucifer?" Kate asked.

"As I explained briefly to Mark yesterday, this is not the commonly known Lucifer—the fallen angel or Satan from Christianity. Anthroposophists refer to Lucifer as the *bringer of light*, the literal translation from Latin. But this does not mean Lucifer is necessarily good. At the other end is Ahriman, a destructive or dark spirit, one who uses deception to tempt humans into the material world. Lucifer represents Satan while Ahriman represents the devil. Paul looked at Chris. "Perhaps you have some experience with Ahrimanic deception? Waldorf teachers are well-versed in the power of Ahriman to negatively influence children—especially with electronic devices like televisions and computers."

Chris crossed his arms and sat back in his chair. "I've heard that some schools make parents sign a NO-TV contract but I had no idea we were supposed to be protecting our kids from a dark spirit."

"What idiots would believe this crap?" Kate asked.

"I think kids watch too much television," Paul said. "So I'll give Waldorf some credit there. Critics of the movement complain that the deeply esoteric nature of Anthroposophy comes as a surprise after children have been enrolled in Waldorf schools. Although Anthroposophy is not taught per se, it forms the foundation of the education and often permeates the culture of the schools. Unlike Catholic schools, for example, with their overt Christian roots, the veiled religious or spiritual base of Waldorf education can leave students and their parents feeling confused. While most people in the world believe in some sort of higher power or deity, Anthroposophists are often accused of not explaining their beliefs to those who deserve to know."

"Like to the parents of children in their schools," Kate said. "Pretty hard to explain some of those beliefs—like the racial stuff."

"Indeed," Paul agreed. "Although parts of Steiner's racism are toned down or removed from reprints of his books, some teachers-in-training drop out when they encounter the first traces of racist content. The good news is that many Anthroposophists now believe it is time to move forward—meaning they are willing to deal with these difficult issues."

Mark watched Kate shake her head, start to speak and then remain silent. Apparently there were some limits to her brash behavior.

3

Ithaca, New York

Chris had not slept much since his wife and son had left, and the three-hour time difference from Oregon to New York only added to his fatigue. His nerves were tight. The past two days felt surreal and although his mind was scattered and tired, he knew he would need to understand this brief lesson in occultism as this was what was motivating his wife. He put pen to paper and listened to the professor.

"So," Paul continued, "we have Ahriman-the-dark spirit on one side and Lucifer-the-light spirit on the other, and between them we find the Christ Impulse, as a sort of mediator, balancing those two powerful forces. I could go on forever about that dynamic but I'll try to condense a heavy academic course into a few minutes here." He sighed and glanced at Chris. "This is where it might relate to your current situation. Rudolf Steiner made various predictions during his life. He considered himself to be an Initiate with clairvoyant abilities."

"More like a racist nut-job," Kate said.

Paul ignored Kate's latest outburst. "And many of his followers today hang onto Steiner's every word as the gospel truth. They believe the world has become far too materialistic—too Ahrimanic—and they see it as their Anthroposophic duty to restore a balance. You see, one of Steiner's predictions includes the reincarnation of Ahriman in this time period, so some might believe that something is needed to counter that powerful event. Left unchecked, Ahriman could lead the world farther down a materialist path."

Chris looked up. "So, if the dark spirit Ahriman is here now, do you think they are waiting for the reincarnation of Lucifer—their spirit of light?"

"I don't think so," Paul said. "Although the influence is still felt today, Lucifer's time was four thousand years ago. Then the Christ Impulse happened two thousand years ago at Golgotha. And now is the time of Ahriman, and regardless of whether or not his physical incarnation has happened yet, his power is very strong; the world is too materialistic for Anthroposophists.

There was no mention of the return of Lucifer in human form but some Anthroposophists are still influenced by Theosophy. Remember, years ago the young Krishnamurti was taken from his village because he was believed to be the incarnation of Christ."

Chris looked up again from his notes. "So you're suggesting some Anthroposophists think another Christ is coming to counter the power of Ahriman? Maybe a white-skinned Christ?"

Paul said nothing.

Kate broke the silence. "Oh shit! They think Mike is the reincarnation of Christ?"

"Oh my God," Chris said. "He's their new Krishnamurti?" He felt his heart pounding hard.

Paul continued: "Christ was to have already reincarnated but in the etheric plane—not the physical. A group of fanatics, however, might have a different interpretation. Steiner also predicted that Ahriman would reincarnate somewhere in the West. Ahriman, the inspirer of materialistic science and commercialism is destroying modern culture with deadening forces. Simply put, spiritual life is currently being crushed by materialism. Anthroposophists want to see a balance restored and to some, a new Christ Impulse would fit perfectly."

Paul stretched his legs and arched his back. "Think about it. Where do we, in the West, get the bulk of our televisions, computers, radios, and stereos? Where is all this *Ahrimanic* stuff made?"

Kate stared. "Mostly in Asia."

"That's right," Paul continued. "Asia is doing Ahriman's grunt work while the dark spirit—reincarnated in the West, denounces spiritual life, leading the masses to fill that void with a perceived need for materialistic consumption. Ahriman is the salesman—the huckster. By denying the spiritual world, his *impulse* is promoting consumerism and materialism. Anthroposophically speaking, this is classic Ahriman at his best—or worst, depending on how you choose to do the esoteric dance.

"I suspect, however, the influence of Ahriman is stronger than some of them expected. Organized religion has failed miserably in bringing the true spirit to the West. Anthroposophy was supposed to be much more influential during these troubled times—Steiner predicted it—and some followers could conclude that an intervention is urgently needed in order to shift the balance and fulfill his prophecy."

"Holy shit," Kate said. "It's like they are from another planet."

"Other planets are, in fact, connected to the roots of Anthroposophy," Paul said.

"I read something about that online," Chris said. "Something about planets and evolution and humans transforming into plants on Jupiter, and Steiner also spoke about Vulcan."

Kate shook her head. "Un-fucking real. Maybe Mr. Spock or Captain Kirk will beam down and save the day."

"That discussion is complex and best saved for another time," Paul said. "Back to the matters before us now: While Steiner was never officially on record as believing in a reincarnated Christ, some Theosophists who followed him into Anthroposophy were not quite so sure. And who knows what went on in private? There was also some talk at that time of Steiner, himself, being the reincarnation of Christ. There was and still is a strong belief, in some occult circles, that the German Folk Soul and the white race, will guide humanity forward."

Chris felt dazed. "Serena's grandparents were both German."

"German-American blood," Paul said. "Makes perfect sense—Anthroposophically speaking." He looked at Chris. "Your son is a white American with German roots." He paused. "There is a Steiner book called *The Occult Significance of Blood.*"

"What about indigenous peoples?" Kate asked. "Native Americans were here before Germans or any Europeans. They are more North American than any of us."

Paul continued: "Anthroposophists believe Native Americans came from Atlantis—"

"Atlantis?" Kate interrupted. "As in the lost continent? This is totally unbelievable."

"Indigenous peoples arrived from Atlantis long ago, to sort of pave the way for Europeans. And then they were destined to die out."

"That's sick," Kate said.

Paul shuffled through new papers he pulled from his briefcase and read another Steiner quote:

> "The American Indians died out, not because of European persecutions, but because they were destined to succumb to those forces which hastened their extinction."

Paul watched the stunned faces around him. "Not all Anthroposophists believe in a spiritually justified genocide."

Mark shifted in his chair. "You told me earlier that you have a friend in the leadership of the Anthroposophical Society. What does he think of all this?"

"We have interesting discussions," Paul said. "He thinks I am misinterpreting much of Steiner but he also believes his movement should not ignore its controversial elements—difficult as that might be."

Mark looked at his notes. "Aryan myth, Judaism is outdated . . . it sounds like some of the Nazi nonsense from years ago. Was Steiner in cahoots with the Third Reich?"

"Short answer—no. Steiner died in 1925, before Hitler's reign of terror. And we know that Hitler was critical of Rudolf Steiner and his movement. Of course, Hitler despised everyone who he considered to be his competition. It is interesting to note, however, that although many of today's Anthroposophists are unwilling to discuss their movement's history, there were connections between Anthroposophy and the Nazi Party. And like Steiner, Hitler also misunderstood the Aryan myth—as do many people today. Lots of Waldorf documents from the Nazi period proclaim allegiance to the fatherland. Many Anthroposophists were themselves Nazis or at least Nazi sympathizers—some holding prominent positions in the party.

"Remember, though, despite their views on Judaism, Anthroposophists did not align themselves with the final solution, nor have they openly expressed hatred towards any particular group of people. They have never seen their movement as being racist or elitist and it would be wrong to liken Anthroposophy to groups like the KKK. It's important to understand the distinction between racism and bigotry."

Chris was hoping to hear more about his son, but he suspected this latest information might be important. "What is the difference?" he asked.

Paul continued: "People can be kind and well-intentioned but if they believe in the superiority of one race over another, they are, by definition, racist. This dynamic is also in evidence with Europeans and missionaries in the Americas and elsewhere.

"Many Anthroposophists today believe Steiner was infallible. If the great man said something a long time ago, it simply must still be true today. They see themselves working with souls as opposed to the bodies used to carry those souls. Skin color reflects the quality of the soul but there is generally no overt hatred of non-whites. A great karmic plan sees souls traveling through the races."

Chris could feel his head spinning. "So you really think this fanatical group believes my son is their new messiah?" The words sounded horribly strange as they left his lips.

"I think it is possible," Paul said. "They could see Michael's arrival as the reason to take necessary action—as if he were drawn to them from a pre-earthly existence. In layman's terms, Michael is the excuse they needed to fulfill their mission."

"What mission?" asked Mark.

Paul paused. "That, I do not know. These people would need to act in secret. There's one more thing you should know."

"Bring it on," Kate said. "Can this get any weirder?"

Paul smiled. "Maybe. Another powerful element in Anthroposophy involves an ancient story of good and bad." He looked at Chris. "Do you recall a celebration called *Michaelmas* in your child's Waldorf School? It takes place at this very time—near the autumnal equinox every year."

Chris knew of the celebration. That was something Mike had enjoyed. "Yes, I never understood the significance but the kids dress up in costumes and there's a dragon and then a knight arrives to slay the dragon." He smiled. "Last year Mike was chosen to be the knight who slays the dragon."

"That does not surprise me," Paul said. "When a student slays the dragon in a Waldorf school, it represents the archangel Michael sending Lucifer— the light being—down to earth. The archangel Michael administers cosmic intelligence and holds a very important place in Anthroposophy. They work with what they call the *Michaelic Impulse*. In fact, they openly refer to their spiritual path as belonging to the *Michael School* or the *Michael Stream.*"

"That's strange," Kate said, "that a kid named Michael was chosen to be the archangel Michael, the dragon slayer. Quite the coincidence."

"Anthroposophists do not generally believe in coincidence," Paul said. "To them, this is karma." He looked around the table and fixed on Chris. "Symbology is very important and I doubt it is mere coincidence that your son, Michael, was taken to the Anthroposophical Headquarters in Switzerland in September, just before Michaelmas."

Chris stared at Paul in disbelief. He dropped his pen on the table and felt his heart sink. "What will they do to Mike?"

Paul sighed. "I'm not entirely sure."

4

Dornach, Switzerland

It had been less than one day but Mike wanted to go home. He had not slept well on the plane and was feeling tired. The food was good but the men who arrived during lunch were strange. They sat and asked him weird questions and then they asked him to paint a wet-on-wet. So boring . . .

After lunch, he was taken to a house not far from the strange Goetheanum building. This is where his mother told him he would sleep for a couple of nights. She would be with Miss Meyer in a small cottage just down the path. He sat on the hard bed in his little room on the top floor at the end of a long corridor. There was a tiny window in the room but he needed to step up onto a little desk in order to see outside. He wanted to get out of the house and go for a hike. Suddenly, there was a tap on his door and Herr Ackermann appeared.

"Hello Mik-eye-ell." The smile was still glued to his shiny round face. "Come and have a look at something special," he said, motioning for Mike to follow him down the hall. "I saw the painting you made and I must say you are truly talented." They walked quickly.

"Thank you," Mike said, "but it's really not that good. In school, we just copy what Miss Meyer does, so my paintings are nothing special." He tried to keep up with Herr Ackermann's quick steps.

"Oh, you are very special," the fat man said. "Very special." He opened the back door of the house and they made their way across a little field of grass and wildflowers towards another strange-looking building.

"What's this place?" Mike asked as Herr Ackermann guided him inside and down some stairs.

"A special place for a special guest," the fat man said. "This is Haus Duldeck and down here is where we keep the most important documents. He opened a heavy door and as they entered the basement room, Mike saw his mother and Miss Meyer and two other men; one wore a suit like Herr

Ackermann's and the other was the man in the brown leather jacket from lunch. The room was full of very old furniture.

"Hello Mik-eye-ell," Miss Meyer said.

Something was wrong. His mother looked at him but she seemed sad. She smiled but her eyes were not smiling. "Hello Mik-eye-ell," she said.

The man in the brown leather jacket spoke: "Please sit down." He was not smiling and Mike wondered if he ever *had* smiled. Mike sat at an old table, across from the man in the leather jacket. He had not been introduced to this man but he heard Miss Meyer call him Karl.

"I would like you to close your eyes for a minute and relax all of your muscles. Can you try to do that, Mik-eye-ell?" Karl asked.

Karl's voice was as smooth as vanilla ice cream. He had a neatly trimmed beard and mustache, lots of dark brown wavy hair, deep-set dark eyes and he smelled like perfume. Some sort of German cologne, Mike suspected.

Close my eyes and do what?

"Can you do that for us, please?" Karl repeated.

"It's fine, Mike," his mother said. "Just give it a try."

It was the first time in months his mother had called him Mike. It felt good. Mike closed his eyes and tried to relax. It was cold in the room.

"Good," the man said, stretching the word out in a soft, soothing voice: "Goooood. Now, take a few nice relaxing breaths. Relax . . . and when I ask you to open your eyes I will show you some pictures and ask that you comment on those pictures. Just say the first thing that enters your mind." The voice was firm but melodic—similar to the way Miss Meyer spoke to the class back at school, but Karl's voice was deeper . . .

Mike felt tired and when Karl finally asked him to open his eyes, it took a few seconds to pull his eyelids up. On the table in front of him was a large photograph of a desert scene. He could see two little huts and a camel standing beside a strange-looking tree.

The soothing voice again: "And what comes into your mind?"

"A dry desert," Mike said. "Camels, huts, trees."

"Not what you see in the picture, Mik-eye-ell. What comes into your mind? How do you feel?"

"Tired," Mike said.

"Let's try another one," said the soothing voice. "Again, just close your eyes and relax . . ."

They repeated this exercise again. And again and again and again. In all, Mike must have looked at two dozen pictures—everything from more desert scenes to black and white photos of an old city, rooms in houses all decorated with old-fashioned furniture and ornaments, photos of people dressed in old-fashioned clothes from a hundred years ago, none of them smiling, some of them sitting sternly around tables as if discussing things of great importance.

"What comes into your mind—into your soul, Mik-eye-ell?"

"I'm not sure."

"How about this one?"

"It's a room full of people and—"

"Yes, but do you know that room and those people? How do you feel about these people?"

Mike felt frustrated. *How do I feel? I feel like I want to go outside and climb a mountain. I feel like going home!*

He was allowed to go outside in the afternoon but only to walk around a garden-like courtyard with high walls behind a house where an old woman was supposed to look after him. Her name was Dott and she wore a tattered old dress and a blanket-like shawl. She was missing lots of teeth and those that remained were brown and yellow.

Dott stood stirring something dark and liquid in an old barrel. She told him to come and watch her work. At first he was a little frightened because she reminded him of a witch but then he realized she was probably just mentally ill. In fact, even though she had a very strong accent and was difficult to understand, he liked her; she seemed kinder and more sincere than the other people he'd met there.

"Ziss is important vork, Mik-eye-ell," she said, staring into the barrel. "Biodynamic preparation for the gardens." She looked at Mike with a nearly toothless smile. "You know all about ziss, ya?"

She spoke as if assuming he knew certain things. He tried to explain to Dott that he was just a kid from Oregon here on holiday but she did not seem to understand.

"Zeeese are vonderful times, ya?" Dott said. "Mik-eye-ell here at za Goetheanum!" Her old eyes beamed like Christmas lights and she went back to stirring her *preparation*.

Mike decided to go along with whatever Dott said. She seemed lonely. She talked non-stop about planets and zodiacs and herbs and he politely listened and pretended to understand. She seemed to enjoy his company and Mike was delighted when she gave him a piece of homemade fudge. It was delicious. "Zeese is our secret, ya?" She gave him another piece and they both sat and ate fudge together in the cool shadows of the little courtyard.

Before dinner, Mike was back in the cold basement room with the strange adults and their old pictures. Some of the pictures were really strange—there were chalk drawings on black cardboard with lots of weird diagrams and numbers and little squiggles that made no sense at all.

"Close your eyes, relax, and now—how do you feel about this? And how about this one . . . ?"

Mike looked at the bearded Karl and then glanced at Herr Ackermann and another man in an old gray suit. When Mike's eyes turned to his mother, she quickly looked away and for a moment Mike thought she was about to cry. Karl did not seem pleased with Mike's lack of *feelings* for the pictures.

Karl finally stood and pushed his chair back against the table. The other men followed his lead and the sound of chair legs scraping on the stone floor echoed in the basement. Miss Meyer stood, his mother stood and both women left the room.

"Mom," Mike said, but she did not look back. "Mom!" The door closed.

Herr Ackermann leaned into Mike and smiled an exaggerated nervous smile. "We can try again another day," he said. "But now I bet you are hungry, ya? Let's go and see what the cook has prepared."

Karl and the other men left the room without a word. Mike followed Herr Ackermann across the field and back into the house where he would sleep that night. They made their way to the dining room where old Dott was pouring soup into bowls while talking to herself about archangels and destiny. When she saw Mike, her eyes opened wide and she smiled.

She scurried out of the room and returned with steaming fresh bread, a bowl of vegetable stew, and another bowl filled with applesauce. She lit three beeswax candles and as soon as Mike sat down, she spoke a pre-meal prayer; it was the same one Mike knew so well from daily recitals at his Waldorf School.

Herr Ackermann sat beside him and they ate in silence. Above the aroma of soup and melting beeswax, he could still smell Herr Ackermann's body odor. It was awful. Mike wanted to leave this room and the stuffy old house, but he knew he would not be allowed. Instead, he sat and ate and tried hard to hide the tears that wanted desperately to escape.

5

Ithaca, New York

Chris sat in Professor Paul Sung's hotel room, taking notes and feeling shocked at what he had learned. He looked at his sister, knowing she was growing increasingly impatient. He felt relieved that Kate was there but was concerned that her blunt comments might not go over well in present company.

"But they won't harm Mike, right?" Chris asked. He needed some reassurance from the professor. "Tell me what you think. You're the expert."

"Until yesterday," Paul said, "I would never have suspected any Anthroposophist capable of murder."

Chris stood, stretched and walked to the window. The sun was trying to pierce through a gray cloud cover but the clouds were winning the struggle.

Paul continued: "My guess is that a fringe group with ties to Anthroposophy's Executive Council, called the *Vorstand*—or how they say in German, the *Forshtandt*—was expecting a significant reincarnation and learned of a boy named Michael from a western state in America. His good school work and general demeanor might have piqued the interest of a deeply esoteric Anthroposophist at the school—probably his teacher." Paul took a deep breath and let it out slowly. "And I'll go out on a limb now and guess that your son is fair skinned, blond and has blue eyes."

Chris could hear his own heartbeat. "Yes," he said. "Yes, that's him."

"Here's more Steiner," Paul said, reading from one of his papers:

> "If the blond and blue-eyed people die out, the human race will become increasingly dense. In the case of fair people, less nourishment is driven into the eyes and hair; it remains instead in the brain and endows it with intelligence. Brown and dark-haired people drive the substances into their eyes and hair that the fair people retain in their brains."

Paul looked up from the paper. "Steiner had dark hair and brown eyes but believed, as did his followers, that being an Initiate meant he had a direct line to the spirit world."

Chris rubbed a hand across his forehead and sighed. "Mike's teacher was always telling my wife that our son is special. But this is unbelievable."

"There is one other possibility," Paul said. "During my research for the book, I discovered that some Anthroposophists are waiting for another very special incarnation—one that they believe to be connected specifically to North America. So, if Mike is not considered to be the reincarnation of Christ, he could be someone else of great importance to this fringe group of occultists."

"And who is that?" asked Kate.

"Their leader," Paul said. "In fact, Rudolf Steiner is reported to have told a handful of his followers that he would reincarnate around the year 2000."

"Holy shit," Kate said. "It's like Alice in friggin' Wonderland."

"OK," Mark said, "so regardless of which incarnation they believe him to be, it seems the boy is in no immediate danger and it should not be too difficult to find him." He looked at Chris. "You go to Europe, find a bunch of loony Anthroposophists at their headquarters and bring your son home. I'll poke around here for a deranged New Age killer who might be involved with that group."

"It's not that simple," Paul said. "If they have connections in the First Class of the School of Spiritual Science, they might be able to keep him well hidden."

"What's with this *First Class*?" Chris asked. He had read references online but did not understand.

"Before his death in 1925," Paul said, "Rudolf Steiner wanted to set up three classes dealing with Spiritual Science—aka Anthroposophy. He was unable to complete the task because he died after initiating the First Class. It's basically a group of Anthroposophists with special initiation rites— nineteen Lessons with secret mantras that Steiner gave to the first initiates in person."

"Oh sure," Kate said. "Their guru is clairvoyant but died before he could finish his job. He can't even foresee his own death?"

"They don't like to be reminded of such anomalies," Paul said. "So, these experienced Anthroposophists meet from time to time to discuss Steiner's special First Class notes, the stenographic records and the near-sacred *tafels*. That's the German word for 'blackboard' but they are more like sheets of heavy black card that Steiner used to record his sketches and mantras. The tafels are jealously guarded in the archive vault in Dornach. Holders of the First Class are able to induct new initiates and hold the nineteen lessons in rotation for their local Class members. Many esoteric groups have such secrets and levels of initiation."

"Can Waldorf teachers be First Class members?" Chris asked.

"Sure," Paul said. "The entire faculty of the first Waldorf School in Stuttgart, signed up in 1924. You're thinking of your son's teacher?"

"It would not surprise me," Chris said. "I feel so stupid. I mean, I thought it was just a nice arts-based private school and now I learn about an international cult-like organization with tentacles everywhere and a headquarters in Switzerland. How are they funded?"

"They are resourceful," Paul said. "The schools are usually self-sufficient, thanks to the financial means of their clientele—generally upper middle-class parents. And the school supplies, like special paint and crayons and paper, come from Anthroposophic companies. There is also a branch of spiritual healing called Anthroposophic medicine; many of their doctors are registered physicians and have established regular medical practices with non-Anthroposophical patients. There is no shortage of eager, anti-establishment types or New Agers looking for unconventional treatments. The movement is also involved in agriculture via biodynamic farming, as well as international banking and it has links to a successful line of health care products. And they are connected politically."

Chris stopped taking notes. "But the vast majority of these folks are harmless, right?"

"I cannot speak for the majority," Paul said, "but it's generally known as a fairly benign spiritual movement."

"What about the murders?" Mark asked. "Where do you think they fit in to this story?"

"Greg Matheson's research and my unpublished chapter," Paul said. "If my theory is correct, this secret sub-group of Anthroposophists would be very concerned that outsiders know about them. They would also need to hide their activities from their peers. I suspect Greg's research distressed this group a great deal."

Mark was taking notes again. "So you think there is an occult hit man on the loose—wiping out all traces of their plan to treat little Mike as the new messiah?"

Chris felt his heart sink.

Paul sighed. "It's a possibility. Remember that throughout history, religion has often been at the root of irrational human behavior. When someone believes strongly in a cause—any cause—heinous acts can be easily justified. These people probably believe they have no choice in this matter. It is their collective karma." He paused for a moment. "Most Anthroposophists would be appalled to learn this might be happening."

Mark flipped through his notes. "You said they have their own doctors? Any chance one of these docs is connected to what we've been calling the surgical murders? Our local medical examiner told me the larynx removal was done by someone with experience."

"A doctor who kills people by nailing their body parts to the ceiling," Kate huffed. "There's a pleasant thought."

Paul's face went blank.

"Something else?" asked Mark.

"Maybe," Paul said. "I just thought of it now. Anthroposophical medicine had support during the Nazi regime. Rudolf Hess, for example, supported Anthroposophy and established a new department of public health in 1933 which, in part, funded biodynamic methods of agriculture and Anthroposophical medicine. A number of Anthroposophical doctors were members of the SS and the Nazi party. Perhaps one of today's Anthroposophical doctors still believes in an ideological overlap of Steiner's mission with that of the Third Reich."

Mark was writing as he listened. He looked up. "So you think our guy is one of these doctors?"

"I'd say it is a possibility," Paul said.

"But for now, Paul," Mark said, "we need to keep you alive. If you are correct with this theory, the killer has more work to do and we all need to be very careful." He stood and handed business cards to Kate and Chris. "I'd like to stay in touch so feel free to call me from Switzerland." He looked at Paul. "And you, Professor—stay put until tomorrow. I'm going to see if we can find you a safer place to live until this is over."

"I think I'm all right, detective," Paul said, "but thanks for—"

"Sorry, Paul," Mark interrupted, "but this is bigger than just you. I'm going to pull in some more resources." He leaned over and whispered to the professor: "The last thing I need is to discover your larynx nailed to a ceiling. It'd be real bad for you and worse for my reputation." He smiled. "Stay put, order food from room service and I'll call you tomorrow."

"OK," Paul said, trying but failing to return the smile. "Where are you going now?"

Detective Julian stood. "I'm going to check out a couple of Anthroposophical doctors. See what they know about the surgical murders."

Chris stood and shook hands with Paul. "Thanks for your help, Professor," he said. "I really appreciate your input." He sighed. "It seems so surreal."

"Welcome to the world of mystics and separate realities," the professor said.

"They're just people," Kate said. "Fucking criminals. And they have Mike."

As they drove their rental car back to the airport, Chris could not help but think of his son in the hands of those mystics and criminals.

Paul sat at the little table beside the bed and looked at his watch. What time was it in Dornach, Switzerland? Late. He picked up the phone and less than a minute later heard a familiar voice ask him if he knows the time?

"I'm sorry," Paul said, "but something has come up and I need your thoughts."

"Now, that's a switch," a friendly voice said. "Doctor Paul Sung asking the advice of an Anthroposophist? Finally deciding to investigate the spiritual world? I'm delighted." The man chuckled. "This is worth waking up for."

Paul smiled. "I did not say advice, Benjamin. I said *thoughts.*"

"Of course," Benjamin said. "But I will still hold out hope for you. A Michaelmas miracle would be most welcome."

"Not likely. I still dwell within the depths of atheism." He could imagine Benjamin rolling his eyes. "But I need some information."

"We have not spoken for quite some time, Paul. What's up?"

Paul thought quickly of how best to phrase his questions. "I'm wondering about the Vorstand, Benjamin. I know there are divergent views within the leadership of the Society."

"Yes, and you and I have spoken of them in the past. Why are you asking me about this again now?"

Paul could hear the curiosity—more like concern—in his friend's voice. How much should he say? "Benjamin, I—"

"I sense apprehension in your voice, Paul. There are problems in the Vorstand but what does this have to do with you?"

Paul pulled himself from the chair, stood for a moment and then sat on the bed. "I'll come out and ask this directly, Benjamin. Do you think there are any potentially violent people in the Vorstand?"

Silence.

Paul pushed the receiver hard to his ear. He could hear breathing.

And then Benjamin's voice again: "Violent? Is this more of your infamous research into Anthroposophy? You always want to discuss Steiner's more controversial beliefs and now you throw violence into the mix . . . on the telephone after waking me up? That's not fair."

Paul knew his friend was feeling defensive. They had been down this road before. "I'm sorry. I realize this—"

"Listen, Paul, as you know we are experiencing growing pains at this time. Tensions are high as many of us have strong feelings about the future of the Society, but we will work them out. I am hoping to see positive change within the Vorstand soon. You know I cannot go into detail with you. As a matter of fact, some of my colleagues and I are meeting tomorrow at a two-day retreat in Zurich to discuss how best to deal with . . . our internal leadership problems."

Unfortunately, that answered Paul's next question. He was hoping Benjamin could help the brother and sister from Oregon when they arrive in Dornach. "Will you miss the Michaelmas Conference at the Goetheanum?"

"We'll be back for the important meetings. Why on earth are you so interested?"

Suggesting that an Anthroposophist might be murdering people in New York would probably result in the end of the conversation, so Paul tried a less threatening approach. He wondered if Benjamin had seen Chris's wife and son. "Did you spend much time at the Goetheanum today, Benjamin?"

"No, there was a team of cleaners in there. Our organizing committee is preparing for the conference. I was told they needed the building empty today."

"So you know nothing about a boy and his mother from Oregon?"

"No. Friends of yours?"

Paul felt the strain of the day pulsing through his neck and shoulders. *Was the Goetheanum closed today so that Mike and his mother could arrive without being seen?* Paul knew his friend would spend a sleepless night if he went any further with his questions. Perhaps Mike and Serena were staying somewhere else—maybe they were not even in Switzerland after all.

"I apologize, Benjamin," Paul said. He sighed. "I'm sorry I woke you."

They chatted for a few minutes, with Paul trying to sound less intrusive, but as he hung up and replayed the very strange day in his mind, he was convinced that something was dreadfully wrong. He lay on the hotel bed and tried to search for pieces to what was rapidly becoming an extremely discomforting puzzle.

6

En Route to Switzerland

The late flight to Zurich was long and uneventful. Kate had been to Europe as a backpacking teenager years ago but this was a first for Chris. They agreed not to dwell on the present and spent time chatting about everything they had missed during the past few years—the years where Kate had been off limits because of Serena's demands. Chris learned that his sister was currently unemployed but had previously worked two jobs as a jujitsu instructor and as an assistant manager in a sporting goods shop. Her needs were few.

She rented a small apartment near Portland's Chinatown district, rode her bike everywhere and had managed to save "a fair chunk of change" over the years. Her health meant everything and although he had to pry the information out of her, Chris learned that she had recently won a few international martial arts competitions.

They reminisced about days long since passed when they would play hide-and-seek as kids, and sneak out of bed sometimes to watch late night movies on TV when their parents were asleep. They did not speak about extended family, nor did either of them mention Kate's sexual abuse from many years ago.

Although Kate was still rough around the edges, Chris sincerely enjoyed sitting beside her and chatting during the eight-hour flight to Zurich. Eventually, they broke their agreement and spoke about Mike and all that they had learned from Paul that day.

"The professor sure knows his stuff," Kate said. "Lots of information but he knows what he's talking about."

"It's weird," Chris said. "I mean, I discover him from an online cult support website and the next day I'm sitting in his hotel room in Ithaca, New York where he's staying because some New Age nutcase might want to kill him and here we are zipping off to Switzerland to look for my son because my wife flipped out . . . I mean, can this get any stranger?"

Kate chuckled and tapped his leg. "Hey, don't speak too soon, little brother. Who knows what might happen when we land?"

Chris stared out the window. The constant hum of the engines reminded him that he had not slept much during the past two days. "I really miss him, Kate."

"I've missed him for a few years," his sister said.

He looked at her and managed a tired smile. "You know how much I appreciate your support, don't you?" he asked.

"Yup," she answered. "But wait until you get my bill." She raised her eyebrows and they both laughed. "Hey," she said, "what are you going to do about Serena? If she's totally into this ultra-weird anthro trip and refuses to budge, what are you going to do?"

"I've thought about that," Chris said. "I guess I'm hoping she'll just wake up and come home with me and Mike."

"Or how about this," Kate said, still smiling. "Maybe you and I take Mike home and Serena can stay with the cult in Europe. If we're lucky, one of her leaders will pass around poisoned Kool-Aid."

"That's not funny, Kate."

"So, why are you smiling?"

Chris managed to get some sleep as his sister listened to Lil Wayne on her iPod. *Just 'cause I'm in my forties doesn't mean I can't get into good rap.* Chris woke up once, opened tired eyes and watched his sister's blond hair bopping to the music. He could hear the thump-thump-thump of the song (it must have been *really* loud through the headphones) but it did not bother him in the least. He closed his eyes again and slept.

Day Five

1

New York City, New York

Detective Mark Julian was happy to be on the road, driving fast on the highway to New York City in his old Ford Explorer. It felt good to be away from his office, away from angry phone calls, away from frustrated crime victims, but it felt especially good to be away from Ithaca, the centre of the surgical murders. No fingerprints and no real leads. The latest revelations from the professor were interesting but speculative. Whatever happened to the good old days when bad guys killed good guys over money or women?

Mark was on the outskirts of New York City in search of an Anthroposophist named Doctor Friedrich Adler at the Rudolf Steiner Wellness Center in Manhattan. After some checking, he had learned that Doctor Adler was considered one of the more prominent Anthroposophical doctors in the United States. Hopefully, it would be worth the four-hour drive. Until that week, Mark had never even heard of an Anthroposophical doctor.

The building sat nestled between huge oak trees on 87th just off of Columbus; it was more like a big old house in a residential area than a medical building. He obeyed the *Please Park at Rear* sign, which meant driving down an old lane and finding a spot in a very tidy carport. He entered the house via a pathway through a garden, up wooden stairs and into a little office that must have been someone's kitchen some years ago. A friendly-looking woman in her mid-fifties sat behind a counter. She wore a plain, light brown cotton dress and a purple scarf. Large wooden astrology symbols hung like Christmas tree ornaments from her ears.

"Hello," the woman said, still smiling. "Do you have an appointment?"

"I'm Detective Julian from Ithaca." He showed his badge.

The smile disappeared. The woman looked down, shuffled papers on the counter and then looked up again. The smile reappeared. "Yes, you called. One moment, I'll see if Doctor Adler can see you now." She stood, walked into an adjoining office and popped out a few seconds later.

"Please go right in," she said.

Doctor Friedrich Adler was a tall, middle-aged man with lots of gray curls on his thin head. Old-fashioned spectacles sat on the bridge of a hawk-like nose. He wore thick dark corduroys and a white lab coat over a sweater. The man exuded confidence and extended a bony hand as the detective entered his office.

They exchanged introductions. The office was not a typical doctor's office. There was a counter and a sink in one corner and a few instruments hung on a wall, but the rest of the room resembled a home office.

"What can I do for you, detective?" the doctor asked. "My secretary did not confirm the nature of your visit so I don't know if this is a visit to the doctor or if it has to do with police business." His voice was deep and strong and slightly nasal.

"It's police business, I'm afraid," Mark said.

"I'm afraid too," Doctor Adler said. "Because now I will not be able to bill you for my time." He chuckled.

Mark smiled politely. He sat and the doctor took his place behind his desk.

"I suspect you've heard about the rash of murders we've had up in Ithaca?" Mark asked.

"Terrible. Yes, I read about that in the newspapers. Terrible."

"You wouldn't happen to know anything about those murders?"

The man removed his thin wire-framed glasses and rubbed his eyes. "No, of course not." He replaced his glasses. "Why would I know about such things?"

Mark detected a slight German accent. "We're checking all possible leads. One lead suggests the killer might have something to do with surgery— maybe works in a hospital or could possibly be a physician."

"You are checking with every doctor in the state of New York? That's a lot of doctors."

"Not every doctor." He watched Doctor Adler closely—looking for a reaction. Although he would never admit it, he enjoyed this part of the job.

The man was visibly upset. Adler stood behind his desk and frowned. "What are you saying? You think I have something to do with murders in Ithaca? Why do you think this?" His voice was loud and packed with anger. "What would compel you to suggest such a thing?"

"Don't get me wrong, doctor," Mark said. "I'm not suggesting you have anything to do with the murders but due to certain circumstances, we think there might be a link to your branch of medicine."

"Anthroposophic medicine deals with healing people, detective!" The doctor's anger had shifted into high gear. "We deal with the whole person in order to heal, not to destroy." His breathing was hard and fast and he slammed a hand on his desk. He glared down at Mark. "I resent this line of questioning!"

Mark stared up at the man across the desk. He did not like to be yelled at and he was now interested in the doctor's angry reaction. *If I can wind him up a little more maybe he'll say something—perhaps he knows something . . .*

"I did not accuse you of anything, doctor. But it looks like someone familiar with your Anthroposophic medicine might have something to do with these murders." *The doc was fuming.* "I mean you must admit there are some pretty odd characters involved in your religion." Mark stood.

"Get out! Get out!" The doctor stormed around from behind his desk and stood toe-to-toe with Mark. "Anthroposophy is not a religion and there are no odd characters here!" His eyes were like flamethrowers behind the old-fashioned glasses.

"I'm not finished," Mark said. He stared into those wild eyes, not six inches in front of his face. "I'd like to know where you were at certain times last week." Mark calmly sat back down and pulled a pad of paper from a shirt pocket.

Doctor Adler's breathing slowed to a normal pace. He blinked hard a few times, tapped a hand on his desk and returned to his chair. He was trying hard to compose himself. "I cannot believe that anyone involved in Anthroposophy or the medical arts would ever commit a murder."

"Lots of pleasant people do terrible things, doctor," Mark said. "I see it every day."

Mark proceeded to gather information from the doctor regarding his whereabouts during the times of the murders. He was pretty sure the man had not killed anyone but putting a suspect on the defensive is never a bad idea. He was saving his key question for the end.

As he finished taking notes, he made a point of apologizing for any misunderstanding, and then he stood and extended a hand. "Thanks for your cooperation." They shook hands and Mark did not let go. He smiled. "Oh," he said quickly, "do you happen to know if any Anthroposophical doctors might be visiting New York now? Maybe from Europe?"

Strike one.

Their hands were still linked and Mark could feel it. Doctor Adler pulled out of the handshake, but not before Mark felt a slight tightening of the muscles in his hand. This was Mark's own little lie detector test; he'd used it many times. Hold the hand and stare into the eyes.

"No, I don't know of any," the doctor said. He shook his head and looked away. "I have not heard of any visiting doctors."

"OK," Mark said. "Thanks again for your time." He left the office, strolled through the kitchen-like reception area, smiled at the receptionist, pulled open the door to the outside and turned around.

"Oh, excuse me," he said to the woman. "Do you know of any visiting Anthroposophical doctors in New York? Maybe from Germany or Switzerland?"

Strike two.

The smile fell fast from the woman's face. Her eyes were afraid. The doctor arrived and stood beside her, pretending to look at some papers on her desk. "No," she said. "I don't know anything about that."

"You sure?"

"Yes, I'm sure," she said, not able to meet his eyes with hers.

As his Explorer pulled out of the little carport, Mark looked back at the house. Doctor Adler was standing at the window, pulling back the peach-colored curtains, and talking on the phone while watching him leave.

Strike three.

Mark had planned on visiting another doctor on his way back to Ithaca but when he stopped at the Steiner Medical Holistic Centre in Scranton, he was told the good doctor had been called away on an emergency—one that the receptionist (who turned out to be the doc's wife) knew nothing about. Mark was not surprised.

Finally! He smiled to himself. *Finally, a break in this case.* Now he needed to look into visiting Anthroposophical doctors from Europe. He turned on the radio, found the classic rock station, pushed the volume to high and smiled again as Stairway to Heaven accompanied him home to Ithaca.

2

Dornach, Switzerland

Karl Heisman sat and stared at the old black rotary telephone on his antique roll top desk. The phone would ring soon. Perfectly trimmed fingernails slid through his neat goatee as two beeswax candles cast a soft light throughout the tiny attic office. It was his favorite part of the house and nobody—*nobody*—except him had been in that room since the death of his father. Old framed black and white photographs hung bunched together on one wall, images of family and friends and distinguished visitors, proud and stoic faces from long ago, staring in earnest at the camera.

As he had done every time he sat at that desk since his father's death, Karl stared hard at one particular photograph, that of his grandfather standing beside the most important figure in his family's life: the great Austrian occultist, Doctor Rudolf Steiner. His grandfather had been under the master's tutelage from 1910 until Steiner's death in 1925. That special relationship had sparked the great mission of the Heisman family for generations.

After Herr Steiner had crossed the threshold, Karl's grandfather had continued to work secretly within the Society. This was important work, spiritual work and Karl knew that the mission to save the soul of humanity now rested with him. Karl Heisman would help fulfill Man's true destiny according to the knowledge and secrets handed down from father to son since the time of Rudolf Steiner.

Karl sighed and stared into the photograph, gazed into Steiner's deep, dark, loving eyes. He knew their karmic connection was very strong. He could feel it. Karl would not let his master down.

When the old telephone rang, Karl tore his eyes from those of his guru.

"Karl Heisman."

"Dave Dunigan in Canada. How are you, Karl?" The voice sounded upbeat.

Karl looked at his watch. "You are on time."

"Science demands precision. Especially Spiritual Science." A muffled laugh.

"Yours is the last report of the day."

"A couple of loose ends but all is well."

Karl did not like loose ends. He hesitated briefly before responding. "You will be here tomorrow as planned?"

"There is no need for concern, Karl. Except . . ."

"Yes?"

"The good doctor is making front page news in New York. Did you know?"

Karl sighed into the phone. "There is nothing we can do about it. He is very good at what he does. He's a professional."

"But why does it need to be so damn public?" There was an edge to Dave Dunigan's voice.

Karl did not like where this was going. "I will not discuss this on the telephone. The doctor is a valuable member of the Group and he knows his destiny. You would be wise to consider your own role in this mission. Your work, I might add, will soon be extremely public." He paused. "A few deaths in New York will pale in comparison. We each follow the path that was put before us." Karl's eyes darted back to the photo of his master. "Karma demands this of us."

"I've got a small problem in Winnipeg."

"I do not like problems, Mr. Dunigan."

"I said it's a small problem. Please be patient."

Karl sighed again. "I will see you tomorrow."

He hung up the phone, blew out both candles, and sat alone in the dark. Tomorrow would be a glorious day!

3

Ithaca, New York

When the plain-clothes cop escorted Paul Sung from his hotel room, through the lobby and to the waiting car, Paul had no idea that someone might be watching them leave. It was only when they began to drive away that he happened to look back and see a big man in a khaki trench coat standing at the hotel entrance.

Paul jerked his head forward and felt his heart pounding. The man resembled the fellow he had seen outside his office the previous day. *The day the policemen were murdered*. Paul turned again and the man was gone.

He was being driven to a safe house in an unmarked police car; he wondered if he should mention the man in the trench coat to the driver. No, he thought, I'm tired and my nerves are tight. Perhaps I'm mistaken—maybe it was a trick of a tired mind. No need to appear paranoid. Let it go.

He had phoned the university earlier to have a colleague cover his classes for the next few days. He planned on using the time at the safe house to prepare for his next semester's course: Myth, Ritual and Symbology in the New Age. *How appropriate*.

The safe house was a tiny bungalow just outside of town. The interior was straight from the 1970s—flowered wallpaper in the kitchen, shag carpet in the living room and chairs that belonged in the past. As he unpacked his things, Paul wondered who else had stayed there over the years. He imagined mafia informants or defecting diplomats during the cold war, but in reality he knew such things were unlikely in the peaceful little town of Ithaca. Of course, until recently, who would have guessed that same little town would host a series of horrific murders?

The two young policemen assigned to stay with him were pleasant but professional. Officers Derrick and Cooper. They both looked like movie marines—short hair and lots of muscle. Detective Julian had handpicked both men for the job.

The only good news that day was the discovery that the kitchen had been well stocked with food and drink. Paul was pleasantly surprised to discover a bottle of decent Bordeaux in the pantry and decided to calm his frayed nerves with a glass of wine, a few wheat crackers and smoked Gouda. He had just sat down at the kitchen table when Mark Julian arrived. He was pleased to see the detective and offered him a glass of wine.

"Not supposed to drink on duty," the detective said. Then he smiled and went to the fridge. "On the other hand, I could use a beer."

"Please try some of this Bordeaux," Paul said. "I was in France a few years ago and visited some wineries." He picked up the bottle. "I was delighted to find this here. Bordeaux is a beautiful place and the locals make very good wine."

"I believe you, Professor," Mark said, "but I'm just a plain, old fashioned beer guy." He grabbed a bottle of Becks from the fridge. "Luckily, I have enough seniority in the department to decide what kind of beer finds its way into this fridge. Call me a snob but I prefer German beer over what we produce here in the US of A." He grabbed an opener from a kitchen drawer, popped the cap and drank from the bottle. He pulled up a chair and sat at the kitchen table. "How's the new home away from home?"

"Just fine," Paul said. He wondered how long this place would be his "home."

Mark suggested they not talk shop right away. "Sometimes it's better to relax frayed nerves for a while," he said. "Take a break from the stress of the moment."

They chatted about their careers. Paul already knew that although they lived in different worlds, there were common threads running through their lives. He had already learned that the detective was divorced and lived alone, and now he learned that Mark was considering early retirement.

"Aren't you too young to retire?" Paul asked.

"Technically, yes." Mark sipped his beer. "But I need a change. I have no idea what that means but it's about half time in the game of life. Time to reassess the game plan. Hell, it's probably just a simple mid-life crisis." He forced a chuckle and drank more beer. "How about you? Plan on staying at Cornell for a while?"

Paul swirled Bordeaux in his glass and sipped. "I could retire now and be comfortable for the rest of my days."

"Define *comfortable*." Mark smiled.

Paul raised his glass. "Touché. I should say *financially secure*. Comfort is another thing entirely. Since my wife left I have had very little interest in anything except my work." Paul realized this was probably the first time he had ever used the words *since my wife left*. When speaking with colleagues or friends he would always use the generic term, *since the divorce*.

Mark finished his Becks. "From what I've seen at Cornell, there is no shortage of lovely ladies."

Paul chuckled. "Please, I have no false illusions. The flirtatious nature of most students is directly related to their academic needs. I doubt grad students are sincerely interested in a short, balding, sixty-two year old man with very few interests other than history and philosophy."

"What about faculty?"

"Sure, there is a vibrant social scene but to be honest, I'm just not interested." Paul popped a cracker into his mouth and wiped his hands on a napkin. "And you? You're younger than me. What's your excuse?"

"Work."

Paul raised his eyebrows, waiting for the rest of the sentence.

Mark smiled. "Well, OK, I don't want to get burned again." He took a deep breath and sighed. "My ex got fed up with my long hours in NYC and she became best friends with a bottle. I'll take part of the blame."

"She's still an alcoholic?"

"That's the good and bad thing. I finally got a transfer to Ithaca—tried to keep better hours and I thought I was spending lots of time with her, supported all her AA meetings. We bought a nice little townhouse, joined a hiking club and went camping sometimes on weekends. She was doing great."

"What happened?"

"She met a guy at an AA meeting and told me she finally understood what love was all about. She moved in with him less than a month later. That was four years ago and last I heard they're still together and both sober."

"Ouch."

"Shit happens. Good news is she's sober."

Paul finished his wine and rinsed the glass in the sink. "What really intrigues me these days is discovering bright young minds. Every once in a while a student shows sincere passion for a subject and I feel that my job is worth something. Working with curious, intelligent students still excites me."

"Like Greg Matheson?"

"Yes."

"Too bad. Such a waste."

"You think this guy will kill again, Mark?"

"Not if I can help it. At least we might have something to go on."

"You got something from an Anthroposophical doctor in New York?"

"I think so."

"Fill me in."

4

Ithaca, New York

Mark opened another beer. "I only met with one doctor. The other guy got a warning call and disappeared. I guess these voodoo docs can do that—simply disappear." He grinned and sipped his beer. "I'm sure Doc Adler in Manhattan knows something—maybe not about the murders but he knows something. My guess is that somewhere in New York there is a visiting anthro doc who might just be our man."

"Really?"

"I played a hunch and got a reaction. Which reminds me . . . is there a way to look for one of these characters online—one who might have experience with larynxes?"

Paul flipped open his laptop. "I'd guess there are not too many Anthroposophical doctors performing that type of surgery. Probably none, in fact. Let's see . . . you've already been to see Doctor Adler in Manhattan."

Paul found two websites and a few clicks later was opening various pages, reading each quickly until he stopped and gazed carefully at one page in particular.

Mark stood and looked over Paul's shoulder. "Got something?"

"There is a reference to an article that mentions a specialist . . . hold on." *Click . . . click . . . click . . .* "Seems there's an Anthroposophical doctor from Austria . . . no, it appears he is not an Anthroposophist . . . this is strange."

"What is it?"

"There are some medical articles at this German site and plenty of links. If I use an advanced search . . ." *Click . . . click . . . click . . .* "I can find a specialist who performs laryngectomies but there is no mention of him being an Anthroposophical doctor . . . so why is he . . ." *Click . . . click . . .* "why does the same name pop up when I . . ." *Click . . .* "when I search . . ."

Mark tried to follow but Paul's babbling, incessant clicking and unfinished sentences were irritating. "I'll wait until you're finished."

Paul seemed lost in thought, travelling back and forth between websites and various articles on his laptop. He had opened seven PDFs, a few word documents and a dozen websites and bounced around them all with experienced precision.

While Mark was impressed with the speed of the uncanny research, he was equally as frustrated at watching something that made no sense to him. Most of it was in German.

Paul eventually pressed his face closer to the screen, reading a scanned document with tiny Arial font. "Strange, it looks like some of these papers are missing a few footnotes—it's as if they have been intentionally removed and some seem to have been altered. Not easy to do with a scanned document—especially when the document is old. You'd need to use photo editing software but it looks like the actual letters are not exactly the same as the original." He turned and looked at Mark. "Have a look."

Mark pulled up a chair as Paul spun the laptop in front of him.

"Look," Paul said, "see the list of footnotes here?" He pointed to the tiny type at the bottom of a scanned PDF. "I can enlarge it—there."

Mark looked at a list of footnotes and sure enough, one of them was slightly different from the others. The letters were crisper, not much but enough to notice. Paul clicked to another document with another doctored footnote. Then he pulled up a PDF that was missing a reference and he showed Mark a sentence from another article and then pointed to another missing reference.

"Interesting," Mark said. "But what is the significance?"

"Somebody," the professor said, "went to a lot of trouble to alter these documents; unless you were specifically looking for them—or at least reading the references closely, you'd never know they'd been changed. Most people don't even look at footnotes."

"So the question," Mark offered, "is why?"

Paul continued to click and a dozen pages flipped up on the screen, one after another and then a website arrived with a photo of what appeared to be a small hospital surrounded by gardens and trees. As was the case with some of the other websites and papers Paul had accessed, this one was in German.

"I take it you are fluent in German?" Mark asked.

"Pretty close," Paul said. "German is necessary if your field of study includes esoteric movements in Europe." He clicked on a link at the side of the page, scrolled down a big block of text and highlighted a sentence in the middle of a long paragraph. He aimed the cursor at the word *Kehlkopf* and then he pointed to a name in that same sentence: *Dr. med Fritz Fleischer.*

Paul sat back and folded his arms. "*Kehlkopf,*" he said, "is *larynx* in German and it seems a Dr. Fritz Fleischer is an Austrian specialist in the fine art of laryngectomy. If needed, he can take out your larynx."

Mark felt a rush of adrenalin. "Or if not needed, maybe he'll do it anyway." He stared at the name on the screen. "But is he an Anthroposophical doctor? Is this our guy? Where is the connection?"

Paul smiled. "The connection is almost not there at all. He is not listed anywhere as an Anthroposophical doctor, nor is he in any physician directory anywhere. Despite somebody's best effort to erase the trail, however, we can see that the good doctor seems to have lectured at a number of Anthroposophy locations a number of years ago. There is at least one online reference to an article he must have written when he was younger. The article has been removed from all online archives. It was about Steiner's views on internal organs and the future of Man. This doctor seems to have disappeared for the past ten years."

Mark could barely control his excitement. Years of experience, however, had taught him to do just that: control excitement. Never show it and always think and act strategically. "Good work, Paul," he said, without a hint of exuberance in his voice. "We have a name. I'm guessing he's been using an alias here in the US but a name is useful." He tapped the kitchen table with a few fingers. "What about typing the name into Google—see if anything pops up?"

"I doubt we'll get that lucky," Paul said. "If someone has gone to this much trouble to rearrange his online biography, he will have made sure the name does not jump out of Google." Paul punched *Fritz Fleischer* into the search engine and watched a never-ending stream of results arrive on the screen. "Very common name, see?" He then typed: *Dr. Fritz Fleischer* and quickly scanned the results—most of them having nothing to do with what they were hoping for. Except for one result that simply read: *Dr. Fritz Fleischer, Impulsive Visitor* and the link was to YouTube.

Mark peered closer at the screen and pointed to the obscure reference. "What the hell is that all about?" he asked.

Paul said nothing. *Click* . . .

The two men silently watched two six-second black and white video clips, looped and repeating four times each. The camera was stationary, as if from a tripod pointing up. The lighting and quality were poor but there was no mistaking what they were watching. They could see the back of a large man in a trench coat, standing on a chair, arms outstretched. Something was dripping from his extended left hand. In his other hand he held a hammer and a long nail. He carefully positioned the nail and after a loud *thump! thump!* the gooey mess was attached to the ceiling.

Mark was the first to react. "God damn," he said. He had spent a couple of hours at that location a few days ago. He recognized Greg Matheson's bathroom. The second video clip simply showed a human larynx dripping from the ceiling of Bob Richardson's bedroom.

"God damn," Mark said, again. "He knows. The bastard knows we're on to him." Mark pushed *play*, and watched the disgusting video clips again.

Paul stood, poured a glass of water and drank quickly. He left the tap open longer and splashed cold water on his face. *I saw that man at the university and at the hotel!* He grabbed a small towel from the counter and sat down again beside Mark.

"Who uploaded the video?" Mark asked.

Paul tapped a few keys on his laptop and looked at his watch. "Only thing I can see is that he uploaded the clips to YouTube about three hours ago. No idea where it came from." He paused for a moment before sharing the news: "I saw someone who resembled this guy—once at the university and I'm pretty sure he was outside the hotel when I left."

"Why didn't you tell me?" Mark asked.

Paul felt light-headed. "I thought he looked suspicious but I also thought I might be paranoid."

"Well, at least we know something about him now," Mark said. "I'll see if our tech guys can trace it." He pulled out his cell phone and walked to the living room.

Paul's stomach was in knots. He wanted desperately to wake up from this horrible nightmare. He stood by the kitchen window, staring out into the late September afternoon. The tiny backyard was partially covered in leaves and twigs. He wanted to go outside to rake the leaves. He felt like breathing cold fresh air. He wanted to do something productive, something that normal people do on cool, crisp days in the fall. He felt like getting away from this craziness. Could he—should he—suggest to Mark that he just pack up and get out of town? But he knew the answer. For his own safety, he needed to stay put in the little safe house on the outskirts of Ithaca.

Mark returned to the kitchen and poured himself a glass of water. "Some bright young computer nerd in NYC is looking into the video source," he said. "You never know. Maybe our doc made a mistake."

But both men knew that possibility was highly unlikely.

"It's been a long day," Mark said. He stood. "You OK here?"

"I'll be fine." Paul paused for a moment. "I've got to be honest though, Mark, I just want this to be finished. It's difficult enough dealing with the death of innocent people, but to know that this surgical killer might see me as his next target . . . it's a little unnerving."

"We'll get him, Paul."

The detective's cell phone beeped. Paul watched him read a text message and shake his head. "Doctor Adler in Manhattan changed his tune. Says he learned of a visiting Doctor Fritz Fleischer from Germany—says the guy used to be a good surgeon but is not to be trusted. Bit of a freak. He's burned a few bridges with his peers over the years. Adler has no idea where he is."

"Interesting," Paul said. "I guess his peers have cut him loose but are probably scared of him."

Mark stopped to speak with the two cops before leaving the bungalow. Officer Derrick asked Paul if he needed anything and walked up the street to a corner store. He returned with magazines: a Sports Illustrated for him and a Scientific American for Professor Sung. Paul flipped through the magazine and then stood by the window in the little living room.

It was late in the day and raindrops were drumming on the glass as gusts of wind rattled the shutters. An hour later Officer Cooper drove away and returned with enough Chinese food to feed a small army. As he sat down to eat, Paul noticed the locks on the kitchen door. There were two deadbolts and the door itself was metal. He then looked again at the windows and realized they were probably not glass. Officer Cooper watched his eyes darting around the room.

"Bullet proof windows," the young cop said. "Nobody gets in unless we say it's OK." He smiled and scooped Chow Mein with chopsticks. "We'll take care of you, Professor Sung."

"Thanks," Paul said, but he was not feeling particularly thankful. He dipped an egg roll into plum sauce but did not feel much like eating. He could not seem to stop the horrible YouTube video clips from playing over and over in his mind.

5

Zurich, Switzerland

Chris and his sister arrived mid-morning in Zurich. Surprisingly, Kate had already arranged for a rental car at the airport.

When he saw the car, he glared at her. "You're kidding, right?" Chris was getting to know his sister all over again.

"Hey, when in Rome."

"We're not in Rome and Porsches are made in Germany. This is Switzerland."

"Close enough," she said. "I've always wanted to drive a Carrera." She pushed a button on the key chain and the little trunk popped open. Their luggage barely fit but Chris had lots of room in the passenger seat.

Within two minutes they were travelling at close to two hundred kilometers per hour through the picturesque Swiss countryside on the road to Dornach, home of the Goetheanum and the world headquarters of the Anthroposophical Society.

It was no surprise to Chris that his sister loved driving the Porsche Carrera. She tore around bends in the highway like a gazelle on speed. Chris grabbed both sides of the beige leather seat with tense fingers and white knuckles. Experience with his sister over the years told him that if he asked her to slow down she would smile and speed up. Occasionally, he peeked at the speedometer, knowing that unlike a German *autobahn*, there actually *was* a speed limit in Switzerland. He wondered what would happen if the local police pulled them over . . .

They made the one-hour trip from Zurich to Dornach in thirty-seven minutes; luckily Kate slowed down at the turn-off and they navigated through the quiet streets of the town center, marveling at the massive building on the hill in the distance. Chris had seen photos of the Goetheanum on his laptop but pictures are never the same as actually being there.

He glanced at a brochure he had downloaded from the Internet, and read aloud as they drove:

> "The foundation stone for the first Goetheanum was set in 1913. Rudolf Steiner was the main architect and supervised construction until the building opened in 1920. Named after the famous German writer, Johann Wolfgang von Goethe—who Rudolf Steiner credited with important spiritual and scientific insight—the first Goetheanum burned to the ground under suspicious circumstances on New Year's Eve 1922. Rudolf Steiner built the model for the second Goetheanum but died before the building opened, unfinished, in 1928. The structure is built from reinforced concrete. The work of many architects has resulted in the magnificent building we see today. The Goetheanum is not only of spiritual significance to Anthroposophists; many tourists also visit the area year after year."

Chris looked up from the pamphlet. "I remember reading Goethe in college."

"He's the guy who wrote Faust, right?" Kate asked.

"And lots of other plays and poetry," Chris said. "Interesting that Steiner was a big fan. Do you remember the professor talking about Steiner's link with Freemasonry?"

"Yeah—Paul said that link was mentioned in his book—or at least in the unpublished chapter. So what?"

"Goethe was a Freemason."

"I guess that's not surprising." Kate grinned. "We should know by now that karma works in weird and wonderful and wacky ways."

Kate slowed the car as they approached the building. They pulled into a gravel parking lot. "So, we are playing tourist today, right?"

"Let's do whatever it takes to get in there and look for Mike," Chris said.

The day was sunny and cold, lending magnificent views of the rounded Jura Mountains near Dornach. Chris had been too busy surviving the drive to appreciate the beauty of the area. He stood beside the Carrera, pulled his eyes from the landscape and gazed up at the huge cement building.

Kate also stared upward, her eyes stopping briefly at the arches and oddly shaped windows and massive cement column-like walls. "This has got to be one of the strangest buildings on the planet," she said. "Holy shit, just look at it!" They had slowly walked to the front of the building and were min-gling with a dozen tourists on the promenade.

"Seems weird to think Mike might actually be here," Kate said. She looked at the smaller surrounding buildings and houses on the property. "They probably put him in one of those houses. I mean, how could he be staying in here when tourists are wandering around every day?"

"You might be right," Chris said. "But Paul Sung suggested we visit this place first. I doubt anyone knows we're here so we might just get lucky and bump into Mike right away." Chris felt a jolt of adrenalin at the thought of seeing his son. He looked at his watch. "It's not too late. Let's go."

It was like walking into a church. As they entered the main foyer, Chris stopped and looked up at the arching ceiling and curved walls. There were leaning and asymmetric arches everywhere and the windows were all different shapes, like strange iridescent, rounded panels from a weird dream. He could hear people speaking softly in German, voices echoing. A handful of visitors stood by a reception desk, listening to an overweight, white-haired woman wearing a long wool skirt, a baggy brown sweater, wool socks and leather sandals.

Chris and Kate joined the group and learned that a tour was about to be-gin. It was a private tour—luckily in English—but nobody seemed to care that they joined uninvited. They dutifully followed the group around the main hall, listening to the guide speak about the first Goetheanum that burned in a fire and the remarkable re-make of this current building by dedicated Anthroposophists in the 1920s. She spoke glowingly about the architecture, and the group marveled at the high, colored windows as they entered the main auditorium, a place where theatre and "eurythmy perfor-mances dazzle the public on a regular basis." The guide explained the spiritual iconography of etched and eerily coffin-shaped slabs of glowing hued glass.

They walked down arched corridors, all covered in an opaque, pastel-type finish called *lazure* that Chris recognized from the walls of Mike's Waldorf school back in Pinedale. He remembered recently reading about the spiritual significance of the *lazure* technique— something about it enabling the spiritual student to see through the material and into the spirit world.

"This is so weird," Kate whispered. They had stopped by a window and the tour guide was pointing to a field below while explaining how biodynamic vegetables are planted each spring using "special preparations and astrological indications."

"Weird and boring," Kate added. "Let's escape and poke around by ourselves." She did not wait for Chris to respond and walked away from the group towards a wooden sign that said: Cafeteria.

Chris caught up with his sister. "We can't just leave the group. I think we're supposed to stay with them—what if someone asks us where we're going?"

"We're going to get a cup of coffee. I've seen people wandering around here by themselves."

"But they belong here. They're Anthroposophists, not visitors."

"So, let's pretend we're Anthroposophists." She suddenly wore a crazy, fake smile. "Our karma is so beautiful . . ."

"Stop it," Chris said. It was hard not to chuckle at his sister's silly facial expression. It brought back memories. She would often mock people she disliked when they were younger. "The last thing we need is to make a scene and get kicked out."

A middle-aged man approached and extended a hand. "Hi folks, I couldn't help but overhear enough to know you speak English. I'm Dave Dunigan from Canada. How are you?"

Chris and his sister told the portly, well-dressed man they were from Los Angeles. They had decided not to tell anyone where they were really from. Just in case.

Dave Dunigan eyed them carefully. "Interesting times, eh? Are you here for Michaelmas?"

"Oh yes," Kate replied. She appeared sincere. "First Class and here for the very special event."

Chris thought: *Here she goes—Kate will try to get some information from this fellow . . .*

Dave Dunigan smiled. "The special event is around the corner. Good to finally meet people face-to-face after all this time. I'm sure you know about me. I'm from AECL—my people have been lobbying our Prime Minister in Ottawa for a couple of years now." Dave Dunigan smiled again, as if he were seeking their approval.

Kate glanced at her brother, as if to say: *don't say a word.* Then she returned her gaze to the Canadian. "It's important work." She nodded approvingly.

"Damn right," Dave said, bursting with pride. "Chinks won't know what hit them."

Chris winced and Kate somehow forced a smile. "Damn right," she said.

What the hell . . .

"I've only met a few members from the other sub-groups so far," Dave said. "I look forward to meeting everyone tonight."

Other sub-groups?

"We're just taking a break," Kate said. "Our group went on without us."

Dave Dunigan appeared confused. "Taking a break? Has your group already met today? Karl said nothing to me about this." His face was deadly serious. "Not with all these . . . people here."

Chris knew the ruse was over. Who the hell was Karl?

Kate would need to improvise. "Our group is here somewhere." She forced a smile.

Dave Dunigan studied them and then his face turned white. He stepped back. "You're with the *tour* group? Damn. We have a misunderstanding. You folks enjoy your visit." He turned, walked quickly across the foyer and started up a winding stone staircase. He looked back once and then ran up the stairs.

6

Dornach, Switzerland

Kate glared at her brother. "Holy shit!" she said. "What the hell was that all about?"

"I need to sit down," Chris said.

He followed her into the spacious cafeteria. The room was beautiful, with a marble floor, dreamy wet-on-wet paintings on paneled walls and wood-framed windows overlooking a field. The sun appeared from behind dark clouds, lending extra light to the place. They stood by a wooden self-serve counter and each plucked a large muffin from glass containers. When they made their way to the cash register, a friendly young woman filled two cups with coffee, took their credit card and wished them a *"bon appétit."*

"See," Kate said. "Nobody cares if we wander around."

"Here in the cafeteria maybe, but there is no way they'll let us go through each and every room looking for Mike."

"So what's up with that nut from Canada? He's lobbying their prime minister and the chinks won't know what hit them? What the fuck?"

Chris sighed. "I have no idea. And what is AECL? Somewhere or something in Canada?"

"Beats me. Talk about racist crap. I know their guru did not think much of Asians but this Canadian is over the top."

Kate buttered her muffin and took a bite. "Whoa, this is really good." She swallowed, took another bite and then sipped her coffee. "These folks are crazy but they sure make good muffins." She looked around the cafeteria. "And this place is spotless, did you notice? I mean, you could eat off the floor."

Chris could not get his son out of his mind. "I just want to find Mike and go home." The novelty of being in Switzerland was wearing off already. "I'm feeling the jet lag and I want my son."

An old pudgy woman arrived and wiped tables that were already clean. She wore a strange assortment of what looked more like old wool blankets than actual clothes. After each swipe of sponge on table, she pulled at her garments, adjusting them as if afraid they would suddenly drop to the floor. Bits of gray hair protruded from a dyed burgundy scarf that covered most of her head. She turned and waddled behind the counter where she checked a few steel pots of soup, and then spoke in whispers to the young woman at the register.

"Check her out," Kate said, nodding towards the woman. "I wonder if the old gal knows about Mike."

The odd little woman returned to wipe tables, mumbling softly to herself and moving from one table to another until she was wiping the already spotless table beside Kate and Chris. They sat quietly, sipped coffee and tried not to stare.

"Looks like the sun is coming out," Kate said to the woman.

No response.

"I said it looks like the sun is coming out," she repeated, much louder.

The woman jerked to a stop, sponge in hand, and stared at Kate with surprisingly clear brown eyes. "Vahss?" she said. "You shpeak in English?" Her German accent was strong.

"Yes," Kate said. "We speak English." The old woman continued to stare. "The muffins are delicious and so is the coffee," Kate added. "Have you worked here long?"

The old woman pulled a chair to their table and sat down as if they were all the best of friends. She leaned into Kate and suddenly seemed quite excited. "Oh yes, I vork here for lonk time." She showed a nearly toothless smile and looked around the cafeteria. "My home is mit Goetheanum and Doktor Steiner." She smiled again.

Kate exchanged a split-second look with Chris, as if to say: *I know this woman has a few missing marbles but here's our chance to get some information.*

"You live here," Kate said. "Lucky you. The spiritual center of Anthroposophy is magnificent—wonderful!"

The woman's eyes swam from side to side as she grinned. "Zeese is best time for visit Goetheanum," she said quietly. "Best time."

Chris felt his heart skip a beat. "Why is that?" he asked. "Why is this the best time to visit?"

The raggedy old woman looked right through him. "Mik-eye-ell-mas!" she said, almost yelling now. She went on to explain in very broken English that Michaelmas is a spiritual time and many important Anthroposophists were in town from all over the world for the conference. "Many from First Class are here!"

"It must be very exciting," Kate said. "We came for Michaelmas, too." She looked at Chris and tried to show a sincere smile. "I can feel the vibration of Rudolf Steiner at this very moment."

The old woman stopped smiling. Her eyes shot wide open and she put a bony old hand to her mouth. "You . . . you are First Class?"

"We are from America," Kate said, not answering the question. "We are here for Michaelmas." She leaned across the table and took a wrinkled hand in hers. "I feel it is my karma to connect with the Goetheanum now at this very minute." She leaned closer and whispered: "Are you able to show us some of the rooms here? I see that you are very connected to this spiritual place and can help us to prepare for Michaelmas. I am sure Herr Steiner would approve."

The woman beamed with pride. "Ya ya ya," she said. "You come. You come!" She stood and motioned for them to follow her from the cafeteria. "I kook here and clean. My nahm ist Dott."

"Nice to meet you, Dott," Kate said.

Chris felt some guilt with this deception. They were, however, there for a reason and what harm could come from accepting the old woman's hospitality? Finding Mike should be their only priority. He followed along, trusting in his sister's ability to play the game—and win.

Dott led them down a hallway, up a spiral staircase and through an archway to another corridor where they stopped by a closed door. She paused for a moment, opened the door, and walked to the end of the small room where she stood and looked back. She pointed to an old desk and bed. "My place," she said. "I schloff—shleeping in ziss room—my room."

"This is your room," said Chris. "Very nice, Dott."

"How wonderful that you can live in the building," Kate said. "Does anyone else stay in the Goetheanum?"

At first it appeared as if Dott had not understood the question but then her eyes shot wide open and she spoke again.

"I shtay here allvays," she said. "Now is shpecial time—gooot time mit Mik-eye-ell-mas and shpecial visitors." She stood beside a small shelf and pulled a few Anthroposophy books out for them to see. "Allvayss shtudy Schteiner books." She smiled her yellow and brown-toothed smile and pulled at her blanket-like clothes.

"What special visitors are here?" Chris asked.

"We've heard there is a very special visitor," Kate added. "A young boy."

Dott replaced the books and sat on her little bed. Her smile disappeared and she stared hard at a beige throw rug covering the tiled floor. She seemed disturbed, as if deep in thought.

"Dott," Kate said, "we've heard there is a special visitor—a young boy. Have you seen him?"

The old woman seemed confused and continued to stare at the floor. She mumbled something under her breath and then looked at Kate.

Were those tears in her tired old eyes?

She sat looking at them, and then her eyes went over their shoulders to the doorway of her little room.

"You have company, Dott," a man's voice said from behind them.

Chris and Kate turned to see a heavy-set bearded man in a brown leather jacket standing in the doorway.

Old Dott shifted her pudgy body on the bed. "Guten Tag, Karl," she said, avoiding his eyes. There was no mistaking the fear in her voice.

7

Dornach, Switzerland

Chris tried to hide his anxiety and was relieved when his sister broke the awkward silence.

"Hello," Kate said. "Dott was showing us her room and her wonderful books."

"Are you with a tour group?" the man asked.

"We *were* with the group," Kate said, "but we stopped for a coffee and met Dott and here we are."

"Visitors are not to wander freely in this area," the man said. He stared hard at Kate and then moved his steely eyes to Chris.

Kate glared at the man. "But as this is Dott's room," she said, "this would be her area. We are not wandering freely—whatever that means."

Dott stood. "First Class," she said to the man. "First Class here for Mik-eye-ell-mas."

The man was not fooled as he looked from Kate to Chris. "You are both First Class Holders?" he asked, sounding scornful. "You have blue membership cards?"

Chris did not want his sister to twist the truth into a pretzel. "Oh no," he said, trying to appear surprised. "I think Dott misunderstood. We are just visiting the Goetheanum."

"And what is your relationship with Anthroposophy?" the man asked, with a slight German accent. He continued to block the doorway.

"I've been interested for some time," Chris said, "and I'm thrilled to be here now." He pointed to Kate and decided against introducing her as his sister. "My friend is quite new to Spiritual Science but has expressed an interest in learning."

"Books!" said Dott, reaching to her shelf again.

"There is an excellent book store on the main level," the man said. His eyes flitted from Kate to Chris and back again to Kate. "Have you seen the book store yet?"

Kate stared at the man. "We'll get to the book store in good time," she said. "For now we're happy to visit with Dott." She smiled and looked again at the old woman. "Which book is your favorite?"

Dott pulled out a book and rattled off the title quickly in German. Then she grabbed another book and started to speak.

The man interrupted. "Dott enjoys reading *Knowledge of the Higher Worlds*," he said. "You know this book, of course?" He looked at Chris.

"Of course," Chris said. He remembered reading an excerpt from it online two days ago. "It is one of Steiner's most important books."

Chris knew his sister was on the edge of letting the charade fall apart. He knew she wanted to get rid of this guy and continue questioning old Dott. But he also knew Kate's lack of tact could easily blow their cover and have them tossed out of the building. Clearly, the man was not pleased with them being there, but something else was wrong—the guy was too cautious, too careful, and too curious. Who cares if a couple of visitors chat with the cook? Perhaps the racist Canadian they met earlier had sounded the alarm.

Surprisingly, the man extended a hand. "My name is Karl Heisman. And you are . . . ?"

"I'm Geraldine and this is Tom," Kate said, shaking the man's hand, and then leaving it for *Tom*.

Tom and Jerry, Chris thought. *Kate is impossible!*

"Where are you from?" Karl asked.

"Just outside of Los Angeles," Kate lied. "United States of America. How about you, Karl?"

"Austria," Karl said, still eyeing them suspiciously. He looked at the old woman. "Dott, I think you are needed in the kitchen."

Dott seemed confused. She looked at a small wooden cuckoo clock on the wall. "Ich habe—"

"Dott," Karl said again, sharply. He frowned at her.

She understood. She pulled at her blanket-clothes and mumbled something softly under her breath. Karl, Kate, and Chris followed her from the room and returned to the lower level where Dott shuffled through a doorway, but not before turning to say something about Mik-eye-ell-mas and special guests.

"She has been with us for many years," Karl said. "She gets confused from time to time." They were at the main foyer now and it was clear that Karl wanted them out of the building. A few people arrived through the big front doors and headed quickly past them down a corridor, talking quietly as they walked—men in suits and a few women in layers of wool and cotton.

"We'd like to look around some more," Kate said.

"I'm sorry," Karl said, "but there is only one tour group in the building now and they have almost finished. We'll be closing to the public shortly."

Chris saw his window of opportunity shutting, but he needed more answers. "I've heard," he said, hoping the panic was not obvious in his voice, "that there are many secret rooms in here and special guests sometimes stay in the building—especially at Michaelmas."

Karl smiled. "I wouldn't know about that." He looked at his watch. "You will excuse me." He opened the main door and motioned for them to leave.

Chris knew Kate would protest. He grabbed her hand and squeezed. He secretly wanted to run right past Karl and look into every little room and alcove in the building. He wanted to scream and shout Mike's name over and over until he found his son. He wanted to hold Mike in his arms and never let him go. But instead he said, "Thank-you for your time, Karl. We enjoyed our visit."

Kate started to speak and Chris squeezed her hand—hard. She got the message, said a polite good-bye and they walked down the steps to the visitor parking lot.

"That Karl is full of shit," Kate said. She looked at Chris. "He knows something, Chris. The ass-hole knows something!"

"I'm not sure, Kate," he said, hoping to calm her down; after all, she would be driving them both to their hotel. "They're all pretty loopy. What about old Dott?"

"She's nuts. At least she's sincere . . . but that Karl—he's just a lying bastard." She started the car and pulled out of the parking lot. "We've got to get back in there, Chris."

"Tomorrow they're probably closed to the public," Chris said. "They have their special Michaelmas conference, remember?"

Chris looked back at the building as they drove from the parking lot. "Hold on," he said. "Stop!"

Walking towards them quickly from one side of the magnificent Goetheanum was a little figure wrapped in blankets. Dott.

Kate slammed the brake pedal and they both hopped out of the car. They met her near the edge of the parking lot; the odd little woman looked once over her shoulder at the building and then stared at Chris.

She seemed disoriented—perhaps frightened? "Mik-eye-ell . . ." she said, her voice trailing to a whisper. Her eyelids stretched wide, and then she took a few short breaths. She smiled and a bewildered expression swept over her wrinkled face. She fell to the ground and her eyes closed.

"Shit!" Kate knelt beside the old woman, grabbed a wrist and checked for a pulse. "Call an ambulance—now!"

Neither of them had a cell phone. Chris took off running and tried the main doors of the Goetheanum. Locked. He pounded hard but nobody came. He ran back down the steps and saw his sister administering CPR to old Dott. He was not surprised to learn that Kate possessed that skill. He ran to the far edge of the parking lot and saw an elderly couple walking towards him from a small hobbit-type house not far away.

"Hello!" Chris ran and waved. "Do you speak English? Yes? Phone an ambulance—ambulance! A woman needs help!" He pointed to Kate kneeling over Dott, continuing to push—push—push . . . on her chest. The old couple stood and stared.

A man came walking towards them from the main building, three others following on his footsteps. One of the followers Chris recognized as Karl Heisman.

"It's Dott!" Chris yelled. "Something's wrong—maybe a heart attack! We need an ambulance. Call an ambulance!"

The first man calmly knelt beside Dott, checked her pulse and heart, and then he looked at Kate and he sighed. "I'm sure you did your best," he said, "but she has left us now." His accent was unmistakably German.

"Call an ambulance," Kate said. "Find a defibrillator and quick!"

"There is no need for that," the man said. "It is too late."

"Too late?" Kate yelled. "She just fell down a few seconds ago." Kate continued to administer CPR. "It's not too late!"

"We have no defibrillator here," the man said calmly. "There is a clinic in town but it is closed now." He smiled at Kate. "You tried your best but it was simply her time to cross the threshold." The man stood and was joined by the other men. They stared at the little old body wrapped in blankets on the gravel.

Kate still knelt over Dott. *Push—push—push* . . . She looked up at the men as she worked. "Are you fucking crazy?" she screamed. "She needs help!"

The men did not move. They did not speak. The old couple from the field arrived and stared silently at Dott.

Kate continued to work on Dott but after two more minutes it was obvious that the old woman was indeed dead.

Karl finally spoke. "She was old and frail and it was her time to cross the threshold. Please accept our thanks for your efforts. We will take care of the body now."

Chris was glad Kate refrained from unleashing a barrage of insults at the Anthroposophists. He stood and looked down at Dott, feeling helpless, sad and more than a little confused.

"A doctor will need to sign the death certificate," Kate said.

Karl pointed to the man who had checked Dott's pulse. "This man is a doctor." He thanked them again for their concern.

Chris looked at the odd little group of Anthroposophists. No remorse, no sadness whatsoever. Their reaction to the death of their friend was no greater than if they had seen her sneeze.

As they got into the Carrera and drove away, Kate let loose: "Un-fucking believable. This man is a doctor—bullshit, he's probably one of their in-house anthro quacks!" She continued with a tirade of expletives and when she'd finally had enough, she asked Chris about his take on the shocking event.

"It was weird," he said. "Sure, Dott was old but the timing is too weird."

"No kidding," Kate said. "Remember what Paul Sung said? There are no coincidences with these people. My guess is that Karl asshole had her poisoned. The old woman was a liability." She slammed a hand on the dashboard. "She wanted to tell us something and they fucking killed her!"

"Maybe she did tell us something," Chris said. "Just before she fell."

Kate took a deep breath. "Yeah, she was nattering on about their Mik-eye-ell-mas conference."

"No," Chris said. He stared out the window as they drove. Cows grazed in pastures and low rolling mountains rose from grassy valleys in the background. It was like driving through a postcard. His mind returned to the present. "She only spoke one word, Kate."

"You sure?"

"I am sure," Chris said. "Just before she fell, she did not say Mik-eye-ell-mas." He paused. "What she said was *Mik-eye-ell*. Michael."

8

Dornach, Switzerland

Mike sat on the bed in his little room at the end of the long hallway on the top floor of the house beside the Goetheanum. He had not seen his mother at all that day and hoped he would see her for dinner. She was acting strange lately. Maybe she was sick.

He had spent hours that afternoon with Karl, repeating the same stupid picture exercises. Sometimes he was shown old desert scenes or people in rooms from the olden days and then the pictures were of symbols like stars and crosses and red roses. Men in suits and strange, silent women in long skirts watched him looking at the pictures and they smiled politely when he returned their gaze. Or they looked away.

Close your eyes, Mik-eye-ell... now open them slowly and look at the picture and tell me... how do you feel... you remember something, perhaps?

There were no other children anywhere and the only person he liked was the funny old lady in the courtyard, when he had been allowed outside. The feelings of boredom and frustration and confusion were nothing compared with the intense feelings of sadness that overwhelmed him as he lay alone in his room at the end of the hall.

He picked up a paper that Karl had given him to study. He would need to memorize all the words on that paper for some sort of speech he would have to deliver at a special ceremony later that night. Some holiday, Mike thought. These people are weird.

He stood on the little desk in his room and peeked out the window. "Cool car," he said to himself. At the end of the road leading away from the Goetheanum, he saw a bright red Porsche Carrera.

9

Ithaca, New York

It had been a long day and Detective Mark Julian was tired. After leaving Paul Sung at the safe house, he stopped to do some shopping and was looking forward to heading home. Unfortunately, his cell phone rang and his boss wanted to see him immediately.

As Mark returned to the station, the always-friendly receptionist was preparing herself to leave for the day. She told him he was to go immediately to the chief's office.

"And the chief has guests."

"Who are they?" Mark asked.

"I'm only the messenger," she said. She pulled on her coat. "You are to report to the chief . . . and his guests." She smiled and raised her thin eyebrows. "Serious suits. The chief was out most of the afternoon and just returned with both men a few minutes ago."

Mark made his way past the little lunch area and into a larger room with three desks and two cops at computers. He exchanged puzzled glances with the cops. One of the uniforms shrugged his shoulders as if to say, *I have no idea what this is all about.*

Mark looked through the glass door, saw two suits and the chief, knocked once and entered.

The men stood. "Hello, Mark," the chief said. He aimed a hand at the two strangers. "Bruce Bander, Ron Martins—this is Detective Mark Julian." They exchanged handshakes and Mark sat down.

"FBI?" Mark asked.

The older man smiled. "Something like that." He wore a single-breasted gray blazer, pinstriped vest and bulky navy blue tie. Although clean and well cut, the style was old and so was the man. He looked to be in his seventies.

The other man was middle aged and also dressed conservatively.

Mark glanced at his boss. The chief avoided his eyes for a moment and then cleared his throat. "They are from a special investigations branch of Homeland Security."

Mark raised an eyebrow. "Homeland Security?"

"Detective Julian," Bander said, "we're interested in your murder investigation."

It was not a question but the man paused as if waiting for a response. Mark said nothing.

"You visited Manhattan this morning and you think the suspect might be a visiting doctor from Europe?" That was definitely a question.

"That's right," Mark said. "News travels fast. I only learned of this today." He looked at both men and then at Chief Bischel. "What's this all about? Why is Homeland Security interested?"

The younger agent forced a weak smile. "I'm sure you understand that we cannot explain our reasons at this time."

Mark did not understand but sat and shared his information—the conversations with Paul Sung, the story of the dad and aunt and their trip to Switzerland in search of the missing boy from Oregon. Both men took copious notes.

"Listen, Mark," Chief Bischel said. "I'd like you to work full time on this case."

"Seems you have a good rapport with Dr. Sung," Bander said.

"He is a wealth of information," Mark said.

"So it seems," said Bander.

Chief Bischel exchanged glances with the agents and then looked at Mark. "He's gone, detective. Unfortunately, Paul Sung has disappeared."

Mark felt his blood run cold. He looked at his watch. "Gone? I was just with him two hours ago."

"There were problems at the safe house," the chief said.

Mark was stunned. "Where is he?"

"No idea." Chief Bischel tapped a nervous finger on his desk. "Both officers were found shot to death in the backyard and the professor is missing."

Mark's pulse was racing. "I can't believe this."

"It's very unfortunate," Bander said.

Mark glared at the agent. "Unfortunate? Two dead officers and Paul Sung missing is not just unfortunate. How the hell could this have happened?"

"We were hoping you might be able to tell us," the other agent said.

"How could I know anything?" *They think I have something to do with the professor's disappearance!* "I just told you—I made sure he got to the safe house and left him there a couple of hours ago."

They were staring at him . . . watching his reaction.

Agent Bander spoke: "What do you know about the brother and sister from Oregon? Did you tell them about the safe house?"

"Of course not," Mark said. He looked at the agents. "What the hell is going on? I only just met the people from Oregon and I'm not sure their problem has anything to do with this case."

"But Paul Sung thinks there is a connection," Martins said.

Mark's mind was buzzing with questions. "Yes, that's right." He wanted to change the direction of this conversation. "Have you checked the house for prints?" Mark did not want to mention the next obvious question but it was necessary. "And checked the surrounding area for Paul's body?"

"All been done," Chief Bischel said. He continued tapping his desk. "Ever been to Switzerland?"

"No," Mark said. He frowned. "Why?"

"You're booked on a flight this evening to Zurich."

"What? How can I work on the Ithaca murders from Switzerland?"

"Go for a few days; see what the Oregon folks are up to. Professor Sung thinks there is a connection, so poke around and see what you can learn. And keep me updated." He looked at the two agents. "I'll forward all reports directly to you."

"Just a minute," Mark said. "I'm at a disadvantage here. I'll need to know more about any parallel investigations or I'll be stumbling around in the dark."

"Sorry, detective," the chief said. "Even if I knew more, I would not be at liberty to tell you."

"Some decisions," Martins added, "are made further up the ladder." He smiled. "We're all pieces of the larger puzzle."

"And too many cooks can spoil the soup," his partner added.

And too many clichés can ruin the day, Mark thought. He was not fond of being low man on the information ladder. The men exchanged awkward handshakes and Mark headed back to his desk with plenty to think about.

Special agents from Homeland Security involved in my murder investigation? I'm off to Europe—what on earth is going on?

For the first time in recent memory, Mark felt very much like finding a bar and sitting down for as long as it took to empty a bottle of decent Scotch.

10

Ithaca, New York

A black Cadillac quietly crept onto the tarmac at Ithaca Tompkins Regional Airport just after dark. It pulled up beside a sleek black Learjet, its bright white taxi lights rhythmically cutting through the night sky. The driver exited and quickly made his way to the rear doors of the vehicle. The giant Doctor Fritz Fleischer stepped out of the passenger side and together they carried an unconscious body into the aircraft.

The driver smiled. "If you ever need me again, sir, please don't hesitate to call." Five thousand dollars was a decent wage for two hours of no-questions work.

The doctor handed the man an envelope stuffed with cash. "You have two children, aged seven and ten. You will speak to nobody of this work. Do we understand each other?"

The man crammed the envelope into a pocket. His hand was shaking. "No problem," he said as he got back into his car. He could not hide the fear in his voice. "You have a nice flight." He started the car and quickly made his way back to Ithaca.

Two minutes later the jet was accelerating down the runway and within ten minutes it was at thirty thousand feet, banking east en route to Basel, Switzerland.

11

Dornach, Switzerland

The little car screeched into the parking lot beside the Enzian Hotel in Dornach. The three star hotel was clean, comfortable and very friendly. They had decided to check in as Mr. and Mrs. Thompson and felt no need to explain to anyone in Switzerland that their relationship was that of brother and sister. Chris found it mildly amusing that people might think he was married to Kate.

Kate tossed her suitcase onto a table and flopped onto one of the beds. "I'm starting to see odd-ball Anthroposophists everywhere. I mean, there is friendly and there is *friendly*. Did you see all the smiles downstairs as we checked in?"

"No need to be paranoid," Chris said. "The Swiss are a friendly lot." He hoped his sister would try to relax. "And besides, even if some folks in Dornach *are* Anthroposophists, remember Paul Sung said they are decent people. He thinks the problem is a handful of hardcore nut bars, so let's not imagine danger around every corner." He lay on his bed, closed his eyes and saw an image of old Dott lying on the ground; he also heard the last word ever to leave her lips.

Mik-eye-ell.

"This is a fucking nightmare, Chris," Kate said. She was off the bed and drinking from a green glass bottle of complimentary hotel water. "We know they killed the old lady and I'm damn sure Mike is there—or at least nearby." She sat on the edge of the bed beside her brother. "What the hell is our next step?"

Chris opened his eyes and stared at the ceiling. "Maybe we should phone the local police."

"And tell them what? Nothing illegal has happened. A mother and son are visiting Switzerland and his dad and aunt would like to find them. Not exactly police business. An old lady suddenly dies and a local doctor signs the death certificate. Heart attacks happen. No need for an autopsy and the cops won't give a shit about two visiting Americans with conspiracy theories."

Chris closed his eyes again. Frustration and fatigue poured through him and his sister's negativism was only adding to the heaviness on his mind. He knew she was right but listening to her was not improving his mood.

Kate finished her water and thumped the bed with a fist. "Tomorrow is the start of their Michaelmas conference, right?"

"That's right."

"We think they brought Mike here because of that event, right?"

"That's what Professor Sung was thinking."

"Then we simply go back tomorrow. We'll wander around and try to find Mike."

"They already know us. Karl will not let us wander around."

"One thing I noticed today," Kate said, "was a lack of security. We push our way in tomorrow and find him."

"Kate, there will be tons of people there tomorrow. There is no way they'll let us push them around. They'll call the police and we'll be on the first plane back to the States."

"God damn it, Chris," Kate said, standing and looking out the window. "He's your son. You must have some rights—even in Switzerland. It's not 1950s Russia!"

"We've been over this," Chris said. "I phoned a lawyer before we left, remember? The law says this is a simple domestic dispute. If I want custody, I'll need to fill in the appropriate papers and blah blah blah. So no, at this point in time I don't have rights."

Kate opened a window and leaned her head outside. "I can see the god damn building from here. This is so frustrating."

They ate dinner at a nice little fondue restaurant and were feeling full but tired as they prepared for bed. "Maybe we should call Detective Julian," Chris said. "He told us to phone any time, remember?" He pulled out his wallet and found the detective's card. "We could call him right now from here—what do you think?"

"And what's he gonna do, Chris? Send the marines?"

Chris could feel his blood boiling. "Why do you have to be so—"

"So real?" She sighed. "Sorry Chris, maybe you're right. You wanna phone him?"

Chris looked at his sister. "Why don't you do it?"

Kate checked her watch. "It's almost 6:00 p.m. in New York." She picked up the hotel phone and dialed the detective's cell phone number.

The connection was good. "Detective Mark Julian."

Kate put him on speakerphone. "It's Kate here. Remember us—Kate and Chris Thompson from Oregon?"

"Hey, how are you? You made it to Switzerland?"

"Yeah, we're both here." She looked at her brother. "Just thought we'd check in."

Chris watched his sister walk around the tiny room as she spoke. She seemed nervous. He lay back on the bed and listened to the conversation.

"Anything wrong? Have you been to anthro headquarters yet?"

"We went there today and there was no sign of Mike but . . ."

"You tell me your news and I'll tell you mine."

"All right. We went to the Goetheanum and an old woman who worked there seemed like she wanted to tell us something—maybe about Mike. Before she could talk to us . . . she died. We think she was poisoned."

"Poisoned? You sure it was not simply an accident or a heart attack?"

"You think we're imagining this, detective? They fucking murdered her before she could talk to us. It happened. We were there."

"Were the local police contacted?"

"Of course not," Kate said. "Like they would believe a conspiracy theory from a couple of Americans? They had their own doctor there to say it was death by natural causes."

"We can talk about it when I get there."

"What?"

"I'm on my way to JFK right now. Tell me your hotel and I'll book a room before I leave."

"Why are you coming here?"

"I've got some bad news, Kate. Paul Sung has disappeared."

Chris felt his heart sink. He sat up on the bed and looked at his sister.

She sat beside him and spoke slowly into the phone. "You mean he left or . . . ?"

"He was kidnapped. And no, I have no idea how it could have happened. It makes no sense. We'll talk more in the morning. I should be there before breakfast."

Kate told him the name of their hotel and ended the call.

"This is unbelievable," Chris said. "It's like a bad dream."

"Fucking nightmare," Kate said. "But our priority is with Mike. He is up there." She pointed towards the strange building on the hill.

Chris tried to push the anxiety and frustration from his tired mind. He said nothing for a moment and watched Kate brushing her hair as she looked in a mirror beside a chest of drawers. He tried to remember when they had spent any real time together. It had been many years. Kate always seemed to exaggerate the hard edge to her tomboy personality but she could—if she so chose—be less threatening.

She caught him watching her in the mirror. "What are you looking at?"

"You. Do you remember mom always trying to get you to wear make-up and lady-like dresses when you were a teenager?"

"I remember. Could you really see me with a painted face and a flowery dress? The perfectly pretty princess?"

"Maybe. You looked great at my wedding."

"And that was probably the last time anyone saw me in a dress." She turned from the mirror and looked at her brother. "Dressing to impress is just not me; you get that, don't you?"

"Of course I get it. And don't think I did not appreciate your effort at my wedding." He lay down on the bed and stared at the ceiling. He remembered the wedding. "It seems like so long ago . . ."

"Before Serena went anthro," Kate said. "She was actually OK back then. Not quite my style but she was OK."

"Yeah, she sure was OK." He didn't want to wander down memory lane. Not now. "So what do you think of Detective Julian?"

"Oh *pull-ease*. You're trying to hook me up with a cop?"

"Hey—I only asked what you think of the guy. He seems like a decent sort, don't you think?"

Kate turned back to the mirror and pulled a brush through her short blond hair. "I refuse to answer on the grounds that I might incriminate myself." She put the brush down, stretched for a minute and fell onto her bed. "And you can take that however you want to take it, little brother."

Chris turned out the light and felt relieved that he was not alone. Kate was extroverted and often rude but she was his sister. She was all the family he had right now and he was glad to have her in his corner.

Later that night, a black stretch limousine crept up the hill and parked near a back entrance to the Goetheanum. Three men helped to unload a passenger and a few minutes later Doctor Fleischer was nudging a heavily sedated Paul Sung down a long corridor and into a hidden room deep beneath the magnificent old building.

12

Dornach, Switzerland

Usually, evening at the Goetheanum was a quiet time. This night, however, was unique. It was the night of the autumnal equinox and a select group of forty-eight members of the School of Spiritual Science was secretly gathered for a very special purpose.

The main auditorium was very much like the inside of a cathedral, with a high painted ceiling, heavy columns and beautiful stained glass windows. Theatre style seats arched back from the stage, but tonight only forty-seven people sat in the first few rows. These specially chosen members of the Society sat in silent reverence, looking up at a solitary figure on the stage before them. He was the forty-eighth member of their group. Dozens of candles illuminated the area at the front of the stage where the small, blond, blue-eyed Initiate would deliver what would later be referred to as *The Michaelmas Sermon*.

Mike looked down through the candles, trying to find a friendly face. He found none. He had been told to repeat a few well-rehearsed sentences and then he could go back to bed. Tomorrow they would leave this place. He could hardly wait until tomorrow.

As he had been instructed, he watched Karl in the first row. The tall, calm-looking man stroked his goatee while staring at an old silver pocket-watch and waiting for the exact moment of the fall equinox. Mike had been told that at exactly eleven fifty-eight and fifty-three seconds, the sun would align directly over the equator and Karl would signal for him to begin.

Karl finally looked up to the stage and nodded his head. Mike felt nervous but did as he was told. He took a very deep breath and spoke:

"I am Mik-eye-ell." His tiny voice echoed in the cathedral.

Karl's instructions had been clear: *Be confident. Sound confident. You are special. Do not hesitate.*

"These are special times," Mike continued, "and we have anticipated this moment for many, many years."

Mike peered through the glow of the candles. Shadows danced on the massive cement columns. The scent of melting beeswax was intense. He spotted Herr Ackermann in the second row, his hairless head still shining, his eyes wide as if telling Mike to *carry on, carry on—you can do it, boy!*

At his afternoon session with Karl, Mike had felt like running from the room in frustration.

I'm fed up with looking at hundreds of pictures and symbols. I don't know anything about the stupid pictures! What do you want from me? I just want to go home. What happened to Dott? At least she was kind . . .

Karl had not been pleased with his attitude. Mike hadn't seen his mother at all that day and Karl had told him he had better change his behavior *now* because he would need to speak later in front of some very distinguished guests. Karl did not exactly threaten him but Mike was smart enough to know what was expected tonight. Although he tried hard not to, Mike had cried tears of frustration that afternoon and neither Karl nor the others watching him had offered as much as a tissue. They simply sat and stared and Karl had said he needed to concentrate harder. Mike stopped crying, took some deep breaths and Karl then gave him a script that he was to practice over and over and over for the rest of the day. He would need to know the script by heart.

We have been told how special you are, Mik-eye-ell. This is your chance to prove it. We paid for you and your mother to come on this holiday and we do not ask for much in return. You don't want to disappoint us now, do you? Think of your teacher. Think of your mother . . .

If he recited the script properly, perhaps they really would leave this place tomorrow. He had repeated it a dozen times from memory to himself and a few times to Herr Ackermann so he should know it well enough now. It made no sense but he did as he was told. He cleared his throat, took a deep breath, looked first to the people seated below and then up to the vaulted ceiling. His small voice continued to echo in the large hall:

> "Here you are, four times twelve human beings, and the Mik-eye-ell
> Thought has become fully alive—four times twelve human beings,
> that is, who are recognized not only by yourselves but by the Lead-
> ership of the Goetheanum in Dornach. We see some members of the

executive council in our midst and together you are all four times twelve such human beings. Leaders have arisen having the mood of soul that belongs to the Mik-eye-ell festival, now we can look up to the light that through the Mik-eye-ell Stream and the Mik-eye-ell Activity will be shed abroad in the future—the now—among mankind."

There were gasps from the audience, and then people spoke excitedly amongst themselves. Karl stepped up onto the stage and stood beside Mike, his deep-set brown eyes gazing pensively out at his peers. He put a hand on Mike's shoulder and squeezed, as if to say: *Well done!*

"Ladies and gentlemen," Karl began. His heavy voice bounced throughout the auditorium. "It is truly an honor to be here with you on this historic occasion. Most of us have not been physically in his presence, yet we have all been chosen to let the Mik-eye-ell Stream fill our souls. We have worked hard over the past few years to be where we are today. Let the Mik-eye-ell Stream Guide Our Work!"

As in prayer, dozens of voices chanted in unison: "The Mik-eye-ell Stream Will Guide Our Work!"

Karl continued: "Despite silly squabbles and misgivings amongst the so-called leadership of the General Anthroposophical Society, there are those of us—and make no mistake, we are all in this room now—who understand the significance of that which draws us here. We are the true leaders!"

Mike did as he had been told and stood as still as a statue. All eyes were on Karl now and Mike stared straight ahead, hoping it would soon be over.

"The majority of those in the Vorstand are weak." Karl smiled but anger crept into his voice. "As we meet now, many of them sleep in comfortable hotels in Dornach, waiting for trivialities of the conference. Some trouble-makers are meeting in Zurich. I made sure we would have our privacy at this time. They call themselves Anthroposophists but are oblivious to the fact that in Rudolf Steiner's last public address on the eve of Mik-eye-ell-mas in 1924, he foretold of our group and of our important work." He looked down at Mike. "And now we have heard the same lecture on this special occasion. It is not a miracle, my friends—it is our collective destiny!"

Karl raised both hands, forming triumphant fists in the air. "We will accomplish great things. Ahriman will no longer hold the upper hand. We will slay the dragon and shift the balance with the Christ Impulse in our souls and the power of Mik-eye-ell at our side!"

A boisterous cheer arose as dozens of hands clapped. Mike saw lots of smiling faces in the candlelight. He did not understand why they were cheering. When he was finally allowed to sit on a small chair on the stage, all he could think about was leaving this place. He wanted to go home—away from these strange people. They were all looking at him. He wanted to be with his dad.

13

Dornach

Karl unbuttoned his old brown leather jacket. He was feeling the heat of the candles and the joy of the moment. He had waited a lifetime for tonight.

"Dear colleagues," Karl said calmly, "it is time for brief reports from the four group leaders." He smiled and his eyes widened. "The first needs no introduction and has just arrived from America on his way to Rome."

Karl raised a hand. "I know there has been some concern regarding recent publicity in the United States, but I can assure you everything is under control." He lowered his hand and continued to smile. "Ladies and gentlemen, Doctor Fritz Fleischer."

A polite smattering of applause greeted the giant Doctor Fleischer as he made his way up onto the stage. His deep voice sounded calm and cold.

"Dear friends," he began, "let he who does not understand the need to express the Will of the Mik-eye-ell Stream with clearly defined symbols in the death of Ahriman's minions, now stand and show his face." His coal-black eyes scanned the audience. "It has come to my attention," he continued, "that some here might not approve of the publicity surrounding my work." He leaned forward and whispered loud enough for all to hear: "This is our time to be bold. The true leaders of the Mik-eye-ell School will not waver in the monumental task before us.

"Dear colleagues," he continued, "let me remind you of the prophetic words of Rudolf Steiner." Doctor Fleischer quoted from memory:

> "The situation is that the souls who have passed violently through the gate of death retain something on account of having lost their life in that way here in the physical world; they have retained certain possibilities of being able to make use of forces which they have had here, for instance the force of the intellect . . . These

people, these activists who murder people, are only doing it in order to draw attention to the misery in the world; it is a means of incitement and so on."

"But if you analyze the matter and try to bring it into the context of social laws, you notice immediately that none of this has any meaning. It becomes meaningful, however, if you know that souls sent up into the spiritual world by such means understand things up there which they ought not to understand yet and which souls who have died in the normal way even shy away from . . . if you analyze the matter and look at the individuals who have been dispatched to their death in this way, you realize that they must have been selected on purpose, though not on the basis of criteria applying to the physical world but rather on the basis of criteria applying to the spiritual world."

Karl looked into the eyes of his colleagues in the Group. He saw fear and respect. This was a good sign. He looked again at the big man addressing them now.

Doctor Fleischer glared at his audience. Nobody made a sound. "Any questions?" he asked.

A nervous voice from the focused gathering asked, "What about . . . him, Herr Doctor?"

The giant stared into the audience and smiled. "He is here."

Gasps and murmurs echoed throughout the auditorium. "Here?" someone said. "Here in the Goetheanum?"

Doctor Fleischer lost his smile as his eyes darted from face to face. "Here? Here?" he mocked. "Do not test my patience with your fear and weakness. Here is where he belongs at this point in our collective destiny."

Doctor Fleischer returned to his seat behind the other First Class Holders. Karl stepped up and spoke with slow deliberation about his own place as the leader of the twelve-member team from Switzerland and Germany, charged with protection and evaluation of Mik-eye-ell. He assured his colleagues that everything was going according to plan.

He finished with a loud proclamation that, "Destiny will unfold according to the indications of Rudolf Steiner!"

More applause and Karl then introduced a fat man from Canada.

"As many of you know," Dave Dunigan began, "Atomic Energy of Canada Limited has become a political quagmire in my country." He smiled.

"The crown corporation has been a drain on Canadian taxpayers. There have been problems for many years, including a recent leak at the Chalk River Reactor. I am sure you heard about this problem, as the reactor was shut down, resulting in a serious shortage of medical radioisotopes around the world. It was a major news story."

The fat Canadian smiled again. "During that particular *accident*, it was easy to arrange for forty-seven kilograms of heavy water to leak from what appeared to be faulty plumbing. I thought you might appreciate the symbology of one kilo for each of you. Of course, being a humble man, I did not include a kilo for myself." He chuckled and muffled laughter arose from the audience.

"Prime Minister Harper recently commissioned the National Bank of Canada to look at the viability of a privatization plan for the beleaguered company. I'm delighted to say that fifty-one percent of AECL—the commercial operations side—is now owned by private interests, one of which has yours truly on its board."

Applause from the audience.

Dave Dunigan beamed. "What this means, dear colleagues, is that our plans are right on schedule. While the Canadian CANDU reactor is ostensibly safe, privatization has many perks for those with special interests. It was not difficult for my team to make certain adjustments to reactor core components before and after recent sales to China."

The overweight Anthroposophist had trouble suppressing his pride. "To our delight—and I'll admit to playing a small role in this—our Prime Minister also fired the president of the Canadian Nuclear Safety Commission, believing her to be too concerned with safety. Fewer watchdogs make our work much easier!"

Hearty applause caused Dave Dunigan to grin from ear to ear.

He chuckled and motioned for silence. "My dear friends, the fate of the Qinshan Phase III CANDU nuclear power plant in China is now, for all intents and purposes, controlled by us—The Mik-eye-ell School of the Future."

Intense applause erupted. When it finally died down, someone asked a question about Manitoba: "Is everything under control in Winnipeg?"

"Almost," Dave Dunigan said. His smile disappeared. "You must understand that unfortunately, the current Premier of Manitoba is neither an Anthroposophist nor a Freemason. Of course, we cannot rely on today's Freemasons, anyway. Nor can we depend on the vast majority of those who call themselves Anthroposophists. They are all weak. We must continue to rely on our slush fund for the Winnipeg Project, but I am confident in the Will of Mik-eye-ell to see us through." He glanced at Mike and smiled again at his audience. "Hard cold cash has its place in the mission of Spiritual Science."

Karl thanked Dave Dunigan and waited for the applause to subside before introducing the last guest of the historic gathering. Things were going very well. Karl felt the joy of the moment flowing through his soul. His father and his grandfather would be proud!

"Dear friends," he said, "years ago when we realized the momentous task before us, we knew we would need experience in certain areas. As karma would dictate, this man came to us from a place of deep spirit and as our souls connected over the years, it became clear that the ties between true Anthroposophy and true Freemasonry are stronger now than ever. Rudolf Steiner told us this would happen in the future and the future is now. This man understands sacrifice. He has spent time in prison and his conviction is stronger because of it. He is a man of the past, a man of the present and a man of the future. Above all, he is a man of action. Please welcome our distinguished Italian colleague, Silvestro Nardo!"

An elderly man in a silk suit took the stage to loud applause. His hair, mustache and goatee were silver-white and perfect and his smile as warm as the Tuscan sun. He grinned and raised one hand to quiet the crowd before speaking slowly with a strong Italian accent.

"Dear friends," he said, still smiling like a loving grandfather. "When I was invited to join this fateful team I knew in my heart we would meet with well-deserved success." He frowned and his expression turned solemn. Silvestro Nardo then shook his head and his brown eyes glistened in the light of the candles.

"The most inappropriate actions of Pope Benedict have strengthened our resolve to bring the real spirit back to humanity. As you know, I have deep connections with the true spirit of Anthroposophy." He smiled again. "Although they have both crossed the threshold, I am sure you know of my dear friends, the Italian Anthroposophists, Ettore Martinoli and Massimo Scaligero?"

Strong applause.

The old man held both hands up until there was silence. "The Vatican had to pay a price for the Pope's insubordination and believe me, my friends, part of the debt has been paid. Our mission needed substantial capital and we still have support within the Vatican Bank. It was important for Pope Benedict to learn that when one is dismissive of occultism, one might need to learn a difficult financial lesson in karma." His eyes narrowed and he chuckled.

Laughter and more applause sprung from his audience.

The old Italian strolled over and stooped beside Mike. "You are a true blessing, Mik-eye-ell," he said. He ran wrinkled fingers through Mike's blond curls. "Blue eyes and blond hair, from German roots and born in the West—the west coast of North America, in fact." He smiled and continued to stare at Mike. "We have been expecting you, young man. Your presence at the Goetheanum is a sign of great things to come."

Silvestro Nardo walked slowly back to his seat to a standing ovation and cheers of *Bravo! Bravo!*

Karl waited for the applause to fade. When there was complete silence, he told the gathering that it had been his honor to host this momentous meeting. He then quoted from their beloved leader, Rudolf Steiner:

> "White humanity is still on the way to take the spirit more and more deeply into its own being. Yellow humanity is on the way to conserve that age in which the spirit is held away from the body, is sought purely outside the human physical organization. This makes it inevitable that the transition from the fifth culture epoch to the sixth will bring about a violent struggle of the white and yellow races in the most varied domains. What precedes these struggles will occupy world-history up to the decisive events of the great contests between the white world and the colored world."

Karl watched his colleagues stand and applaud his work—the work of generations of the Heisman family. He imagined his father and grandfather at his side. He imagined Rudolf Steiner standing with him on the stage and Karl smiled and felt his soul brimming with pride. *Glorious times are about to unfold!*

Day Six

1

Dornach, Switzerland

Mark finished his shower and wondered what the hell he was doing in a little hotel in Dornach, Switzerland. Following orders, it seemed, and trying to catch the bad guys. But in Switzerland? He got dressed and shaved and looked in the mirror. He was pleased to see that jet lag had not taken too much of a toll on his face. It was still early and he hoped Chris and Kate were awake. He walked down the hall and knocked on their door. It opened just a sliver but enough for him to notice Kate's soft blue eyes peering out.

"Can I come in?" Mark asked.

Kate opened the door wide. "Speak of the devil."

"I'll take that as a compliment," Mark said. He tried not to stare at Kate as he walked past her into the room.

Chris stepped out from the bathroom, his hair still wet from the shower. He grinned and shook the detective's hand. "Am I glad to see you," he said. "We were just wondering when you would arrive."

"I just got in." Mark's eyes darted from Chris to Kate. "I'm in a room down the hall. How about we head downstairs for some food?"

The complimentary breakfast of coffee, buns and fruit salad left Mark craving bacon and eggs.

Kate reminded him they were not in New York and a greasy American breakfast would be hard to find in Switzerland. "It's not good to eat greasy crap for breakfast, anyway," Kate said.

Mark frowned and finished the light meal in a few bites. "I wonder if I can order a few more of these." He smiled and looked across the table at Kate.

She wore faded jeans and a baggy sweater. Her straight blond hair barely touched her shoulders and the turquoise top made her blue eyes seem more beautiful than Mark had remembered. He tried to make himself believe this woman was too butch for him. But he could no longer ignore his feelings. She was tall but pleasantly proportioned, and as he had learned back in Ithaca, she was outrageously extroverted. Maybe it was the eyes. Given half a chance he would disappear into those soft blue eyes forever.

"So what happened to Paul?" asked Kate. "You're suggesting the surgical killer simply murdered two cops and kidnapped him? That's a bit of a stretch."

"We don't know exactly what happened," Mark said. "It looks like Paul had gone outside for some air and someone was waiting. Both policemen were shot—something new for our surgical killer, assuming it was him. Until now he's been using a blade. There was no sign of a struggle. We've got some very good people looking for him."

"So far the very good people leave a lot to be desired," Kate said.

Mark wondered why he found her brash behavior so appealing. "I knew both officers," he said.

Chris sipped his coffee. "I'm sorry. But how would the killer know that Paul was at the safe house?"

"Good question," Mark said.

"Do you think Paul is alive?" Chris asked. "I mean, if they'd wanted him dead, why not just kill him and leave the body like the others?"

"At this point in time, we're treating it as a kidnapping. I stopped by the safe house and found some of Paul's notes in the kitchen. I can't make sense of everything but I suspect they have to do with our surgical killer." He finished his coffee before continuing: "My boss told me to come to Switzerland—check in with you, poke around and report back."

"How does a police chief in Ithaca know about us?" Kate asked.

"I told them about you. The agents were curious." Mark explained his meeting with Chief Bischel and agents Bander and Martins.

"What the hell?" Kate said. "Special agents from Homeland Security—this is getting complicated."

"I am sure this *is* more complicated than a missing child and a few murders," Mark said. "The Ithaca Police Department does not normally pay for cops to travel to Switzerland. I'm not even supposed to tell anyone I'm here. Pretty clandestine operation for a lowly detective like me." He looked at Kate and managed a grin.

Kate returned his smile. "Or maybe someone just recognizes your super-cop skills and is waiting for you to crack the case?"

Mark suspected a trace of sarcasm. He changed the subject. "Paul Sung is convinced of the connection between the Ithaca murders and Mike's disappearance."

"So what do we do now?" Chris asked.

Mark thanked the waitress for another continental breakfast. "I took the liberty of arranging a plan for today. I told you I stopped by the safe house yesterday. One of the professor's notes included the name of an acquaintance of his in Italy—and that fellow has a connection with an important officer in the Pontifical Swiss Guard."

"The guys who guard the Pope?" Kate asked. "With the funny uniforms?"

"That's right. I phoned them both this morning. Paul's friend works at a university in Rome and was very helpful. I didn't tell him the whole story but when I told him I was coming here, he suggested I phone his contact with the Swiss Guard—which I did. Although the Swiss Guard is based in Rome, he has some clout here in Switzerland and sounded very interested in helping us."

They left the hotel restaurant and walked towards the parking area. It was a cool, cloudy September morning with very few people on the streets. The tourist season had almost ended and Mark could see a fresh dusting of snow on the low, rolling mountains around Dornach.

"You told the officer the entire story?" Chris asked, as they walked.

"Not everything, but it seems his organization has its own concerns about some people at the Goetheanum. A Special Ops team will meet us there in an hour."

"I don't get it," Kate said.

Chris frowned. "Why would they want to help us?"

"He wouldn't go into detail," Mark said, "but apparently the Swiss Guard has its own reason for wanting to look around inside the building."

"A Swiss Guard Special Ops?" Chris said. "I didn't know such a thing existed."

"Me neither," Mark said, "but we have nothing to lose by accepting their help. I think the professor's university colleague is legitimate. And the officer from the Swiss Guard sounded sincere, as well. At this point in time, I don't think we have many options."

"I agree," Chris said.

Mark felt relieved to know they were on board with the plan. He continued. "They will use an excuse to get in—something about a report of suspicious activity; they will go in fast, look around for Mike and get out without too much disruption. We must stay outside."

"Karl will be pissed," Kate said.

Mark looked at his watch as they arrived at the hotel parking lot. "We might as well head up there together. What are you driving?"

Kate pointed to the Carrera and unlocked the door. "Only seats two," she said.

Mark chuckled. "Nice car. My rental can take all of us. It's a little less exciting than yours but certainly more practical." He walked towards a black Jetta, motioning for them to join him.

"You boys go together. I need to get my money's worth with this beauty." Kate hopped into the Carrera and revved the motor. The window slid down. "See you at the cement monstrosity!" The Carrera tore out of the parking lot as if Kate's life depended on driving too fast.

2

Dornach, Switzerland

The Jetta pulled in beside Kate's Porsche near the building at 8:47 a.m. She was standing beside her little car, watching them arrive. There were only a few cars in the little lot. The Goetheanum loomed before them on the crisp September morning.

Mark looked up at the massive columns and rounded concrete forms of the huge building. "Amazing," he said. "It's like something from a weird dream."

Kate stood beside him, following his eyes across the facade. "Or a nightmare—compliments of their guru, Rudolf Steiner. This building was his idea."

Chris joined them, eyes glued to a pamphlet in his hands. "So, this is the first day of what they call the Michaelmas Conference. There will be different meetings in various rooms here for the next few days."

More cars were arriving and people were walking towards the front of the building. "So far—so good," Chris continued. "There were only a few Anthroposophists here when we got tossed out yesterday. I'm sure our pal, Karl, is inside."

"But just so we're clear," Mark said, "when the cavalry arrives, we let them do their job, right?" He looked at Kate.

Suddenly, two black panel vans arrived and parked directly in front of the main entrance.

"Gotta love the Swiss," Mark said. "I was told they'd be here at 9:00 a.m. and it's exactly 9:00 a.m. The commanding officer knows we might be here but we need to keep our distance."

Ten uniformed military men shot out of each van and marched up the front steps of the Goetheanum. They were neat, organized and each had a holstered handgun. Bewildered Anthroposophists stepped aside and mumbled amongst themselves as the twenty-man team entered the building.

"Wow," Kate said. "I just gotta see this." She jogged to the front entrance and hopped up the stairs.

"Kate!" Mark ran after her; Chris followed. Mark looked over his shoulder as he ran. "Your sister is driving me crazy."

A group of men and women were gathered in the foyer, huddled around the paramilitary team. The commanding officer was holding a paper and motioning for his men to disperse and begin their search. He spoke in German—loudly. Chris and Mark caught up with Kate as she stood with a group of distraught Anthroposophists, watching the commotion. The commanding officer was a tall man with a no-nonsense face and determined light brown eyes. He handed the paper to a man Kate and Chris knew all too well.

Although most of the First Class Anthroposophists were wearing suits, Karl was dressed in gray corduroy pants, a green turtleneck sweater and his old brown leather jacket—casual wear, but the there was nothing casual about the man now. He was visibly upset. He snatched the paper, read it quickly and screamed something in German. Kate tried to listen to the words; she was sure he was cussing. Karl threw the paper back at the commanding officer and yelled in his face. Two Anthroposophist suits arrived, frowned and spoke loudly to anyone and everyone.

"Let's get out of here," Mark said. "We need to stay outside. That was the deal."

"Karl is totally pissed," Kate said, smiling. "Look at his face—he's going to explode!"

More Anthroposophists arrived and stood in a semicircle around Karl. The military team hurried off in all directions, the echo of their boots on stairs bouncing off the massive walls. Karl looked around the foyer in disbelief at what was happening to his beloved Goetheanum on this most special of spiritual occasions.

He yelled at the commanding officer again and then peered over his shoulder, his eyes flitting from one visitor to the next, his facial expression one of both shock and apology to his distinguished guests.

Three younger Anthroposophists arrived in the foyer and were joined by two older women in long cotton dresses. They conferred for a moment and then approached Karl, speaking quietly while trying to calm him down. Karl ignored them and continued to verbally assault the Swiss Guard officer in charge. When he finally spoke to his colleagues, his voice was still loud, still hostile. They argued for a minute and Karl started to storm away. Suddenly, he stopped.

Karl's eyes fell on Kate and Chris and Mark. "You!" He pushed past the crowd and strutted towards them. Fury burst from his eyes and he screamed again: "You! This is your fault! This is because of you!" He continued towards them, seething more with every step. His eyes then stopped on Mark. "And this—this American detective! You have no authority here!" He was breathing hard and stood toe-to-toe with Mark.

Kate smiled. "Hi Karl, nice to see you again."

Karl ignored her and continued to stare at Mark. The two men glared at each other from inches apart.

Mark immediately knew he disliked this man. "We're just visiting," Mark said, "but it looks like it might not be the best time, so we'll wait outside." He glared at Kate, and waited for her to leave before he turned and walked to the door. Chris was right behind them.

"These bastards have Mike," Kate said, once they were outside. "This is ridiculous—we should just get him and take him home."

"We agreed that we would stay outside, remember?" Mark said. "That was the arrangement and now the plan has been compromised."

"I'm sorry," Chris said.

"I'm not sorry," Kate said. "This is fucking stupid!"

Mark felt frustrated and angry. Kate had possibly caused an international incident by bursting into the building. She acted on impulse and that was a real problem in his line of work. She showed no remorse and was still fuming. He looked at her now and his anger faded away. There was something special about the woman—she was still attractive, even when she was angry.

Kate followed Mark and Chris down the steps and through the geometric landscape to the parking lot. She slammed a hand on the roof of the Jetta and looked at her brother. *Were those tears in his eyes?* She wanted desperately to help him find his son—her nephew. She felt like the older sister again, needing to take care of her little brother. Her mind spun back in time . . .

The last time Kate had felt this close to Chris was when their parents had died in the car crash some ten years ago. She then thought of her wonderful little nephew and a camping trip she had taken with Mike the summer before Serena had shut her out of his life.

She missed being with Mike, missed his laughter and innocent curiosity about everything. One night they lay together in sleeping bags outside the tent and Mike kept his eyes open long enough for both of them to marvel at the star-studded night sky.

"So what lies beyond the farthest star?" Mike had asked.

"More stars," Kate said.

"And what's behind those stars?"

"Even more stars."

"And what's behind—"

"A huge brick wall," Kate replied and they both laughed until Mike finally drifted off to sleep and Kate carried him back inside the tent.

One night the two of them had spent an hour slicing tiny bits of wood with Swiss Army knives, hoping to make a campfire only using one match, just to see if it could be done. It was a painstakingly long task but well worth the effort when a tiny flame licked their wood slivers before finally igniting the carefully placed larger twigs above. As the campfire grew, they roasted marshmallows and Kate's first feeble attempt resulted in a fireball of black goo on the end of her stick, and Mike laughed so hard he fell off his tiny camping stool and accidentally dropped his own marshmallow into the fire. They both laughed until they cried. She had loved spending time with her nephew . . .

Kate stood in the parking lot and looked again at her brother. "You're not the only one who misses him, Chris," she said. "I missed him when Serena kept him from me and I miss him even more right now."

Chris stared up at the building and then gazed at the odd-shaped houses bordering the Goetheanum. "He's here somewhere," he said. "I know it."

3

Dornach, Switzerland

Mark watched a group of Anthroposophists forming on the front steps leading into the foyer. Most of them seemed shocked at the strange disruption. A few minutes later, the Swiss Guard team filed down the stairs and into the waiting vans. One van drove straight back towards the town but the other stopped beside the Jetta.

The commanding officer hopped out and looked at Mark. "You are Detective Julian?"

Mark nodded.

The man's English was perfect—straight from Oxford with only a hint of an accent. "I'm Major Daniel Kappel. I'm sorry, but we were not able to find the boy." The major then looked at Kate and Chris. "There might be some complications. You should not have entered the building."

"I'm sorry about that," Mark interrupted. "I might not have made it clear to my colleagues that we were to stay outside."

"Bullshit," Kate said. She glared at Mark. "Don't make excuses for me!" She looked at Major Kappel. "They have my nephew." She pointed to the surrounding houses. "He must be here somewhere."

The officer seemed calm as he glanced at Kate, and then returned to Mark. His hazelnut eyes were pensive, intelligent. "You must understand there are laws in this country and it would be wise for you to know that this group of Anthroposophists is not without connections. Apparently, you have connections as well, but I'm afraid there are limits to what any of us can do." He paused and looked at Chris. "I understand your situation, sir, but I trust you understand mine."

"Thank-you for looking for my son," Chris said. "I will not stop searching until I find him."

"One question," Mark said. "It looked as if Karl had some problems with his colleagues a few minutes ago. Who were the Anthroposophists trying to calm him down? They seemed to have some authority in the building."

"Like Karl," the major said, "they are also part of the Vorstand— members of the Executive Council. There has been acrimonious division within the Vorstand recently. Some of the other leaders of the movement are in Zurich now, preparing for meetings here tomorrow. Suffice to say that Karl Heisman does not represent the vast majority of Anthroposophists."

"Interesting," Mark said.

"Very," the major said. He met Mark's eyes for a moment. "And now, I really must be on my way." He shook their hands and hopped back into his van.

Mark stood by the Jetta, drumming fingers on the roof while reflecting on the major's words. The sun appeared and then disappeared and a cool wind whipped up dirt in the parking lot.

"It seems as if we have someone else in our corner," Mark said.

"But he was not very helpful," Kate huffed. "We might even be worse off now because Karl and his gang know who we are and what we want."

"That's not necessarily a bad thing," Mark said. "Karl is scared. He was angry as hell but he was also scared. I could see it on his face. When people are afraid they make mistakes." He looked back at the Goetheanum. The building was now officially closed to the public. "And Karl made at least one mistake today."

Chris frowned. "What mistake?"

"You don't remember what Karl said when he saw us—when he saw me?"

"Yeah, he was pissed to see us there." Chris frowned and then his eyes lit up. "Oh, I see what you mean. How did Karl know about you?"

"Exactly," Mark said. "He certainly knew the two of you from yesterday but he should not have known that I was a detective from the United States. Someone told him about me. His mistake was in sharing that knowledge with us today."

Chris stared up at the Goetheanum. "Mike is here somewhere."

"I think so, too," Mark said, "and I am starting to believe there really is a connection with the murders. Karl must know about my investigation. It would not surprise me in the least if he knows the surgical killer. And for our own safety, we need to keep that in mind."

"Another sobering thought," Chris said. "And I'm sure they killed the old lady yesterday."

Mark looked at Chris. "After what happened this morning, my guess is they'll move your son today."

"So, what do we do?" Chris asked.

Mark zipped his black leather jacket up to his neck. It was cold outside. "We wait until they make a move. Not here in this parking area but just in behind that smaller building to the south of the Goetheanum." He pointed. "Regardless of which road they take to leave, we'll see them from there. We sit there and we wait."

"A stake-out," Kate said. "Just like in the movies. If they drive out with Mike, we follow them."

"That's right," Mark said. "It's only a five minute drive back to the hotel. I'll stay here but how about one of you goes back to town to bring some food? We might be waiting here for a while."

Kate offered to drive back to the hotel and return with lunch. "Any excuse to drive this car is fine by me."

Mark tucked the Jetta in behind a storage shed near the Goetheanum. He played the events of the morning twice in his mind, looking for clues—anything that might help with the investigation. He thought about Major Kappel and wondered what his role might be in this sordid affair. Finally, Mark turned to Chris and attempted to nonchalantly learn more about his fascinating sister.

4

Dornach, Switzerland

A friendly, chubby woman in the hotel restaurant told Kate the boxed lunch would be ready in fifteen minutes. Kate decided to head up to her room to freshen up.

As she unlocked the door, she stepped back and kept a hand on the doorknob. A well-built young man in coveralls was sitting at the little table beside the bed. Her brother's laptop was on the table. The man appeared startled but immediately smiled.

"Guten Tag," he said. He then stood, walked to the window and opened and closed it twice. There was an open toolbox at his feet.

"Hello," Kate said. She entered the room. The door closed automatically behind her. "Was the window broken?"

"You shpeeek English?" the man asked. He turned and looked at her.

"Yes, I'm from the United States."

"Oh ya. I vant go to America vun day." The man opened and closed the window, testing it again.

Kate looked at the back of his head. His hair was neat, trimmed in a perfect line above a muscular neck. "It looks like the window is fine," she said. "You're finished now, right?"

The man was silent and continued to fiddle with the window. Something was not right. Kate walked to the table and touched the bottom of the laptop. It was warm. She felt a sick feeling in her gut.

As if sensing her anxiety, the man reached into his toolbox, grabbed a large knife and spun quickly to face her. He was no longer the innocent hotel maintenance man. A smile appeared on his face, the dark eyes became cold and confident and the German accent disappeared. "You ask too many questions." The blade was long and thin and moved in small circles as the man stood a few feet away, staring at her. He was still smiling. "You are far too curious." He took a step towards her. "And curiosity kills more than just cats." He lunged.

Kate had never been forced to use her martial arts skills for anything other than in competition between like-minded athletes. This was different. Adrenalin pumped through her body like wildfire. She stepped back and planted one foot, raised the other high and quickly kicked hard at the knife. The blade flew to the carpet. The man's face showed surprise and fury.

Kate took up a defensive position. Karate was the first discipline that came to mind.

"What the fuck?" he said. He shook the pain from his hand, jumped to the floor, and grabbed the knife. He bounced back to his feet and stood staring at her from across the bed. "You wanna play rough, bitch? OK, I like it rough. That's why Uncle Sam kicked me out of the Marines. I was too rough with the ladies." He pulled his hand back and quickly released the knife.

Kate had anticipated this move and with well-honed reflexes she grabbed a massive pillow from the bed, held it as a shield and felt the blade rip through thousands of feathers, the tip stopping just in front of her chest. She grabbed the knife's steel handle, her eyes never leaving the man on the other side of the bed. Her knees felt weak. She tried to stop her hands from trembling. The man stood frozen, a strange look of fear and bewilderment glued to his face. He slowly raised both hands defensively.

"Hold on now," he said. "I'm just doing my job here. I don't even know the dudes who hired me. I just need to copy the hard drive from that laptop and nobody gets hurt."

"So that's why you're trying to kill me?" Kate flipped the knife in the air and caught it by the tip—a trick she had practiced many times in her little apartment back in Portland. She suddenly thought of the small Chinese instructor at her knife-fighting course, his kind round face, soft voice and words of wisdom:

Always use practice knives and avoid a real knife fight—resist the primal urge to kill.

"Nobody told me a ninja-woman would be here," the man said. "Who the hell are you? Let's just talk this over, honey. Nobody needs to get hurt, right?"

Kate felt her emotions boiling over. Was the man lying? Was this one of Karl's goons? She suddenly saw her young nephew's face and she wanted nothing more than to hurt this guy. She played it quickly in her mind—what she would say after the fact.

I entered the room and this intruder attacked me. I managed to disarm him but he kept coming and I had to defend myself . . . Did he say "bitch?"

The man stuffed a hand into a pocket of the coveralls and pulled out a small handgun. Kate reacted. With lethal force, she tossed the knife. He flew onto the bed and the blade sunk into the wall behind him with a *thud*. Kate used that split-second to hurl herself at him before he could steady his weapon.

Her rigid right hand met the gun as he pulled the trigger. The explosion was muffled by a thick silencer that covered the barrel. Bits of drywall fell to the bed as the bullet met the ceiling.

Two bodies wrestled for a moment on the bed like a kinky sex scene gone terribly wrong. Kate felt a fist hammer into her stomach and she winced at the sudden pain. She felt dizzy, unable to breathe.

He was big, full of muscles and obviously not averse to fighting. His wild eyes told Kate he had killed before. He rolled on top of her with both hands on her throat. She struggled, trying to push hard against his chest but his bulk was too much. She felt blood rush to her head as her throat constricted. Powerful fingers dug into her neck and she heard herself gasping for air . . . and life.

"Yeah, that's right," he said. "I'll bet you like it rough, bitch." His sweaty face was inches from hers. She could smell BO and bad breath. To her horror, she could also feel his erection growing against her stomach as his mouth descended to meet hers.

God damn—he wants to rape me!

Somewhere in the back of her mind was a lesson from her martial arts training. Then, in a flash, it was gone. While she could not recall the appropriate reaction to this situation, she dug down deeper and let her instincts dictate the response. As if in a terrible nightmare, she slowly managed to let her body relax. Nightmares and memories . . .

Are you awake Katey . . . Uncle Brad likes you very much and he wants to show you something. Look Katey, look at this—touch it sweetie, go ahead and touch it. Don't be shy. You're almost a teenager now and this is what teenagers should learn. Uncle Brad can touch you too. Isn't that nice? Your brother is fast asleep and mom and dad will be home very late tonight so we have some time to ourselves. Don't cry, Katey. Uncle Brad would never hurt you . . .

The man's erection was rock hard now and he relaxed his grip slightly on her throat. Despite her revulsion to this thug, their lips met, and she closed her eyes. As if in a nightmare, she found herself surrendering.

Survive. Then, a sliver of light forced its way into her mind. She realized her right leg was slowly—very slowly—moving between his thighs as he pinned her to the bed. Her body quivered as his tongue entered her mouth and despite her best effort to be strong, she felt tears running down both cheeks.

He pulled back from the kiss and struggled awkwardly to unzip his coveralls. "That's better now," he said. "You want me and you know it. Good girl."

Those were his last words. She only needed a second. As he pulled at the coveralls, she jerked her leg up hard between his thighs. She felt his body lurch with the force of her knee on his crotch. He was off balance. Her hands were free. Rage coursed through every fiber of her body and mind as she spun and delivered a succession of quick, hard blows to his stomach, neck and face. He never knew what hit him.

Blood gushed from his suddenly malformed nose. His body twisted awkwardly on the bed. He was missing his front teeth. He fell to the floor gasping for breath, the smug expression of a bully replaced by one of shock and pain and humiliation.

Kate stood over the man now. She gasped for breath, sucking air back into her burning lungs. She looked down and sent him off the floor with a strong kick to his groin and another to his chest. The pain in his eyes told her that she had broken either his ribs or his testicles. He coughed and tried desperately to breathe. She kicked him one more time. He would not have sex for a very long time—if ever.

She stared at the pathetic, beaten man. Hatred and adrenalin controlled a voice inside: *Do it—kill the bastard!* She knelt over the broken body at her feet. Her face was close to his. His eyes opened slightly—begging her to stop. He coughed and made gasping noises through a face full of snot and blood.

"Sorry," Kate said. "But I thought you liked it rough."

There was a loud knock at the door.

"Hallo! Hallo!" A man's shaky voice. Then a fist pounded at the door. "Please open the door!"

Kate stood. Someone must have heard the noise. Questions fired through her mind. What would she say? Would anyone believe her story? What if the hotel staff had connections with Karl? Maybe they helped this man get into her room. Or did they call the police? There would be reports to file, paper work. It would take days, weeks maybe. This guy could play the victim and it was his word against hers. She didn't have a mark on her body and he looked like shit. He might press charges. Nobody would believe her . . .

> But mom, Uncle Brad touched me and he did it over and over and
> I told him to stop and he said it was OK and it was our little secret
> and . . . and . . . mom why don't you believe me? No mom, it's not
> just a misunderstanding and no I am not exaggerating and I know
> Uncle Brad is daddy's brother but . . .

Kate ran to the bathroom and splashed water over her face, then squeezed too much toothpaste on her toothbrush and scrubbed her teeth and tongue and lips with trembling hands. Her heart would not slow down. She stared at herself in the mirror. Her eyes seemed cold and hard and distant.

One more deep breath in. Hold it . . . and let it out, slowly . . .

She grabbed a towel, dried her face, and forced herself to walk calmly to the door. She opened it slightly. The elderly concierge stood beside another man in a suit. Security, she guessed. They both stared at her with wide eyes.

"People in the next room phoned the front desk about strange noises," the concierge said. "They said there was a fight?" Both men tried to peek past her into the room.

Kate managed a weak smile. "I'm very sorry," she said, trying to appear calm. "My husband and I were too loud." She faked another smile. "We have not had time alone for many weeks—you understand? I'm so sorry. We'll try to keep it down." A muffled groan came from the bedroom.

Both men smiled. The concierge blushed. "I see," he said. "Yes, yes, I see." They stepped back from the door, both seemingly embarrassed at interrupting a mid-day lovemaking session by the feisty American couple.

"We'll try to be quieter," Kate said.

"Thank-you," said the concierge. He grinned and the two men walked back down the hall.

Kate locked the door and returned to find the thug dragging himself towards the bathroom. She had a sudden pang of guilt. And fear. What if he had an accomplice in the hotel? She quickly threw all their belongings into suitcases.

Two minutes later, she strutted through the hotel lobby carrying their luggage and Chris's laptop. The concierge gave her an odd look as she passed. She tossed the bags into her little car and returned to the restaurant where she paid for a good-sized box of Swiss-lunch-to-go.

As she sat behind the wheel of the Carrera, she saw that her hands were still trembling. She filled her lungs with fresh mountain air, turned the key and got the hell away from that place as fast as the little sports car would take her.

As she drove up the hill to the Goetheanum, Kate imagined her attacker making his way to a local hospital for treatment, trying to invent reasons for his substantial injuries. He would be a fool to tell the authorities the truth, but a lie would sound equally suspicious. Kate tried to push it from her mind. He was in bad shape but the asshole deserved it.

She wrestled with whether or not to mention the incident to Chris and Mark. If she brought it up, they might feel sorry for her and that would make things worse. Kate despised pity. She slowly relaxed her grip on the steering wheel. This was not the time for anyone—including her—to feel sorry for Kate. The three of them needed to be there for Mike. They needed to stay disciplined. She would somehow find a way to explain the incident but would need to hide her feelings. Years of practice would help. Sympathy was the last thing she needed—not now, not ever.

5

Dornach, Switzerland

Mark was pleased to see Kate finally return and was equally delighted when she opened the box of food. The three of them sat in the Jetta and enjoyed the lunch of thick sandwiches full of cold cuts and crunchy gherkins, carrot sticks and aged Edam cheese cubes, complete with a thermos of strong coffee and freshly baked apple strudel.

"This makes up for the lousy continental breakfasts," Mark said. He started in on another sandwich but noticed that Kate seemed distant and had remained uncharacteristically quiet since her return. Something was not right. Then he saw Chris staring at her, as well.

"Something's wrong," Chris said. "What's the matter, Kate?"

Kate smiled but Mark could see through it. "What's wrong?" he asked.

Kate then told of the incident at the hotel. It came out in short bursts, with no tears. She understated the size and strength of her attacker; she also downplayed his injuries. She never met their eyes with hers, nor did she mention the attempted rape. But Mark knew. Years of police work and he just knew.

"You're sure you're all right?" Chris asked. "Maybe we should get you to a doctor."

"I'm fine." She glared at her brother.

"But just for a check-up, maybe we should—"

"I'm fine!" Then her eyes moved to Mark. "He only wanted access to the laptop." Kate had already given it back to her brother.

"We'll stay together from now on," Mark said. He felt stupid for letting her go to the hotel alone.

"I have our bags in the Porsche," Kate said. She looked at Mark. "But I couldn't get into your room."

Mark was still digesting news of the attack. "I'm not worried about my luggage." He watched her closely—*what a remarkable woman*. "I can get my things later," he said. "We'll need to change hotels and hope there are no problems with the authorities. Reporting the incident might not work in our favor. Maybe not worth the risk."

"I agree," Kate said. She changed the subject. "Didn't Paul Sung say he knew someone who worked at the Goetheanum? An ex-Waldorf teacher from New York—remember? It seems Karl and his pals are not very popular with many of their peers. Maybe Paul's contact here can help us."

"I thought about that," Mark said. "But I have no name or contact information." Mark finished his coffee and pulled some papers from an inside jacket pocket. "But I have Paul's notes from the safe house. The professor wrote something about the anthro doc—there are references to some lectures and something about a conference in Berlin. I guess Paul was doing research online from the safe house." He read quietly again from the notes. "But I think this is interesting."

"What's that?" Chris asked.

"He wrote some letters and numbers that might be important. G-A-9-3-0-4-1-2-2-3. Does that mean anything to you?"

"Sounds like a car license plate," Kate said. "I've seen some like that over here."

"Me too," Chris said. "Maybe Paul discovered the anthro doc's license plate number. Or maybe it's Karl's license plate."

As they finished lunch, they discussed strategy and tried to make sense of the past few days. No cars came or went from the building. Mark wanted to avoid the subject of Mike's well-being as he knew that topic was emotional for both Chris and his sister. But Mark was concerned. Things seemed to be unraveling and he had no idea what to expect next. The boy could be in serious danger.

Mark's police experience had taught him important lessons. Keep it rational, stay focused and never let emotions interfere with the job. He reminded himself to ignore his own feelings whenever Kate's eyes met his. They sat for another three hours until finally, a dark-colored car rumbled slowly down the road.

"Hold on," Mark said. "We've got a green BMW coming from the complex. When it passes, try to get a look inside. I'll try to catch the plate number."

The BMW was travelling slowly and as it passed, not more than twenty feet away, there was no mistaking the occupants.

The driver wore a brown leather jacket, had a neatly trimmed goatee, moustache and deep, dark eyes. Mark immediately recognized Karl. Beside him was a tall woman dressed in a baggy wool sweater and wearing a light purple scarf. In the back seat was a bald man with a pudgy face and a smaller woman wearing a tightly knit dark blue sweater. And beside her, Mark saw a small head of curly blond hair.

"It's them!" Chris said, as the car drove onto the feeder road toward the center of Dornach.

Mark started the car. "We'll keep our distance," he said.

"Let's just go get him!" Chris pounded his seat as their car pulled out slowly onto the main road. "Please, let's just cut them off now!"

"Think about it," Mark said. "For all intents and purposes, the boy is with his mother on a holiday and you are the troublesome father. Your wife has new friends here and you'd be on the next flight back to the States. Guaranteed."

"Stop!" Kate put a hand on Mark's shoulder. She opened the door and Mark slammed on the brakes. "I'll take my car," she said.

"Forget it." Her hand felt good on his shoulder but Mark was not about to change the plan. "We just talked about staying together, remember?" He could feel his pulse soaring.

"It's better to have two cars following in case there's a problem," Kate said.

"Oh sure—and one of the cars is a fire-red Porsche Carrera?" Mark huffed. "The idea is to be inconspicuous, Kate, not to show off. Close the door and let's stay together."

"Two cars are better than one," Kate said. "I'll follow you and I won't get in the way." She smiled at Mark. "I promise." She hopped out, slammed the door and jumped into the little sports car.

Mark considered going after her, but shook his head and drove onto the main road. Kate was not about to change her mind and Karl's car was barely visible on the horizon. The Jetta quickly pulled out and followed the BMW.

With Kate now gone, Chris climbed into the front passenger seat. "Sorry, Mark. She's always been strong-willed. She's a good driver, though. She once trained to do stunt driving for movies, but quit half way through the course— she said the instructor was an asshole."

"Why does that not surprise me?" Mark saw Kate's Carrera in his rear view mirror. "Her car sticks out like a very sore thumb."

They followed Karl through the narrow streets of Dornach, making sure to stay one or two cars behind, weaving in and out of traffic all the while. Kate stayed right behind the Jetta, aggressively edging other cars out of the way.

They turned off the Goetheanumstrasse onto another street with an equally long German name and then quickly turned onto a side street.

"Where the hell are they going?" Mark said. "I don't like this."

"Why not?" Chris asked.

"Because they are not going anywhere. He's checking for a tail."

The BMW was two cars ahead. Mark looked in the rear view mirror. "Damn! I wish your sister had chosen a less conspicuous car." He pulled to the side of the road and stopped. "I'll put three cars between us and Karl. He looked again in the mirror. "It's hard not to notice the Porsche."

Kate's Carrera pulled in behind the Jetta. Mark saw her waving her hands frantically as if to say, *hurry up—Karl is too far ahead!* She honked and pedestrians stared—some frowning at the Porsche. This was a quiet, peaceful little town, not used to Americans honking the horns of red sports cars while racing through the quaint streets.

"Is she nuts?" Mark said. "The whole town can see her now." He slowly pulled his Jetta back into the street. He could see Karl three cars ahead. The BMW turned left at the top of a crest and then accelerated.

"God damn! They made us." Mark pushed the accelerator hard and the car lunged ahead, tires screeching as they sped up the street, avoiding other cars by inches on each side. Kate followed in the Carrera, managing to stay close by honking warnings to pedestrians and drivers alike.

Mark spun left around a corner and saw Karl veer right two blocks ahead. Mark rammed his foot on the accelerator for two blocks, braked hard and spun to the right, down another narrow street, scraping the wall of an old building as he tried to keep Karl in view.

"Careful!" Chris said.

Mark felt an adrenalin rush. "I still see him."

"Get him to stop!" Chris shouted. "Mike is in that car!"

Mark's eyes flashed up and down the street. "Don't they have cops in this town?"

"Maybe we should let them go!" Chris yelled. "They're going too fast—it's too dangerous!"

Mark ignored the warning. The Jetta sped up a hill and flew off the crest, landing hard on the other side. The BMW was right in front of them.

"If we lose them now, we can say good-bye," Mark said. He glanced in the mirror; Kate was there and honking the horn like a crazy woman.

The three cars were racing through the maze-like streets of the picturesque little town at ridiculous speeds. People stood and stared and jumped out of the way.

Finally. The unmistakable hee-haw-hee-haw of Swiss police sirens filled the air. Just like in the movies, Mark thought. A blue and white police Smart Car shot out of a side street, missed the BMW and swerved in front of the Jetta, siren blazing and lights flashing.

Mark thought for an instant of trying to plough through the little car but quickly decided against it. Smart Cars are not too smart when hit by larger vehicles. He cursed and slammed on the brakes.

Chris slowly loosened his grip on the leather seat. His face was as white as the fresh snow on the local mountains. The BMW disappeared in the distance.

"Shit!" Mark hammered the steering wheel with two fists.

"We didn't see the license plate," Chris said.

"I got it," Mark said. "It's not the same as the one from Paul's notes." He took a deep breath. "God damn! The cop misses Karl and gets us. We've lost them now. God damn!"

It took Kate less than a second to make up her mind. She would not let her nephew disappear—again. Her bright red Carrera flew past the parked Jetta, braked and skidded and slammed sideways into the police car, denting it badly on the driver's side. Kate looked in her rear view mirror to see a Swiss cop scrambling out of the passenger side and staring at her as she sped to catch up with the BMW. A few seconds later, the Carrera disappeared into the distance.

6

Dornach, Switzerland

Mark was prepared for an onslaught of verbal abuse from the Swiss cop as he walked to the Jetta. The officer was upset, but surprisingly cordial and professional. He had just witnessed a dangerous car chase through the narrow streets of Dornach, ending with his car being smashed . . . and yet he strolled up to the Jetta with a polite smile and a little leather-bound book in his hands.

"Guten Tag," the cop said.

"Pardon me?" Mark said.

"Parlez-vous Francais?" the cop asked.

"I only speak English."

"You are American?"

Mark wondered how many languages the guy spoke. "Yes, we're both American."

"And why do you drive so fast?" the cop asked. "You were racing with the Porsche? You have a name for the driver of that car?" He put his pen to the paper of his notebook.

"No, we were trying to keep up with the BMW."

"I saw only you and the Porsche," the cop said. "Where is this BMW?"

"Gone," Mark said. Thanks to you, he thought.

A dark car pulled in behind the Jetta. A well-dressed man got out and joined the policeman. He said something in German and the Swiss cop replied. Then, the newcomer pulled out his wallet and showed something to the cop. The sun poked through the gray clouds behind the two men and Mark was not able to see the face of the stranger.

The cop looked in at Mark and Chris, shook his head and walked back to inspect his Smart Car. He checked the dents and then climbed in through the undamaged passenger door. He shook his head again and drove away.

The well-dressed man bent down and looked in the car. Mark could see his face now.

"Now what do we have here?" the man asked.

Mark stared at the face in his window—a face he had seen that morning. "Major Kappel," he said. "From the Swiss Guard."

"How are you?" the major asked.

"Been better," Mark replied. "What are you doing here? And how the hell were you able to send the police officer away like that?"

"There is a time for explanations," the major said. "The short answer is I followed you. The red Carrera made it easy." He smiled. "But now, may I suggest you park in the lot around the corner and join me in my car?"

"We need to find my son," Chris said, leaning across Mark as he spoke. "And my sister is —"

"Yes," the major said. "I know. Please—I will meet you around the corner and we will try to find your sister. Unfortunately, finding your son will be more difficult but let us take one step at a time, shall we? And I suggest we hurry."

The two cars turned the corner into a parking lot and in less than a minute, Mark and Chris were in Major Kappel's dark brown Mercedes and driving onto Highway 18 north out of Dornach.

Mark sat beside the major. Chris was in the back, laptop in hand. A thousand questions formed in Mark's mind but for now he was content to accept the major's help as he drove through the streets at a good clip. It was evident this man was a very experienced driver.

"If you don't mind me asking," Mark said, "where are we going?"

Major Kappel kept his head straight, and his brown eyes glued to the road. "I am—how you say in America—playing a hunch. I already made a call to make sure your sister will not be arrested."

Mark was intrigued. *Just who is this guy?* They shot past other cars on the highway. Mark peeked at the dashboard. They were travelling at two hundred and fifteen kilometers per hour. After a few minutes, the car slowed and turned off the highway onto an off ramp and then onto another four lane street. The signs were nothing more than blurs as they sped by, but Mark was able to see one that announced "Basel," and further along there was another sign with a picture of an airplane.

"We're going to the Basel airport?" Chris asked.

The major said nothing as he screeched to a stop near an airport security gate. An overweight, uniformed man sauntered over to the driver side window. Major Kappel flashed his identification and the man immediately jogged back to his station and raised the gate. As the Mercedes drove into a VIP parking area, the major finally spoke.

"I am allowed to be here," he said. "Most people must park back there." He pointed to a larger parking lot fifty yards back.

"Kate!" Mark saw her running along the side of the road towards them as the major pulled into an empty space.

Chris jumped out of the car and ran to meet his sister. The two of them then walked quickly back to the Mercedes.

The major pulled out a tiny cell phone, pushed a button, said a few words in German, listened for a moment and then slipped the phone back into a pocket.

Mark felt torn between conflicting emotions. He wanted very much to scream at Kate for pulling such a stupid stunt—following them too closely while honking her horn; but he also wanted to take her in his arms and let her know he felt relieved that she was safe.

Kate was fuming. As she walked past the big security man, she let loose with a string of profanity the man did not seem to understand. The guard simply raised both hands as if to say, *I'm only doing my job.*

"Those assholes drove right in here," Kate yelled, standing in front of Mark. "Karl is welcome. No questions asked! And then I arrive right on their tail and he stops me!" She pointed at the guard. "He shuts the fucking gate and I almost ram it—and him!" She looked at the men and then her eyes scanned the parking lot. "Where are they now? They've got to be here somewhere." Her eyes left Mark and then settled on the major.

"I know you," she said. "You're the guy from this morning. Major . . ."

"Major Daniel Kappel," the major said. He extended a hand. "Nice to meet you—again."

Kate shook the hand quickly and looked around the parking lot. An airplane descended and landed, its engine forcing them to shout in order to be heard. A helicopter took off from a nearby pad.

"Where are they?" Kate yelled.

The major leaned back against his car, still staring at Kate; he pointed to the sky. "They are in that helicopter."

"How do you know?" Chris yelled above the noise. "They could be anywhere."

"Their car is at the end of the VIP lot," the major said. "In the Heliport area. They often travel by helicopter."

"How do you know all this?" Chris asked.

"All in good time," he replied.

"Can't we stop them?" Chris shouted.

"No," the major said. "They have done nothing wrong—officially. They drove too fast but so did you."

"You have a point," Mark said. "But I'd like some answers."

"This is so fucking stupid!" Kate was furious. "I almost kill myself following them here and now we watch them fly away over our heads?" She slammed a fist against the roof of the Mercedes. "Damn it!"

Major Kappel rubbed a hand over his car—checking for damage from Kate's latest tirade. "Come," he said, "let's go into the VIP lounge and have some coffee."

"I take it," Mark said, "you know where they are going?"

"Yes," the major said. "I'm afraid there is not much we can do but it seems they don't know that. They are nervous and when people are nervous—"

"They make mistakes," Mark added.

The major looked at him as they entered the VIP lounge. "Exactly, detective," he said. "Exactly."

7

Basel Airport, Switzerland

The little lounge had high ceilings and big leather chairs. Plate-glass windows looked over the tarmac and Neil Diamond sang *I am I said*, through a good sound system.

Mark sat back and looked at Major Kappel. "So, where are they going?" he asked.

"They are flying to Rome," the major said. "Italy." He looked at his watch. "They will be there in a couple of hours."

Chris frowned. "How do you know?"

"I called the tower. Although they are secretive and evasive, they still must file a flight plan."

"Why Rome?" Mark asked.

"They have friends there," Major Kappel said. "Very good friends who help with their financing and will do anything to keep their secrets safe." He eyed Chris. "Why is your son so special?"

So there is something the major does not know, Mark thought.

Chris started to speak: "Because they think he—"

"It's not important now," Mark interrupted. He was not entirely sure they could trust this Major Kappel.

The major smiled again and looked at Mark. "I help you but you do not answer my questions, detective. Is this fair?"

"Nothing personal, major," Mark said, "but I only just arrived here and I have some catching up to do."

"I see."

A moment of uncomfortable silence was broken by Kate. "The license plates don't match. The plates on Karl's car do not match the one from Paul's notes." She leaned back into the folds of the big chair. "So Paul's notes are just another fucking mystery."

The major's brown eyes fixed on Kate. He motioned for the waitress and ordered coffee and pastries.

"I could have told you the license plate number," the major said.

Mark sat back and cleared his throat. "I have a feeling you can tell us more, as well." He managed a smile. "And how the hell can I get one of those *get out of trouble for free cards* you have in your wallet?"

Major Kappel smiled. "It is my identification." The coffee arrived. He took his black, no sugar. "My Swiss Guard ID is practical."

"Interesting," Mark said as he bit into a sweet bun. "Did you know I spoke with a colleague of yours yesterday?"

"Yes, you spoke with my commanding officer."

"I don't know much about your organization," Mark said.

The major sipped his coffee. "The Swiss Guard was formed in the fifteenth century and has undergone a few changes over the years. There are various sub-groups within the Guard—some are known, some not; as you can see, for example, I am not in Rome guarding the Pope at the moment."

Mark had a hundred questions but settled on one for now. "So, what are you doing here?"

Major Kappel stared at Mark. "To be honest, Detective Julian, for the past few hours I have been on my own time. In fact, I would be reprimanded for using my Swiss Guard status while not officially on duty."

Chris finished his pastry. "That Swiss Guard status sure carries a lot of weight. You flash your ID and the rest of the world bends over backwards."

Major Kappel smiled. "My organization is highly respected. Especially in Switzerland."

"So what exactly are you doing here?" Kate asked.

"The Swiss Guard is a dedicated force. We look out for the Pope and the interests of the Vatican. Wherever those interests might be."

"And you are very well trained, I've heard," Mark said. "The best of the best. But what are you doing in Switzerland when the Pope is not here?"

"When we are not involved in security at the Vatican or with the Pope abroad, some of us have other duties. In this case, I was asked to look into some anomalies within the Anthroposophical Society. By the way, you would be wise to understand the politics involved. Despite my Swiss Guard status, I am not able to simply march into the Goetheanum and poke around at my leisure. So, when my orders came to take a twenty-man unit and execute a fifteen minute search of the building—ostensibly looking for suspicious activity based on a tip—I was delighted but perplexed about the real reason for the order."

He looked closely at Mark. "This was the excuse we had wanted for a few months. But why on earth was I asked to look for a young American boy? It makes me very curious about you and your role in this affair." His eyes were glued on Mark.

Kate broke the silence. "What does guarding the Pope have to do with Anthroposophy? What are these anomalies that concern the Vatican? And what are we going to do about finding Mike?"

Mark thought: *And how will I solve the Ithaca murders from over here in Europe?*

"I trust there will be a reciprocal sharing arrangement soon," the major said, still staring at Mark. And then, surprisingly, he added: "Do you know the whereabouts of your Doctor Fritz Fleischer?"

"Now, how the hell do you know about him?" Mark asked.

"We were following his . . . career until he disappeared. Be very careful with this individual."

No shit, Mark thought. *He sneaks up and drugs you and then nails your larynx to the ceiling.* Mark was interested in this news. "So you know he's in the US?"

"Actually, we think he's back in Europe. We know he's done some horrible things in your country and we know he is very difficult to find. He has connections."

"What the fuck is going on?" Kate boomed.

Mark suppressed a smile. Straight to the point. That was Kate.

"My interest is both professional and personal," Major Kappel said. "First and foremost are the interests of the Vatican. Secondly, my father was killed by terrorists in a 1980 act of terror at a Bologna train station in Italy. I suspect Doctor Fleischer was involved in that bombing—eighty-five people were killed. You might remember it?"

"I remember," Mark said. "It was all over the news in those days. Sorry to hear that your father was killed. You must have been very young."

"It was a long time ago." The major's face was tense. "But I will never forget. Even after all these years, the guilty will be brought to justice. I will see to it. "

"But wasn't a weird cult responsible?" Mark asked.

"It was a fascist group," the major said. "Fascists with a quasi-spiritual leader named Licio Gelli, the Grand Master of Propaganda Due or P2 as it is more commonly known—a Masonic Lodge in Italy. They had links to organized crime and the Italian government. Gelli's P2 Lodge was eventually closed by Italian Masonic authorities in 1976 but the group continued to function in secret. They allegedly conspired to destabilize governments and were involved in a major bank fraud, and unfortunately, we suspect they had connections inside the Vatican."

"Quite the spiritual group," Kate said, sarcastically.

The major continued: "You might remember the 1982 incident of the Banco Ambrosiano president found hanging under Blackfriars Bridge in London? The Vatican Bank was Banco Ambrosiano's major shareholder. Gelli was not convicted of any murders but he spent twelve years behind bars for other crimes. He mysteriously escaped from a Swiss prison by helicopter. He is very old and not active today. The fact that he is alive and enjoys near celebrity status in Italy is both surprising and disturbing to many of us."

Major Kappel sipped his coffee. "But we have reason to believe that at least one of his colleagues has carried on with illegal activities. The man's name is Silvestro Nardo. Fleischer and Nardo go way back—right to the Bologna train station bombing. In fact, their family trees read like a who's who of shady characters—especially their links to the Third Reich. We think Nardo has joined a fringe Anthroposophist group."

"With Doctor Fleischer?" Mark asked.

"And others." The major paused. "Although I am interested in their contacts in the Vatican, I also believe they are planning a significant event. They must be stopped."

Mark stared hard at the major. "Significant event, as in an act of terror?"

"It is a distinct possibility," the major said. "And one we cannot afford to ignore."

Outside on the tarmac, a black limousine pulled up beside a waiting helicopter. A wheelchair appeared and a large man pushed an anesthetized Paul Sung into the helicopter. Two minutes later, it disappeared into the darkening sky.

8

Basel Airport, Switzerland

Mark sat back and processed what he had just learned. He had suspected this case was more involved than the Ithaca murders. And now he was certain.

"What do you know about cults or new religious movements?" the major asked.

"We're certainly not experts," Chris said, "but this last week has been a crash course on the subject."

"Anthroposophy has an interesting foundation," the major continued. "Its members occasionally revise their movement's history—especially in Europe where some of the biggest players were racist, anti-Semitic and pro-Nazi during the 1930s and 40s. Anthroposophist leaders in Italy like Ettore Martinoli and Massimo Scaligero openly supported Nazism and considered Rudolf Steiner to be a precursor to Mussolini and Hitler."

"Was he?" Chris asked.

"I certainly don't think so," the major said. "While many of Steiner's beliefs include racial hierarchies, his main message was steeped in occultism and had nothing to do with fascism.

"Anthroposophy's link with Freemasonry in the 1930s was non-existent, possibly because the Nazis saw Freemasons as a threat. Hitler eventually saw every fringe group as a threat and although some high-ranking German members of the Nazi party were supporters of Anthroposophy, it was a time of fear and paranoia in Europe and everyone needed to be careful in making public their spiritual and religious beliefs."

Mark watched as the major sat back and stretched his long legs. The man sounded convincing but where was this going? Could he be trusted?

The major continued: "Although some of their beliefs are controversial, most Anthroposophists today are quite harmless."

"But a handful or two," Mark said, "are connected to murder and chaos because they believe it to be their karmic duty. Right?"

"Apparently," Major Kappel said. "History is fraught with examples of secret societies within societies—some harmless, others not. But for all intents and purposes, I think we need to treat this fringe group as suspected terrorists. Recent activity at the Vatican, the murders in New York and now the boy at the Goetheanum tell me something very important is happening—and potentially devastating."

"What activity at the Vatican?" Mark asked.

Major Kappel shifted his lean body in the chair. "Pope Benedict is a . . ." He paused, as if searching for the appropriate words. "Pope Benedict holds certain conservative values. Before his election in 2005, for twenty-three years he was the head of the Congregation for the Doctrine of the Faith. The CDF is the oldest of all Vatican departments and deals with subjects that many people find troubling." He paused. "One such subject is exorcism."

Kate rolled her eyes. "Oh give me a fucking break. How weird can this get?"

Chris glared at his sister. "Can we let him finish?"

"Two years ago," Major Kappel continued, "Pope Benedict instructed bishops to offer courses to priests about the need to steer people away from Satan. The Pope believes all occult activities to be evil, and when required he supports having specially appointed bishops perform exorcisms.

"Pope Benedict also wanted to restore a prayer—a controversial prayer—as protection against evil. This prayer was traditionally recited at the end of Catholic Mass but it was dropped in the 1960s by Pope John XXIII. The current Pope would like to revive the prayer."

"What prayer?" Chris asked.

"A prayer to Saint Michael, the Archangel," said the major.

"Saint Michael?" Chris frowned. "Michael the Archangel? But that's—"

"Let him finish," Mark said.

"Pope Benedict's conservative plans did not go over well within some circles at the Vatican." Major Kappel pulled in a deep breath and let it out slowly. "I'm sure you know that although Anthroposophy is founded on occultism, it also has roots in Christianity. Despite the misgivings of many, some Catholics consider themselves Anthroposophists and have connections in the Vatican. These people are displeased with the current Pope's position on occultism.

"When certain Anthroposophists learned of the Pope's plan to revive the prayer to Saint Michael with the goal of combating occultism, they were outraged. The archangel Michael is very important to Anthroposophists. They tried to explain that the Anthroposophist Lucifer is not evil in the Christian sense. There was much heated debate within the private walls of the Vatican. Some felt the Pope was living in the past and being disrespectful to other spiritual paths. Out of fear of reprisal, these Anthroposophists felt compelled to conceal their occult inclinations. After all, the Church had condemned Anthroposophy as far back as 1919—the same year the first Waldorf School opened in Germany." The major looked out into the darkening sky. "And once again, substantial amounts of money have gone missing."

"Missing?" Chris said.

"There have been problems in the past," the major continued, "including during the time of the Licio Gelli Masonic Lodge scandal. Millions went missing then—that scandal was public in the 1970s and 80s. This latest . . . discrepancy is why I am here. I am investigating the links between the Vatican, some Anthroposophists, Silvestro Nardo and over six million US dollars that has mysteriously disappeared from the Vatican Bank."

"Holy shit," Kate said. "How can someone steal that much money?"

"Connections," the major said. "Creative bookkeeping. Look at recent activity on Wall Street in your country. When one has connections, anything is possible."

Mark was busy joining the dots. "And you think the money will be used for terrorist activities." It was not a question. "And this involves the Ithaca murders because the terrorists were afraid some people at Cornell University might discover their plan. And that plan—whatever the hell it might be—somehow involves ten-year old Michael from Oregon."

The major sat back in his chair. "And that is what has me curious." He looked at Mark. "What about the boy?"

Mark studied the man. *Perhaps I should trust him. He knows about Doctor Fleischer so maybe this is the break I need to find and arrest the surgical killer. Indeed, why not share information and resources? Maybe I should check with Chief Bischel in New York . . . ?*

Kate broke the silence. "If you have this much clout in Europe, let's go to Rome to get Mike."

Chris leaned forward. "I agree. I need to find my son."

Mark stared out through the big plate-glass windows. The afternoon was quickly turning into evening and the few planes left on the tarmac were becoming shadows in the dusk. "Seems like a good idea," he said. "Let's go to Rome and catch some bad guys." He looked at Chris. "And find your son."

9

En Route to Rome, Italy

Mike had never been in a helicopter. Only minutes before, for some unknown reason, their car had been speeding through the streets of Dornach, like a stunt car in a movie. Mike's mother was screaming and crying and Miss Meyer kept telling her to be quiet.

Everything will be fine, Serena—you'll see.

Mike was strapped in and his mom held his hand tight as they sped through the narrow streets. He was sure they were going to crash a couple of times and once they caught the edge of a patio table on a sidewalk and sent it flying. Luckily, nobody was sitting at the table. Mike was sure Karl was not only mean—he was also crazy. It was all Mike could do not to throw up as they twisted and turned until the car finally stopped at an airport. It was not the Zurich airport.

"Is someone chasing us?" Mike asked. He looked back and saw nobody. "Where are we going?"

Not surprisingly, nobody answered his questions.

He was hurried into a waiting helicopter where a young man wearing overalls made sure their seatbelts were secured. Mike's mom had almost stopped crying when they left the ground.

As shaken as he was at the strange events of the day, Mike enjoyed the feeling of flying in the helicopter. Helicopters always reminded him of his favorite insect and as they lifted off and tilted sideways before gaining speed, Mike smiled and felt very much like one of the dragonflies he loved to watch back home in Oregon.

Karl seemed very tense. Herr Ackermann looked more nervous than ever. His jacket was off and Mike could see huge perspiration patches on the white shirt under his arms. Miss Meyer still had the familiar smile glued to her face. Just like every day back at the Loving Sun Waldorf School.

All right now children, everyone in nice neat rows and repeat after me . . .

Mike's mother sat beside him and would not let go of his hand. Even though the helicopter vibrated, he could still feel her hand trembling. Mike suddenly felt really sorry for his mom. "It's all right," he said to her. "We'll be fine, mom." He squeezed her hand but she cried again.

10

Basel Airport, Switzerland

The VIP Lounge was almost empty. Mark saw three men at a table, drinking beer and sharing a laugh with the young waitress. He looked at Major Kappel. The man was immaculately dressed and could have passed for a successful businessman waiting for a late flight. As the major shifted in his chair, Mark spotted the bulge under his jacket. Cops instinctively notice such things.

"Let me guess," Mark said, nodding and staring at the bulge. He had once attended a conference on handguns used by police forces around the world. Mark had been impressed with what he learned about the Swiss Guard. "It's a SIG Sauer nine millimeter?"

The major appeared surprised. "Close. In fact, that is standard issue these days but not many of us carry weapons. I am an exception."

The three men at the other table left the lounge. The major glanced around the empty room and pulled out his handgun. He handed it to Mark. "This was my father's gun. It's a SIG P210. Swiss made—old, but still very good."

Mark cradled the weapon in both hands. It certainly looked old but felt very comfortable. The most redeeming quality was the solid wood handle. He held the gun in one hand and passed his other over the barrel.

"Beautiful," he said. He handed it back to the major.

"Indeed." He slipped the gun into its holster beneath his jacket.

Major Kappel quickly changed the subject. "I'm curious about the boy."

"We want to go to Rome," Mark said. "Find him and arrest the bad guys."

"But why is the boy so important to them?" the major asked.

Mark looked briefly at Chris and Kate and decided to confide in the major. "They think Mike is a reincarnated Christ or perhaps Rudolf Steiner."

Major Kappel sunk back into his big chair, looking like someone who had just learned of a death in his family. His light brown eyes were wide open. He appeared to be deep in thought.

Mark then proceeded to tell him all he knew. Chris and Kate interjected from time to time. The major listened carefully. He asked a couple of questions about the professor and seemed very concerned at his disappearance. When they had finished, the major stood and walked to the window. The lights had been dimmed in the lounge and stars could be seen sparkling in the darkening night sky.

Mark felt tired but his mind was busy. He hoped they could trust this man. His eyes met Kate's; he could sense her frustration.

Kate pounded the little table. "Let's just go to Rome and find Mike," she said, almost yelling. "He must be scared shitless!"

"I agree," Chris said. "I want my son back. Period."

Major Kappel returned to the table. "I'm afraid that will be difficult. It is not a simple matter of going to get him and taking him home. What you have told me is very disturbing. We really do need to look at the big picture."

Kate took a deep breath and looked at the major. "Maybe you can make sense of the license plate," she suggested.

Why not? Mark pulled the paper from his jacket pocket. "I found this in Paul Sung's notes—it's underlined so maybe it's an important license plate. Are you able to run a plate here in Switzerland?"

"That should be no problem," Major Kappel said. He took the paper and read: G-A-9-3-0-4-1-2-2-3.

Major Kappel smiled. Then he chuckled.

"What is it?" Kate asked. "What the hell is so funny?"

"It's not a license plate number," the major said. "It refers to a lecture. The letters and numbers refer to catalogued lectures and dates. The letters 'GA' refer to the German word, 'Gesamtausgabe,' which simply means 'the entire works' and the number '93' is the number of the lecture. The '04-12-23' tells us the lecture was given on December 23, 1904."

Mark sat back in his chair. "A lecture? Whose lecture?"

The major looked at Mark. His smile disappeared. "A lecture by Rudolf Steiner."

11

Basel Airport, Switzerland

Major Kappel leaned back in his chair. "This is how Anthroposophists catalogue the entire works of Rudolf Steiner," he said.

Mark felt a little sheepish, but really—how was he to know? "So, if Paul thinks it's important," he said, "how can we find this particular lecture?"

"That's the easy part," the major said. "Most lectures can be found in the Steiner archives online." He looked at Chris and pointed to his laptop. "May I?"

Chris pushed the little computer across the table. "Be my guest."

The major flipped it open and tapped some keys. "Good, there is wireless Internet here."

Mark stood and looked over the major's shoulder. The screen displayed a busy website full of buttons and what Mark had already learned was Anthroposophic font. At the top left corner, he saw "Steiner e.lib" and farther along, "Steiner archives."

"The entire site is in English," Kate said.

"It also exists in the original German," the major said. "Anthroposophists take Steiner's work very seriously. Lots of time goes into translating much of what Steiner said and wrote."

The major scrolled down to the search button for lectures and typed: GA93. There were two results, but only one from December 23, 1904. He clicked on the link. "And there we have it," he said. The title of the lecture was clear:

The Work of Secret Societies in the World
The Atom as Coagulated Electricity
A lecture by Rudolf Steiner
Berlin, December 23, 1904   GA 93

"What the hell is that all about?" Kate asked. She looked at the masses of text under the title. "What does this have to do with anything?"

"Let's have a look," Major Kappel said. "Steiner was not the most succinct of lecturers. I've learned to scan his excessive verbiage and can usually pull out the pertinent information."

The major leaned in, his eyes darting across the screen. "This lecture is about occult knowledge and immortality . . . laws of evolution . . . man's spirit and the atom and electricity . . . higher degrees of Freemasonry . . ." He stopped, a surprised look formed on his face. "Steiner also talks about the destruction of the fifth root race through the *War of All Against All.*"

Kate shook her head. "I gotta be honest. I don't have a clue what most of that means. But it sounds bad."

"Are you familiar with this lecture?" Mark asked.

Major Kappel was speed-reading the entire lecture. "Not this particular one." He was still reading. "Wait a minute, please."

Mark stood beside Kate. Her short blond hair was inches from him and he resisted the urge to lean in and breathe deeply. He pulled his attention back to the laptop and tried to read the text on the screen.

Major Kappel finally pushed his chair back. "Interesting."

"Refresh my memory," Chris said. "Steiner divided history into epochs, right?"

"That's right," the major said.

"And in this lecture he speaks about the destruction of the fifth epoch through a war?" Chris looked again at the screen and continued to address Major Kappel. "Professor Sung mentioned this *War of All Against All.* And isn't this current time period the fifth epoch?"

"That's right," the major repeated.

"Well, that's not good," Kate said. "Steiner is predicting a war?"

"Steiner does not simply predict this war," the major said. "In other lectures he says the War of All Against All is necessary. He taught that such violence is needed from time to time." He scrolled down the lecture. "This is troubling." He read aloud:

"Before the end of the fifth epoch of culture, science will have reached the stage where man will be able to penetrate into the atom itself. When the similarity of substance between the thought and the atom is once comprehended, the way to get hold of the forces contained in the atom will soon be discovered and then nothing will be inaccessible to certain methods of working.

"A man standing here, let us say, will be able by pressing a button concealed in his pocket, to explode some object at a great distance—say in Hamburg! Just as by setting up a wave-movement here and causing it to take a particular form at some other place, wireless telegraphy is possible, so what I have just indicated will be within man's power when the occult truth that thought and atom consist of the same substance is put into practical application."

"Sounds like he's nuts," Kate said.

Major Kappel sighed. "Steiner was many things, but there is no questioning his intelligence. Misguided perhaps, but he was certainly no fool."

"How could he have known about atoms in 1904?" Chris asked.

"Steiner borrowed many ideas," the major said, "and nuclear fission had been discussed by scientists like Einstein well before it became a reality many years later. Our problem now is that a number of Steiner's followers today take everything he said and wrote as the gospel truth. And they can twist his words to fit their own agendas. Listen." He read again from the lecture:

"A tiny handful of men will make good and thus insure their survival in the sixth epoch of civilisation."

Chris shifted his body in the big chair. "So, some Anthroposophists believe they will survive this catastrophe?"

"That is how it could be interpreted," Major Kappel said. "Or their souls will survive. But something is not right here."

"And that is?" Mark asked.

"Steiner speaks elsewhere of this War of All Against All, but the timing seems off. We are not yet at the end of the fifth epoch."

"Maybe they think we need a trial run before the big one," Mark said.

It was completely dark outside. They sat in silence for a moment as the sound of a jetliner faded into the distance.

Mark pushed his chair back and stretched. He felt exhausted. "There is no point in trying to catch a flight to Rome tonight," he said. "Mike could be anywhere by now."

"Agreed," the major said. "I've already booked us a flight for tomorrow morning."

"You're always one step ahead," Mark said. "And you're coming with us?"

"Rome is home to me," Major Kappel said. "I took the liberty of booking all of us into a hotel here in Basel. I hope you don't mind. There will be no charge."

Kate stared at Major Kappel. "You what?"

"Under the circumstances, none of you can return to your hotel in Dornach," the major said. He stared at Kate.

"But my things are still there," Mark said.

"No," the major said. "I had your things taken to where we will stay tonight."

Kate's face flushed. "How did you—"

"Forgive me," Major Kappel said, "but I am sure you'll understand my concerns about what happened back at your hotel a few hours ago. If we are all being honest here, you'll have no problem explaining this event?"

"She was attacked," Mark said, defensively. "She had to defend herself. How do you know about this?"

Major Kappel looked at Kate. "After you burst into the Goetheanum today, I had one of my men make sure you would not have unwelcome visitors at your hotel. It seems my officer arrived just after you left with your luggage and lunch. Suffice to say, my man was surprised to find a half-conscious thug spitting blood and bits of teeth into your bathroom sink. The fellow was an American living in Switzerland. Ex-Marine—big with lots of muscles." The major continued staring at Kate. "He had barely started his work when you surprised him." He paused. "He was very badly beaten."

Mark looked at Kate. She avoided his eyes and said nothing.

The major continued: "He needed very little persuasion to explain that he had been hired to copy a laptop hard drive in your hotel room. He had no idea who he was working for—he was to be paid in cash and never saw his employer."

Mark raised an eyebrow. "So it's probably best if we stay clear of Dornach."

The major smiled. "Yes. And another reason to leave Switzerland early tomorrow. Please, we can take my car. I'll see that your rentals are repaired and returned to Zurich tomorrow."

"You're a man of influence," Mark said.

"For now," the major replied. "Let's just hope it lasts."

The five-star hotel in Basel included a luxurious private room for each of them but Mark had no desire or energy to admire the decor. He felt exhausted but knew there was something he needed to do before collapsing into bed.

12

Basel, Switzerland

Mark dialed the number, hoping to catch his boss before he left the office for the day.

After a few rings, the phone was answered: "Chief Bischel."

"Chief, it's Mark Julian."

"How are you, detective? How's Switzerland?"

Mark told the chief about the visit to the Goetheanum and meeting Major Kappel of the Swiss Guard. "But I have nothing in the way of a solid lead."

Chief Bischel was curious about Major Kappel.

"He seems legit to me, chief," Mark said.

"Keep it to yourself, detective, but agents Bander and Martins think there might be problems over there in Europe. Seems nobody can be trusted. Be careful."

Mark was curious. "Have they heard about a terrorist group?"

Silence.

Mark frowned. "Chief?"

"I'm here. Terrorists? As in Al Quaeda?"

"I don't think so but Major Kappel says it might have something to do with a secret Italian-German cult."

Chief Bischel sighed into the phone. "Sounds farfetched."

Mark's mind was whirling, still looking for connections between the Ithaca murders and international terrorism. Yes, it did sound farfetched and he did not want to appear obtuse during a long distance phone call with his boss.

"Major Kappel is experienced and well-connected over here."

"Listen Mark, this is not your area of expertise."

Mark knew the chief was not buying the terrorist angle. He changed the subject. "Any news on Paul Sung?"

"Nothing. The professor simply disappeared. And how about the folks from Oregon?"

"I'm with them now. We're all flying to Rome in the morning."

"Watch them and keep an eye on this Major Kappel, detective."

The conversation ended and Mark replayed it again in his mind. Twice.

Day Seven

1

Rome, Italy

Paul Sung awoke in total darkness. His breathing was slow and his mouth was dry. Gradually, he managed to open his eyes and move his head slowly to one side, then the other. He took a deep breath and let it out—nice and easy.

He was lying on his back on a hard surface in a pitch-black room. His head was spinning and he felt sick to his stomach. Only one thought came to his waking mind: *I am alive.*

The voice was like something from a bad dream: Deep. Guttural. Near. "Hello Dr. Sung."

Paul tried to find the voice in the darkness.

"I trust you had a good sleep?"

Where am I? Slowly, as if reaching for something tangible in a fog bank, his mind came to life. *Ithaca. A house—a safe house—safe from a madman. The surgical killer.* Images flashed through his lethargic mind—*the kitchen in the safe house, leaves in the backyard, breathing fresh air, sharing a joke with a young cop. Then noises—like muffled firecrackers. Two gunshots. Two bodies on the ground, one of them on a pile of leaves. Pain. Falling and then darkness. Noise—like a jet engine, then vibration and more sleep. How long have I been unconscious?*

Paul felt his pulse quicken. He raised himself onto one elbow.

He tried his voice. "Where am I?" He was barely audible.

He heard a muffled sound, like shuffling feet on pavement. And then the deep, raspy voice. Very near. "Welcome to Italy."

Suddenly, a bright light overhead shocked his eyes into closing. He grimaced, tried to roll over to avoid the light but quickly realized he was unable to move. Straps around his legs and waist bound his body to something hard—maybe a table or a bench. He squinted for a moment before the halogen bulb burned his eyes shut.

"Italy?" Paul said. "I am in Italy?"

He was breathing fast now—too fast and he could feel nausea turning in his stomach. He needed to think, needed to survive. Breathe in . . . breathe out . . . in . . . out . . .

I am with the surgical killer. I am with the man who killed Greg Matheson. This man also murdered the Richardson family.

Fear poured through his veins and he tried to think only of survival now.

I am still alive so he must want something. I know his name but he knows that I know his name. He led me to the YouTube video. He's an Anthroposophic physician. And a madman. I need to use my knowledge and wits in order to survive.

Paul cleared his throat. "How are you, Dr. Fleischer?" He thought again of Greg Matheson and then of Bob Richardson and his wife and children.

Silence, then laughter and the deep voice: "Fine, and you Dr. Sung?"

Paul knew he needed to stay calm and not show any emotion. "Nicht Gut," he said. He was not sure why he chose to answer in German.

More laughter. "There is no need to speak German. My English is fine and I am not easily impressed by arrogant Americans."

Paul's eyes were becoming accustomed to the halogen. He blinked twice and glimpsed a very large man bending over and peering at him, as if he were studying a specimen in a lab. Paul wanted to ask the man how he could call himself a doctor when he took so many innocent lives, but he knew the answer. This Anthroposophist did not see people as anything more than vessels needed for carrying souls. If the soul was not working with the spirit of Anthroposophy, the life of the body was of no consequence.

Paul tried to clear his throat again, hoping to appear stronger than he felt. "What can I do for you, Dr. Fleischer?"

2

Rome, Italy

A door opened and Paul heard more muffled footsteps. Whispering . . .
"I trust you are feeling better?" It was another male voice, not nearly as
deep as Doctor Fleischer's, and it contained traces of an accent—but not
German. Perhaps Italian?

"I'd be feeling better if I could move," Paul said. His voice felt stronger
now. "And I could really use some water."

The bright halogen disappeared and Paul heard matches being struck.
The room now glowed in soft candlelight. Much better. A man stood beside
him. Late-seventies, tall, slicked back silver-white hair, with a mustache,
goatee and thin-rimmed glasses. He wore a dark, pinstriped suit and burgundy silk tie.

"So," the man said. "You are Dr. Paul Sung of Cornell University. You
are the *expert*." The word *expert* came out hard and dripped with sarcasm.

"I am Paul Sung but I don't know that I'm an expert at anything."

"Oh but you are an expert. We all have our roles to play and your particular role is very important, but of course, you know that."

"We are in Italy?" Paul was hoping to steer the man away from his anger.
"Why am I here? What is this all about?" He shifted his weight, still leaning
on an elbow. He saw now that he was strapped to an old wooden bench. He
was in what appeared to be a basement—cement floor, another bench against
a far wall, a few tools here and there, wooden stairs leading up to the next
level of the house.

"What is this all about?" the man echoed. "We brought you to Italy, of
course. You are too modest, Dr. Sung. *You* are what this is all about."

The accent was definitely Italian. The man moved and Paul tried to get a
better look at his captor.

"In your work," the man continued, "you use words, plenty of words,
written and spoken. You fill young, eager minds with these words." He

approached the bench and stared into Paul's eyes. "Your clever words, Dr. Sung, are nothing more than dead sounds."

"Can you explain?" Paul said. *Keep him talking . . . and I'll prolong my life. Gather information and use it wisely . . .* The pointed face was inches away. Paul could smell garlic on the man's breath.

"Little is accomplished," the man said quietly, "if one tries to understand these words theoretically. Much more can be gained when one creates sacred moments in life during which one is willing to use all one's energy in an effort to fill one's soul with the living content of such words." The man smiled. "That is a direct quote, Dr. Sung. Do you know from whom?"

"It sounds very much like Rudolf Steiner."

"Very good." The man grinned. "Question: Why do you not fill your own soul? Why do you waste your time dealing only with empty words instead of the essence of those words?" He smiled knowingly. "Don't tell me, Dr. Sung—I know the answer: Because you have your role to play."

The man was breathing hard and the smile quickly vanished. Paul had had enough experience with disturbed esotericists over the years to know that now was not the time to argue. He lay still and remained silent.

"You speak to your students about matters of karma as if they are games of baseball on sunny afternoons. You ruin young minds and destroy the spirit in those students. You deaden their potential to develop spiritual skills needed for . . ."

"The future," Paul said. Although he was afraid, he was also curious. This man's argument was typical of many esotericists who believe it is impossible to study a spiritual discipline without first accepting the foundation on which that discipline is based. Anthroposophists, in particular, feel their guru's lessons can only be learned by those willing to abandon critical thinking skills—their rational minds—before entering into the realm of the occult.

Before one can understand, one must believe.

"The future," the man said. "Yes." Suddenly, he seemed calm and almost friendly again. His eyes widened and he smiled. "We are talking about the future. Forgive me. I should introduce myself. I am Silvestro Nardo." He handed Paul a small glass bottle of water.

Paul shifted awkwardly, took the bottle and spilled as he drank. He doubted he would live long enough to tell anyone about this discussion. Signor Nardo seemed conflicted, manic—bouncing from one mood to another in a heartbeat. Paul searched his mind for something useful—anything that would convince this man to let him live.

"You are Italian," Paul said. "I spent some time in Trieste a few years ago—and Rome." If nothing else, discussing topics of mutual interest might prolong his life. "Are you a member of the Anthroposophical Society in Italy?"

Paul recalled well-known Italian Anthroposophists from the past. Ettore Martinoli and Massimo Scaligero came to mind. Both were still held in high esteem by many Anthroposophists and both were considered racist by historians and embarrassingly anti-Semitic.

"Do not try Ahrimanic tricks on me. I am a member of nothing you can truly understand," Silvestro Nardo said. "I work with moral people, spiritual people and you cannot possibly comprehend the importance of our work. I work with the Mik-eye-ell Stream. The Christ Impulse guides us into the future."

"The future?" Paul said. "Tell me, Signore Nardo, what do you have planned for the future?"

Nardo smiled and shook his head. "You are clever, Paul Sung, but your words are empty."

Paul looked over Nardo's shoulder. He could see Doctor Fleischer standing a few feet away, watching. Paul had noticed something on the wall earlier and his eyes came back to it now. It was a small framed poster and he recognized it as something he had seen many times in books and on the front doors of buildings all over the world. It was a picture of a square and compass—the Masonic Symbol. Pieces of the puzzle were slowly coming together.

Paul's mind flipped through his history lessons. Italian Freemasonry's most infamous character was the fascist, Licio Gelli. His Masonic lodge—known as P2—eventually lost its Freemason Charter in the 1970s because of scandals and alleged terrorist activities. Gelli had long since retired but there were rumors of the secret Lodge's continued existence.

Although he went through a Freemason phase, Rudolf Steiner was never on record as being a Freemason, but in 1904 he received his own charter from Theodore Reuss of the Ordo Templum Orientalis. This group eventually transformed into one that lay the foundation for Steiner's work with Theosophy and then on to Anthroposophy. Although often critical of Freemasonry at that time, Steiner always held that it would play an important role in man's future.

Silvestro Nardo seemed calm again. He smiled. "It is all unfolding according to the laws of karma. The Group of Forty-Eight is the catalyst for all that will happen in the future." Nardo wore a crazy grin. He passed some fingers through Paul's hair and then patted his head as one would do to a beloved dog. "But you know all this, of course."

Paul recoiled at the touch of fingers on his head but was fascinated by what Nardo was saying. The reference to the *Group of Forty-Eight* seemed vaguely familiar.

There was no longer any doubt in Paul's mind that the strange events of the past few days—from the missing boy to the Ithaca murders to his own abduction—were connected to a fringe group of occultists. To his horror, Paul was beginning to put the puzzle together. These people were planning something, but what? He needed more answers. He also needed to find a way to stay alive.

3

Rome, Italy

Nardo glared at Paul. "Why do you think you ridicule Spiritual Science?" Paul searched for a response. "I respect Rudolf Steiner and I —"

Intense pain suddenly ripped through the bottom of his left foot, then his right foot, burning the nerves up both legs. He stretched his neck enough to see Doctor Fleischer standing near his bare feet, holding a hammer.

Fleischer smiled. "Physical discomfort is your karma, Professor," he said. "Do not speak of Rudolf Steiner and your karma will know less pain."

Paul closed his eyes tight and fought the throbbing in his feet and legs.

Nardo strutted to the corner of the room and pulled a thin book from a shelf. He walked back to the bench and stared down at Paul. "I will read a passage from Rudolf Steiner." The little man was still visibly upset; his hands were shaking but he opened the book and flipped through worn pages with the conviction of an alcoholic choosing his bottle.

He held the book open, stared into Paul's eyes from inches away and said slowly: "I . . . know . . . you!"

Paul recognized the title of the book and listened as the strange occultist read aloud from Rudolf Steiner's *The Incarnation of Ahriman, The Embodiment of Evil on Earth*:

> "Just as Lucifer reincarnated at the beginning of the third pre-Christian millennium and Christ incarnated at the time of the Mystery of Golgatha, so there will be an incarnation of Ahriman in the West not long after our present times in the third post-Christian millennium, in fact. To gain a right conception of the historical evolution of mankind of approximately 6,000 years, one must grasp that at the one pole stands the incarnation of Lucifer, in the center the incarnation of Christ, and at the other pole the incarnation of Ahriman."

Nardo shut the book and stared hard at Paul. "Oh yes," he said, nodding his head, "born in the West with your Asian roots. A backwards race best left in the past. You attended synagogue with your mother when the true Initiate knows that Judaism is outdated and useless. There were signs at ages seven and fourteen. As your incarnation progressed, you passed your twenty-first year and showed disdain for all spiritual work by proclaiming yourself an atheist. At twenty-eight, the incarnation was complete and you began your *materialist* teachings while mocking the spirit with your so-called *intellect*. So many empty words. Oh yes . . . we know you!"

Paul felt stunned. *They believe I am the physical incarnation of Ahriman!*

He tried to clear his mind—tried to understand the significance of what he had just been told. His entire career had been spent studying religion and occultism and now his lifelong work had come to haunt him.

"You fool nobody," Nardo said. He strolled around the musty basement blowing out candles, taking the last one to guide the doctor and himself through the darkness and up the old wooden stairs. He stopped once and looked back at Paul in the dark room. "You are Ahriman!"

4

Rome, Italy

Mike sat at a large mahogany dining room table, slurping spaghetti noodles one at a time and listening to the crackling fire in a stone fireplace against the far wall. The house was old but solid, stone masonry style with hardwood floors and thick, faded tapestries on the walls. He finished his spaghetti and stared into the fire, replaying the incredible events of the previous day in his mind.

The car ride through the narrow streets of Dornach had been scary but very exciting and the helicopter trip to Rome was fantastic. He wanted to tell his dad about that amazing day. He watched the flames dance and crackle in the fireplace and when he thought of his dad again, he felt a queasy feeling in his stomach. Mike missed his dad very much.

They had arrived late last night in Rome and after dinner, Mike had gone straight to bed. The men slept in rooms on the top floor; his mother and Miss Meyer shared a pullout bed in the living room. Mike was in a tiny room just off the kitchen. His room was more like a large closet than an actual bedroom, containing only a small cot and a big thick duvet. When he woke up that day, Mike had seen two of the men from that strange late-night event at the Goetheanum. One was the very old, well-dressed Italian man named Silvestro Nardo and the other was that big, scary Doctor Fleischer.

There was no breakfast that day and Mike was told not to leave his room until he was called for lunch. The adults needed to discuss important things. He sat on the cot, looking at a photo album Karl had handed him before shuffling him back into his room and closing the door. Mike flipped through page after page of old black and white pictures of well-dressed men, some in military uniforms and wearing shiny black boots—all looking very serious.

When he was finally called for lunch and took his place at the table, Mike thought he heard groaning noises coming from the basement. He asked his mother if someone was sick downstairs, but she just told him not to be concerned with other peoples' business. But she looked upset—as if she was very worried about something.

His mom and Miss Meyer sat together and ate silently. Herr Ackermann sat across from Karl at the head of the table. A grumpy fat woman served the adults wine and brought more garlic bread from time to time.

Doctor Fleischer and Signor Nardo suddenly appeared from the basement and ate in silence. Mike was tempted to ask them who was down there but one more look at Doctor Fleischer convinced him to remain silent. Nobody spoke for a few minutes.

The massive doctor finished his meal in about two minutes and stared at Mike from across the table. His bushy gray eyebrows came down hard when he frowned. Mike thought his eyes looked like dark, scary pools.

"You do not convince me," the giant said. He leaned his big body forward, glaring at Mike.

Mike felt like running. He looked at his mother for support. She avoided his eyes and continued eating her salad, as if everything was fine. Miss Meyer forced a smile and looked into the fireplace.

The deep voice continued: "Do you feel special? Do you understand what this is all about—the sacrifices made for you to be here?" Doctor Fleischer's dark eyes never left Mike.

Karl cleared his throat. "Please, Doctor Fleischer, I can assure you the mission is following its path according to—"

"The mission is one thing," Fleischer said, "and an incarnated Initiate is quite another. I have seen no proof that this boy—"

"Please!" Karl slammed a fist on the table. His long-stemmed glass tipped and red wine spilled across the lace cloth. "It is as it should be!" The pudgy woman appeared from the kitchen with more wine and refilled the glass.

Karl motioned towards the two women. "Sophia has monitored the boy for years. His biography fits and certain tests have been undertaken."

Doctor Fleischer stared at Mike but spoke to Karl. Mike did not understand the conversation.

"I've heard the tests were not conclusive," Doctor Fleischer said.

Mike noticed his mother's hands shaking slightly as she picked at her spaghetti.

Silvestro Nardo smiled and looked at the doctor. "The signs are all favorable. And here we are, friends—all together in Rome and preparing for a spectacular event."

Nardo accepted more wine from the Italian woman. "This is a time for celebration," he said, forcing his eyes around the table and holding his glass high. "We will soon be travelling west in accordance with the laws of karma." He paused and they raised their glasses.

Herr Ackermann looked at Mike, motioning for him to raise his glass of water.

"To Rudolf Steiner!" Nardo said.

"Rudolf Steiner!" they said in unison.

Mike had heard the name *Rudolf Steiner* a few times and mumbled it now under his breath. He sipped his water and watched Herr Ackermann empty his glass of wine. These people are really weird, he thought.

"Has the transportation been confirmed?" Ackermann asked.

Karl sipped wine and managed a weak smile. "A generous colleague has secured the use of a corporate jet for this momentous occasion. The flight to Winnipeg will not take long."

Doctor Fleischer glared at Karl. A giant finger pointed to the basement.

"The laws of karma must be respected," Karl said.

Doctor Fleischer slapped the table, scowling at Karl, "We must finish it now! If we wait—"

"No!" Karl was furious. "Ahriman's demise is not now! You, of all people, Doctor Fleischer, must understand the laws of karma!"

"You are afraid," Doctor Fleischer said. "The deception of Ahriman has weakened you, Karl."

Karl shook his head. "The Group of Forty-Eight decided this long ago. Ahriman's blood cannot—will not—be on our hands. It is not our destiny and he still has a role to play."

Doctor Fleischer tore his eyes from Karl and stared into the fireplace. "You had better be correct," he said.

Mike felt relieved to be out of Doctor Fleischer's piercing gaze but he was terrified at what he had just heard. He was also curious about the person in the basement. Is he sick? What is all this about Ahriman and blood?

Mike was also curious about something else he had just learned. After a few minutes of silence, he decided to inquire. "Did you say Winnipeg?"

Miss Meyer spoke. Incredibly, she answered his question. "Yes, Mik-eye-ell. We'll be going to Winnipeg soon. It's a lovely city in Canada."

"I know where it is," Mike said.

"How do you know?" Doctor Fleischer glared again.

Mike was about to say that he saw a television program once, explaining that Winnipeg is where Winnie-the-Pooh got his name. Mike had enjoyed reading those wonderful books with his mother when he was younger, until Miss Meyer told all the parents to keep such things away from the children. They were not part of the Waldorf program.

After the TV show, Mike had looked at a map and discovered that Winnipeg was the capital city of the province of Manitoba in Canada and happened to be right in the middle of North America. He thought about sharing this information now but decided against it. Doctor Fleischer gave him the creeps and Miss Meyer would be angry. He was not supposed to watch television.

Miss Meyer spoke on his behalf. "Mik-eye-ell knows many things, Doctor Fleischer. It is his destiny."

5

En Route to Rome, Italy

The flight to Rome would take less than ninety minutes. Although Mark had no reason not to trust Major Kappel, Chief Bischel's words echoed in his mind. Be careful.

Their Learjet carried only a few Vatican officials in transit and the four of them. The other seats were empty. The major sat alone, speaking Italian on a cell phone. Chris tapped away at his laptop and Mark sat across from Kate, a little table separating their padded swivel seats.

Mark looked at Kate and then followed her gaze out the window to the snow-capped Alps and red-tiled houses and barns that lay scattered across endless green valleys below. The scenery was beautiful, dream-like. Mark was hoping she would open up and talk, but it seemed Kate was trying to avoid the inevitable conversation.

"You want to talk about the guy you beat up at the hotel?" Mark asked.

She continued to stare out the window. "Do I want to? No."

"I might be more sympathetic than you think."

Kate turned to face him. "I'm not looking for sympathy." Her eyes were suddenly like cold, steel marbles.

"What I'm trying to say is —"

"Forget it. Just forget it." She spun her head quickly and looked outside.

Mark tried to think of the right thing to say. He felt tired and the strain of the past few days was catching up with him. Maybe try a stronger approach. "Listen, Kate, you cannot just beat the crap out of someone and tell me to forget it. You're damn lucky our major friend has some clout in Switzerland or you could be facing charges."

Mark realized his concern was much more than that of a cop trying to solve a mystery. For the first time since his divorce, he had that inexplicable feeling in his gut, the one that defied logic but could not be ignored. Before he could convince himself of the need to choose his next words strategically, they escaped in a rush of unfettered emotion.

He watched her reflection in the window as her blue eyes wandered over the mountains. "Plus," he said, "I guess it might be obvious that I care about you." He immediately regretted this statement and prepared himself for the dismissive reaction. He was shocked when he saw a smile spread across Kate's face. Her eyes became soft again, turning his mind to mush. He searched for the next line. "I mean—"

"Thanks." She tilted her head slightly and studied him for a moment. "There's some baggage I carry that I'd rather not get into now. I hope you're OK with that because you really have no choice." She met his eyes with hers and for a brief moment no words were needed for each of them to know that something special had just occurred.

Mark broke the silence. "Fine, but—"

"But nothing." Kate leaned closer and smiled. "We need to find Mike and the rest can wait. Agreed?"

He felt very much like kissing her but he knew the timing was not right. He returned her smile. "And I need to solve some murders. Agreed."

Rome was very much as Mark had imagined it to be: a beautiful, bustling city of locals and tourists and bad drivers. Narrow cobblestone streets wove endlessly through open-air markets and residential neighborhoods. A black Cadillac took them from the modern Leonardo da Vinci airport to a modest house in the city. The Vatican owned many such places and this particular house, Mark learned, had been used for decades by the Swiss Guard as they saw fit. It came complete with bulletproof windows and a tall, thin Italian woman who loved to cook.

Major Kappel sat back in a well-used armchair and sipped espresso from a tiny white cup. They had just eaten an excellent home-cooked Ragù alla Bolognese and were enjoying Tiramisu and coffee in the living room.

The major had been trying to convince his guests to relax for the time being as there was nothing they could do until the telephone rang with the latest information. Major Kappel told them his colleagues in Rome had tailed Mike and his captors from the airport the previous day and he was now awaiting orders.

Mark wiped his sticky fingers with a serviette and licked cocoa powder from his lips. "If your people followed them from the airport, why don't we go and deal with them now?"

The major placed his coffee cup on a side table. He frowned. "Because there are certain protocols we must respect." He looked at each of his guests in turn. "And apparently, there were complications yesterday."

Mark leaned forward. "Complications?"

Major Kappel sighed. "We're not sure of their exact location here in Rome."

"But your pals followed them!" Kate yelled.

"I don't quite understand what happened," the major said. "It's unfortunate."

Mark glanced at Kate. Her hands were clenched fists. His own frustration was boiling over. "Listen Major, I appreciate your cooperation and hospitality but I'm sure you can understand our predicament."

"Of course I understand," the major said. "When the telephone rings, I will know what to do."

"*We* will know what to do," Mark said.

The major smiled. "I'm sure you understand that you have no jurisdiction here, detective. If I were to officially involve you in this investigation, my career would be over." He looked at Chris. "As you know, the boy is with his mother and no law has been broken. But I also want you to know I will do everything in my power to retrieve your son."

Chris sighed and sat back in his chair. He seemed resigned to the fact that Major Kappel was in charge here. "Thank you," he said. "I believe you are doing all you can do."

I want to believe you, Mark thought.

As if on cue, the telephone rang. Major Kappel walked calmly to the kitchen and picked it up. He listened carefully, muttered a few words, listened again and hung up.

"I must go now and yes, you may come but you cannot be too close." His face was solemn, deep in thought.

"Where are they?" Mark stood and stared at the major.

"I'll soon find out," the major said. "And it seems we just might get lucky today. Perhaps we can solve a few crimes at the same time." He glanced at Kate and then at Chris. "Your son must be very important. He has a new bodyguard."

Chris and Kate exchanged a troubled glance. Chris spoke. "What does that mean?"

Mark ventured a guess. He could feel his pulse exploding at the thought. "Doctor Fleischer is here in Rome?"

"Apparently so," the major said.

Kate stood. "Fucking hell. We've got to go—now!"

"I doubt they will harm the boy," the major said. "Fleischer is here to protect him."

Chris stood. "We don't know that. All we really know is that Fleischer is a killer."

"Please," the major said, "one step at a time. We need to be very careful as we proceed. I have wanted Doctor Fleischer for years. I'll have more information after I meet my contact in the piazza in an hour."

Chris stood. "The piazza? What is that? Where is it?"

The thin cook carried dessert dishes from the living room. Major Kappel thanked her in Italian and then looked at Chris. "I'm sorry. Piazza San Pietro. St. Peter's Square in Vatican City. It's a good meeting place. Open and very public. We often meet at the obelisk in the square." He grabbed his jacket from the hallway. "It's not far from here. Come, we can walk."

6

Rome, Italy

Mark, Kate and Chris followed Major Kappel out onto Via della Conciliazione. As they walked, the major seemed pleased to talk about his home turf:

"Vatican City is a tiny landlocked sovereign city-state and at just over one hundred and ten acres in size, with a population of only 900, it is considered the smallest country in the world. This is an ecclesiastical state and is ruled by the Pope."

"And they don't mind all the tourists?" asked Chris.

"Not at all. While the area is often full of gawking tourists with cameras, it is a deeply religious place and the blessed home of the Catholic Church. Tourism fuels the economy and who knows—some of the visitors might be converted to the one true religion." The major smiled.

"It's beautiful," Chris said. "I'd love to return one day as a regular tourist—spend some time and see the sights."

It was hard to miss the dome of St. Peter's Basilica, so prominent in the distance. It was late afternoon and the September air was cool, almost damp. Although summer was the busy tourist season, there were still handfuls of visitors strolling the ancient cobblestone streets, filing in and out of tacky souvenir shops and little cafés while heading to and from the Vatican.

As they approached St. Peter's square, Major Kappel stopped. He was in his element here in Rome and Mark sensed the man was excited. Or nervous.

"You must not be seen with me from this point on," the major said. "By all means, walk around the piazza. When I am finished I will find you."

"How long will you be?" asked Mark.

"Not long," the major said. "I will probably be given an address and a plan of how I am to proceed." He glanced at his watch. "I must go now."

Major Kappel wished them a pleasant visit and turned to walk away. "Make your way to the entrance of the Basilica. I'll find you there in an hour."

As the sun broke through layers of dark clouds, Mark watched the major stroll into the piazza. St. Peter's Square stretched out from a tall, red granite obelisk to reach colossal Tuscan colonnades, four columns deep at the perimeter of the plaza.

Mark, Kate, and Chris tried to appear inconspicuous as they mingled with dozens of tourists and locals out to enjoy a September stroll in this historic place of worship. They walked in silence, listening to the murmur of different languages being spoken around them.

Chris finally broke their silence. "Does anyone else have stomach cramps?"

"It's just nerves. Take a deep breath and hold it," his sister said. "Then let it out slowly. Calms the stomach muscles."

"Sound advice," Mark said. He looked at Kate and smiled.

"Hey, check those guys out." Kate motioned with her head towards three Pontifical Swiss Guards, dressed in ceremonial blue and yellow-striped uniforms and red-plumed helmets.

"They are well-trained soldiers," Mark said. "The uniform has history."

"I would have a hard time wearing that outfit to work," Kate replied. "Different strokes for different folks."

They stopped walking and Mark gazed towards the obelisk. "I'm trying to find Major Kappel in the crowd."

"I feel like I'm in a spy movie," Kate said. She followed Mark's eyes with hers.

"What if someone knows we're here?" Chris asked. "I mean, they knew we followed them to the airport in Switzerland."

"I doubt they could know we're here," Mark said.

They were standing about sixty yards from the obelisk, peering into the dozens of visitors wandering the square.

Kate stepped up onto the stone steps of an old building. "I can see him now. He's standing alone beside the obelisk."

"Don't make it obvious that you're watching him," her brother said.

Mark stood beside her. "It's all right. There are so many people here, nobody could possibly notice us." Mark was also curious to see who the major was meeting. "I see him now." He looked at his watch. It was exactly 4:00 p.m.

"Well, what do you know?" Kate said. "His contact is a woman."

Mark saw her, too. A tall, beautiful woman stood beside Major Kappel near the obelisk. She wore a long red-flannel coat, burgundy scarf and sunglasses. Her hair was shoulder-length, wavy and copper red. Mark saw her speak with the major for a few minutes and then, surprisingly, the woman leaned in and kissed him. Kissing in public is not unusual in Italy but this kiss was full of passion and not simply a polite peck between friends. They continued to embrace and then sat together on the stone steps leading up to the obelisk.

"How romantic," Kate said. "I guess he knows his contact intimately."

Mark felt his pulse increase. "Something is wrong." He continued to stare.

The woman slowly stood, looked from side to side, and then quickly walked away from the obelisk. She did not look back. Major Kappel sat alone on the steps, head down.

Mark sprinted, oblivious to the angry cries of those he pushed aside. Kate and Chris followed. As Mark arrived at the centre of St. Peter's Square, a few curious people were already looking at the major. His head leaned forward as he sat alone on the steps. A woman screamed. Blood was leaking from a massive gash under the major's rib cage.

Mark pushed a hand over the messy wound and yelled for someone to call an ambulance. He put his other hand to the major's neck, feeling for signs of life. There were none. The detective yelled again for an ambulance but he knew there was no point. Major Kappel was dead.

7

Rome, Italy

Mike lay alone in the dark and wondered aloud: "Why are we going to Winnipeg?" He was unable to fall asleep that night. The weather had gone from fair to bad. Rain pelted the house and gusts of wind rattled the windows. He had not spoken with his mother much lately. She seemed distant, dreamy or afraid, and it bothered him very much. He had spent the afternoon by himself in the living room with thick paper and watercolor paints. Miss Meyer had told him to complete seven wet-on-wet paintings before nightfall. Boring.

He had never been fond of Miss Meyer, even back in Oregon. He was beginning to seriously dislike her now. He did not like any of the men—especially the scary Doctor Fleischer. He wanted to go home.

After a light dinner, he was back in his tiny room, and trying to fall asleep. The thick duvet kept him warm as thoughts of home swirled in his tired mind. After closing his eyes tight a few times and trying to drift off to sleep, he heard a noise coming from the basement. He opened his eyes wide in the dark and strained his ears while leaning on one elbow. There it was again—like a weak groaning sound.

Maybe it's just the wind outside . . .

He heard it again—someone upstairs snoring maybe? No, it was definitely coming from the basement. Mike spun out of bed and opened the door to his little room. He stood as still as a statue and he heard the soft groaning sound again.

It must be the person in the basement. Does he need help? Should I wake someone up?

Mike crept barefoot through the dark kitchen to the door leading downstairs. He heard the muffled noise again and although he could hear his own heart beating, he slowly opened the door and peered into the blackness below.

He felt a cold draft from the basement cut through his pajamas and for a moment he considered running back to bed and burying himself in the warmth and safety of the thick duvet. But he could not leave. His dad had always told him to do what is right and *when in doubt, just take a few seconds until the answer becomes clear*. Mike did not trust any of the adults in the house. If he were to wake his mother, Miss Meyer would interfere and maybe things would be worse for the person in the basement.

Mike needed to know who and why this person was there, groaning in the cold, dark basement. As his eyes became accustomed to the dark, he noticed a plate of leftover garlic bread on the kitchen counter. It was covered with cellophane wrap. Maybe the person down there is hungry? No harm in offering some food. He grabbed the plate and slowly began to tiptoe down the old wooden stairs. He felt for a light switch, found nothing, and continued to descend into the darkness.

As he reached the cold cement floor he could see dark shadows in the basement. It smelled musty. A street lamp shone through a small dirty window high on one wall, casting enough light for Mike to see something he would never forget for as long as he lived. He felt very frightened.

On an old wooden bench near the middle of the room, was a man. He was tied down with leather straps. He wore ripped pants and he had no shirt and no socks or shoes. The man appeared weak and lay perfectly still. Mike wondered if he was even alive.

Again, Mike resisted the urge to run back to his room. Instead, he slowly made his way closer, as if somehow drawn to this poor fellow, as if he needed to know if the man was alive or . . .

The man groaned, turned his head and their eyes met.

Mike's heart jumped to his throat. He tried to speak but his voice was stuck. He tried again. "Are you OK?"

Incredibly—unbelievably—the man smiled. His voice was barely a whisper but there was no mistaking what he said: "I'll be fine. You must be Mike."

Mike stepped back from the bench. "How do you know my name?"

Paul stared at Mike. So this was their reincarnated Initiate, their modern-day Krishnamurti. Paul studied Mike closely and imagined his predecessor, the young Krishnamurti from a century ago. The Indian boy had been taken from his village by his mentor, the flamboyant Theosophist, Charles Leadbeater. Although today's Theosophists didn't like to speak about such things, there was no arguing Leadbeater's reputation as a pederast. Paul cringed at the thought.

"Has anyone hurt you?" Paul asked.

"No."

Paul looked over Mike's shoulder. "You should not be down here. It's not safe. The others are upstairs asleep?"

Mike nodded and held out the plate. "Are you hungry?"

Paul grabbed a piece of garlic bread and stuffed it into his mouth. When did he last eat? He took another piece and coughed quietly as he ate. He was very hungry. He wolfed down the remaining bread and licked his lips. "You need to go back upstairs, Mike."

"Why are you down here? How do you know my name?"

"There is no time to explain," he said. "But you cannot be found down here—please go back to bed." Paul had no idea what they would do if they discovered this special boy with *Ahriman*—secretly speaking together in the middle of the night.

"Some of these people are dangerous," Paul said. "They cannot be trusted. Pretend you were never here."

Mike's eyes were sad, lonely. "I don't like them," he said.

Paul needed to ask the question again. "You sure they haven't hurt you?"

"No, but they're strange—especially that doctor. He's really creepy."

"Is your mother with them?"

"Yes." Mike sighed. "But I think there's something wrong with her. She's not the same as she was back home."

Paul shifted his weight on the bench. His body ached and his head was still throbbing. He could only imagine what Mike must have gone through, being whisked away from his home and now staying with Doctor Fleischer and his ilk. He tried to smile as he told Mike that everything would be all right.

"My name is Paul."

Surprisingly, Mike's eyes lit up. "I can undo those straps if you like."

That idea had not occurred to Paul. The thought of being able to move his body was very appealing . . . but what if someone heard them? He looked at the window—too high and too small for an escape. If the straps were off, perhaps he could creep upstairs and sneak away from the house.

"The straps are buckled from underneath," Paul said. "But hurry."

Mike slid under the bench and struggled with buckles. "I think I can do this," he grunted.

"Keep your voice down." Paul's own voice was coarse and dry. When he felt a strap loosen he immediately bent his right leg. It felt good to be free but the leg cramped, sending a sharp pain shooting through its nerves. A moment later the other leg was freed and then the strap across his chest also went limp.

Mike reappeared, smiling. "That's gotta feel better."

Paul slowly stretched both legs and began to lift his body from the bench when he heard something that forced him to lie back down quickly. His heart exploded in his chest. He stared at Mike. Someone was coming down the stairs.

8

Rome, Italy

They would have less than a few seconds. Paul whispered to Mike: "Get down. Now!"

Mike slipped back under the bench. He saw huge, brown leather shoes coming slowly down the stairs. He knew who owned those shoes. Fear forced rapid breaths in and out of his open mouth. He felt dizzy. Then he thought of Paul. The awful doctor would notice the loose straps!

From his hiding spot under the bench, Mike gently pulled on the straps, trying to make them tight again, hoping Doctor Fleischer would not suspect anything.

The giant descended the stairs and walked slowly to the bench. His massive feet were inches from Mike's face.

"Hello Doctor Fleischer," Paul said.

"I heard a noise," said the raspy voice.

"I was coughing," Paul said.

"I will not hesitate to end your pathetic life."

Mike continued to slowly tug on the straps as he listened to the conversation. They were almost tight again and the giant had not noticed—so far.

"Your demise is imminent," the deep voice said.

Mike saw the big brown shoes turn. Then, one of the huge feet accidently connected with something and sent it skidding across the floor and crashing against a cement wall.

The plate. It was the empty garlic bread plate. Mike watched in horror from his cold hiding place under the bench. Doctor Fleischer walked towards the wall and bent down to see what had broken. Maybe there was not enough light in the basement. Hopefully, he would not notice the plate. Mike saw the big knees slowly fold, followed by massive hands reaching to the floor. For an instant, the doctor's head was in full view, both dark eyes scanning the floor. With luck, the man would not notice him lying there under the bench. Mike could see the bushy gray eyebrows above those horrible eyes. He tried to stay perfectly still but felt himself trembling with fear. He closed his eyes and hoped Doctor Fleischer would not turn his head. *Just go away! Go away! Go away . . .*

The big man slowly stood and walked back to the bench. Mike knew he held bits of the broken plate.

The deep, horrible voice: "Where did this come from?"

"Someone brought me garlic bread," Paul answered.

"Who is this someone?"

"A woman," Paul lied. "I don't know her name."

Mike was scared, but felt relieved that Paul had not told the truth.

The doctor's breathing was heavy. "You were not to have food!"

"You do not want me dead, Herr Doctor."

Fleischer whispered loudly: "You think you are clever, but Ahriman cannot deceive me!" He slowly made his way up the stairs.

The basement remained silent for a minute before Mike decided to slide out from under the bench. He took a deep breath and stood beside Paul. "See, I told you that guy is creepy."

Paul tried to smile, tried to appear calm in front of the boy, but his hands were shaking and any pretense of confidence was not sincere.

"Yes, Mike, that guy is not nice." Paul removed the straps and stretched again. Each muscle felt immediate relief as he massaged his legs and arms, feeling blood begin to flow, feeling warmth return to his limbs.

"You should get out of here," Mike said. "I bet you could escape."

Paul could not find a reason to disagree with the boy. "We'll both get out of here." He sat up on the bench and found his shirt and shoes.

He thought about trying to find a phone and calling the police but he quickly imagined a disastrous result: A mother and son are visiting friends in Rome and who is this unkempt American intruder with his wild story? Besides, what if Nardo had connections with the local authorities? No, Paul had a better plan and was about to let Mike know about it when the boy spoke:

"I think I should stay," Mike said.

Paul felt surprised. "It would be safer for you to leave. I'll help you get home, Mike. You need to trust me. We'll head straight to the American embassy."

Mike stood by the bench, looked briefly at the floor and then at Paul. "It's just that my mom is still here and I need to stay with her."

Paul considered taking Serena with them, but he suspected the woman would not want to leave. He and Mike would have to sneak out quietly.

"Mike, these people are dangerous. We'll send help back here for your mother."

"I can't leave my mom," Mike said. "I just can't do it."

Paul started to protest but then he put himself in Mike's position. Should the boy leave his mother and run into the dark streets of Rome with a stranger? Not likely. Perhaps he could slip out now, contact the embassy and send help for Mike and Serena before anyone in the house wakes up. Of course, if the mother refused to leave . . .

Paul changed tactics, sat on the bench and spoke quietly and quickly with Mike. He asked him a few questions and was delighted with the articulate answers. He was surprised to learn that the Anthroposophists were planning a trip to Winnipeg, Canada.

"Why Winnipeg?" Paul whispered.

Mike shrugged his shoulders. "I have no idea."

"When are they planning on leaving?"

"Don't know that, either. Sorry."

"That's all right."

He suggested Mike get back to bed and he told him a few times never to mention that he had helped Paul to escape.

"I might just be a kid," Mike whispered, "but I'm not stupid. Of course I won't say anything."

Paul liked the boy. He suddenly realized he had never spent any time whatsoever with anyone younger than eighteen years of age. Speaking with young Mike felt surprisingly refreshing.

"Of course you're not stupid," Paul said. He smiled. "In fact, you're very bright and certainly brave. I owe you."

Paul stepped onto the cement floor and almost collapsed. His legs were weak and painful and his feet were still aching after being hammered by the deranged Doctor Fleischer. He winced as they both crept slowly up the stairs and past the living room where Miss Meyer and Mike's mother lay fast asleep on the pullout bed.

When they were in the hallway near the front door, Paul put both hands on Mike's shoulders and whispered. "You be careful, Mike. Someone will come to check on you soon. Let's hope your mother will want to take you home. Then everything will be fine."

He spotted a large, gray overcoat hanging on a peg and within seconds he put it over his ripped shirt and quietly slipped down the stone steps and into the rainy night.

Mike gently closed the door and made his way back to his tiny room where he quickly buried himself in the thick duvet. He felt afraid—he imagined Doctor Fleischer's horrible voice—until he heard another voice that pushed the fear away. He could hear his dad, telling him he was brave. He smiled but a tear rolled down his cheek. What would happen tomorrow?

Day Eight

1

Rome, Italy

It was dark outside. The early morning air was cool and fresh and the rain did not bother Paul in the least. After being drugged and dragged around Europe, the sense of freedom surpassed anything the elements could throw at him now.

He had been to Rome before but he had no idea where he was in the city or how to find the American embassy. He thought of trying to contact an old colleague, a university professor he'd known for years. The man lived somewhere in Rome but Paul had no cell phone or directory. He had wanted to contact his Italian colleague from the safe house back in Ithaca, but his abduction ended that plan.

The pain in both legs was intense and he tried not to stumble as he limped along a dark sidewalk beside rows of neat, small houses. With no cash or credit cards, a cab was out of the question—not that he had seen any cars at all since leaving the house thirty minutes ago. Not surprisingly, the streets of this Rome suburb were empty at 4:00 a.m. on a weekday.

Paul was thinking of approaching a house and begging a ride to the embassy when another solution presented itself. A sleek, black police car rolled up beside him. Two cops were inside. A window slid down and the beam from a flashlight forced Paul's eyes shut.

"Chi siete?" The cop kept the light on Paul's face.

Paul covered his eyes with a hand and approached the car. "I'm American and I need—"

"No, no, no. You stop." The cop with the light got out and stood over Paul. The man was big. "You Americano?"

"Si, si." Paul's Italian was far from perfect—especially under the circumstances. He searched his exhausted mind for the best way to ask for help in Italian. Suddenly, the cop with the light leaned closer and sniffed at Paul.

"You drunk, Mr. Americano?" He looked back at his colleague in the car and laughed. "You walking ees no good. You drinking too much vino Italiano, yes?" He laughed again. "Maybe you take narcotic?"

"No, no," Paul said. "Please, I need to get to the American embassy. Per favore. Molto importante."

The cop aimed the light at Paul's ripped pants and then at the overcoat. Clearly, it was much too big for his small frame. "Where you get coat, Mr. Americano?" He pulled on the sleeves. "You steal in Roma?" He grabbed Paul's arm and marched him to the car.

"No!" Paul felt his stomach turn. "No—please! American embassy, per favore!"

The two cops ignored his protest. They searched him and took him to the local police lockup where nobody spoke English. Although Paul's Italian was decent, his request to speak with someone at the American embassy was not a priority.

Paul felt tired, frustrated and helpless. He shared a small cell with an elderly man in a cheap suit. The man smelled like booze and spent the better part of two hours vomiting into the only piece of furniture in the cell—an old, dirty toilet.

Paul sat on the concrete floor, thinking about Mike and silently cursing his incompetent captors. A few hours passed until the night shift ended and a well-dressed man arrived, expressing interest in his new American guest.

Capitano Bianchi's English was decent and before long he seemed convinced that Paul was neither drunk nor drugged. He came close to apologizing for the confusion and offered to drive Paul to the American embassy—later. He handed Paul a small cup of espresso.

Paul felt immensely relieved, but now was not the time to sit and drink coffee. "I don't want to be a problem," he said, "but can we please go now?"

"I have telephoned," the captain said. "Your embassy opens at eight-thirty. Nobody is answering the telephone until that time—only answering service now." He sipped espresso from the tiny white cup. "But I drive you now—no problem."

Twenty minutes later Paul and Capitano Bianchi stood outside the black cast-iron fence surrounding the American embassy in central Rome. The rain had stopped, but heavy gray clouds still covered the sky.

Paul found it odd that dozens of people were gathered outside the gate. Something was wrong. Sirens pierced the early morning and cops were everywhere. More police cars arrived and then the gates swung wide for two large black panel vans. A television truck pulled up beside them.

The captain spoke in short bursts into his cell phone. Paul could understand bits of the one-sided conversation. The word "bomba" needed no translation. Capitano Bianchi stared at Paul. "This is not your lucky day."

Paul avoided the captain's eyes. A bomb threat meant nobody goes in or out of the embassy. Paul felt sick.

They knew where I would go. The threat was most likely false, a simple ploy to keep Paul out of the embassy for the day.

He borrowed the captain's cell phone and managed to find his old colleague's number at the university in Rome. There would be no point in explaining things to Capitano Bianchi. Paul needed more help than the local authorities would be able to offer. He thanked the captain, assured him he would be fine, and walked away from the embassy.

One hour later, Paul sat at a round table in a small café near the Pontifical Gregorian University. The man sitting across from him was an Italian Professor of Religious Studies from the Gregorian. Professor Costa had stayed with Paul in Ithaca a few times and although they had divergent views in most areas of theology, they had always enjoyed each other's company.

The elderly Italian was delighted but surprised to see him. "If I did not know you to be a man of reason, I would suspect you to have a mental disorder." Only a slight accent accompanied the words. "Really, Paul—you have no passport, no money and have just come from a police cell? You look like a disheveled beggar, my friend."

Paul was reluctant to share his entire ordeal. He trusted Alfonsa Costa, but he did not want to inadvertently put the man's life in danger. He forced a tired smile. "It has been a very difficult few days."

A waitress brought coffee. She greeted and smiled at the Italian professor and then frowned at Paul, shaking her head as she walked away.

Signor Costa sipped his coffee and leaned across the table. "Paul, I am very glad to see you—after what happened to you in New York. You simply vanished, no?"

Paul felt stunned. "How did you know about that?"

"I received a very strange phone call two days ago from an American detective. He was reluctant to share information but I know you were missing. The detective sounded very concerned for your safety."

Paul's confusion intensified. "How did he get your name and number? Why would he phone you?"

"So, you know this Detective Julian?"

Paul nodded. "I met him a few times."

"It seems he found my contact information in some of your papers . . ."

At the safe house, thought Paul. *Of course.*

". . . and he wondered if I knew anything about your whereabouts. He also asked if I knew about an Anthroposophical doctor from Germany. Imagine that. Why would he ask me such a strange question? The detective said your disappearance might involve this doctor."

Paul frowned. "It's a long story."

"Well," Signor Costa continued, "as it happens, a dear old friend of mine here in Rome has also been speaking with me recently about possible problems with a group of Anthroposophists. Quite a coincidence, no?"

Paul felt exhausted but his mind churned with curiosity. "Your old friend is with the police?"

"The Swiss Guard. His concerns regard the Goetheanum and the Vatican and . . . missing money. Lots of money. There is an ongoing investigation. Very hush hush, you understand."

"Interesting," Paul said. He was both shocked and fascinated at this news. Was there a connection between Doctor Fleischer's gang and this investigation?

"This American detective was on his way to Switzerland when he phoned me. He's probably there now. I gave him my friend's phone number."

Paul tried to digest this latest revelation. *Detective Mark Julian is in Europe? Why?*

Alfonso Costa stared at Paul. "It seems you have more than a few secrets. Perhaps you will share them?"

"I'd like to, Alfonso. Later. Please trust my reasons for needing some time."

"Then I can only assume you have come to ask for my help." He smiled. "And of course, a good Catholic will always help his fellow man—even if that fellow is a grubby, homeless atheist."

Paul returned the smile. "I'm afraid I don't have the energy or time to discuss the merits of atheism and the pitfalls of Catholicism."

Signor Costa rubbed his hands together and stared at Paul. "How can I help?"

Paul needed to choose his words wisely. "What do you know about Propaganda Due?"

Costa frowned. "The old Italian Masonic Lodge? Corrupt, fascist, and not considered legitimate by any Masonic organization. They had friends in government and, unfortunately, they also had friends in the Vatican. They've been out of business for years—ever since the bombing and scandals in the 1970s and 80s."

"Have you heard of a man named Silvestro Nardo?"

"Nardo was one of the more . . . passionate members of P2. He spent time in prison. Why do you ask?"

Paul finished his coffee. "Sorry Alfonso, I can't get into details now."

"If you're in trouble, we should contact the police."

Paul stared across the table. "It's complicated." He was about to ask the Italian professor for a substantial favor when the man seemed to read his mind.

"You'd like me to speak with my contact at the Swiss Guard? Is that it?"

"Do you trust him—completely?"

Alfonso Costa tapped his coffee cup with thin fingers. "Yes." He looked over his shoulder and lowered his voice. "This all sounds so—how do you say—cloak and dagger, but the timing of your visit is interesting. If there is corruption in the Vatican and if Nardo happens to be involved again, it is a very dangerous affair. I've heard he is terribly unbalanced."

Paul knew all about the unbalanced Silvestro Nardo. He also knew this discussion was not easy for his friend. Costa was not only a respected university professor; he was a deeply religious man. Another Vatican scandal would be painful.

Costa produced a cell phone. "I will try my old friend in the Guard. He is a Lieutenant Colonel now—a man of some influence. What shall I say?"

Paul cleared his throat. "Ask him to send someone to check on a house here in Rome. An American boy and his mother are there and they might be in danger." Paul had memorized the address and jotted it down quickly.

The old Italian tapped numbers into his cell phone and spoke Italian for less than a minute. He referred to the address, then waited a few seconds, spoke again and finished with "grazie" and a smile.

He looked at Paul. "Two officers will visit the house. They will meet us in an hour with news of their investigation." He tossed some Euros on the table. "Come—my car is just around the corner."

Paul frowned. He did not want to involve his old friend in this sordid business, but he felt grateful for the support. They walked along an old cobblestone street towards the university parking lot and found Alfonso Costa's car just as the sun poked through thick gray clouds.

"A good omen," the Italian said, pointing at the sun.

Paul glanced up but could only see the sun in an Anthroposophic light:

Christ is the Being who comes from the Sun and who sends Michael with his hosts on ahead . . .

"A good omen," he said quietly. "Let's hope."

2

Rome, Italy

At first, Mike thought it was part of a bad dream. Someone had screamed and then he heard a crash, as if something big and fragile had been hurled at a wall. He opened his eyes and lay perfectly still in the little cot in the room by the kitchen. It must have been very early—it was still dark outside. He heard someone yelling in German. Karl. Then he heard the unmistakable deep, raspy voice of Doctor Fleischer—also yelling. Another loud crash and more shouting and Mike covered his ears with the pillow.

He remembered what had happened—the nice man named Paul in the basement and the secret escape into the night. Mike pulled the pillow tighter around his ears, wondering if the angry men knew of his role in Paul's daring escape. He let the pillow fall slightly and could hear muffled voices outside his room. At least the yelling had stopped. A light rain tapped at his bedroom window. The voices disappeared and he breathed a sigh of relief. Then, his bedroom door opened.

"Mik-eye-ell?" It was Miss Meyer.

He ignored the voice and pretended to sleep.

"Mik-eye-ell?" She was in the room now, standing beside his cot.

He kept his eyes closed, hoping she would leave. Fingers brushed through his hair and he jumped, instinctively opening his eyes. Miss Meyer was smiling above him. She wore a peach-colored nightgown and her hair was a mess. The smile was insincere. *Always.*

"Oh, hello," Mike said, as if just waking up.

"Did you sleep well?"

"Yes."

"Mik-eye-ell, I need to ask you something and you must be honest with me, all right?"

"OK." Mike felt scared because he knew what was coming. He could imagine Doctor Fleischer standing in the doorway, listening to his response.

"Were you in your room all night long?" Her voice was smooth but he knew she was nervous.

"Yes." Mike had never lied to an adult before. He lied once to a boy at school but never to his parents or teacher.

"Are you sure?"

"I brushed my teeth and then I went to bed."

"And you did not leave your room after you went to bed?"

"No."

Miss Meyer turned and looked back towards the kitchen, and then she stared again at Mike. She was not smiling. "Did you hear anything last night, Mik-eye-ell?"

"No." For some reason it felt good to lie to Miss Meyer. He had never liked the woman. "Did you hear something, Miss Meyer?"

A few minutes later Mike sat at the dining room table, eating a boiled egg and buttered toast. Nobody spoke during breakfast and Doctor Fleischer watched him closely. They ate quickly and quietly. It was obvious to Mike that the adults were pressed for time.

At one point, Doctor Fleischer started to ask Mike a question but Karl interrupted with a wave of his hand and one word: "Please!"

When breakfast was finished, the adults packed the bags in a hurry and two big black sedans arrived to pick them up.

"Are we going to Winnipeg now?" Mike asked his mother.

She barely met his eyes with hers as she helped him with his coat. "We're very lucky," she said, trying to smile. "Such a wonderful holiday." Her voice was quiet, monotone.

"So we're going to Canada?" Mike asked.

Miss Meyer pulled a wheeled suitcase to the open front door. "Winnipeg is a special city," she said.

"Yes," Mike said. He was feeling a little more confident today. "It's the capital city of the province of Manitoba. And if you look at a map, it is directly at the centre of North America."

Doctor Fleischer stared at Mike. Then Herr Ackermann squeezed his pudgy body and a suitcase through the narrow hallway. He looked approvingly at Mike and glanced at Doctor Fleischer. "He is such a bright boy." He aimed a nervous smile at Mike. "So insightful and intelligent. This is no accident, Doctor Fleischer." He hurried out to the waiting car.

A short while later, the chubby housekeeper had finished cleaning up and sat outside on the front steps with coffee and a pastry. The day was gray and cool, but the sun was trying to poke through thick clouds. She had not liked her recent visitors and although she was sworn to secrecy, the old woman was glad to see this bunch finally leave her house. She was certainly not pleased to have hosted such a strange guest in her basement. She was glad he had somehow managed to escape. Indeed, if Silvestro Nardo had not been her husband, she never would have let any of them stay in her house.

A shiny black Mazda Miata pulled up in front of the house and two well-dressed young men approached the front steps. Signora Nardo smiled but felt nervous. The men introduced themselves as being with the Swiss Guard and within less than a minute the old woman had convinced them she had no idea what they were talking about. She laughed at the suggestion of an American boy staying in her house and no—she had not seen her husband, Signor Nardo, for a very long time. She had no idea where he was.

3

Rome, Italy

Paul Sung and Alfonso Costa were parked a block away from the house, watching the conversation unfold on the front steps. Then they drove to a parking lot around the corner and waited for the Miata. Paul was anxious for news of Mike and his captors.

When the little sports car arrived and introductions were made, Paul could not help but marvel at the Swiss Guard officers. Both men spoke perfect English with virtually no accent.

"The old woman is lying," one of the young men said. "We know she is Silvestro Nardo's wife and I suspect her husband was recently at the house."

Paul felt tired but adrenalin kept his mind alert. "There was no sign of a boy?" he asked.

"None," said the officer. "But . . ." He looked at his partner, as if wanting permission to continue. His partner nodded. "Do you know about Silvestro Nardo?"

Alfonso Costa answered. "I know of him. Why do you ask?"

"Because," said the young man, "one of our experienced officers was involved in a recent investigation of Signor Nardo and another man—a German named Fleischer."

Paul was tempted to tell them that he knew all about those two men . . . *and Doctor Fleischer is known as the surgical killer. The psychopath kills people and nails their larynxes to ceilings. Fleischer and Nardo had me strapped to a bench in that house last night.*

But Paul said nothing about his ordeal because he did not know whom to trust. "Has your officer learned of their whereabouts?" he asked.

"We have no idea," the officer said. "Our man was knifed to death in Vatican City yesterday."

"This is terrible," Alfonso Costa said. He looked at Paul. "Is there a connection with your . . . situation?"

The two young officers stared at him.

Paul knew he looked like a mess. "I'm sorry. I've had a difficult few days and really need to rest."

The two men frowned, and then hopped into their Miata and drove away.

Alfonso Costa was quiet as he and Paul sat in his car. Finally, Costa turned the key, pulled the car onto the street, and spoke. "I called in a favor for you, Paul. You could have at least filled them in on what you know. What on earth do you have to do with an officer being killed?"

"I don't know," Paul said sharply. Fatigue was ripping at his mind and he was worried about Mike. "I'm sorry. There is a lot going on and I'm exhausted."

"The Pontifical Swiss Guard can be trusted."

"Maybe, but I don't want to put lives in danger."

"They can handle danger. They are well trained."

"I was thinking more about you."

Signor Costa's cell phone rang; he listened as he drove and then flipped it closed and looked at Paul. "Strange."

"What's that?"

"That was my friend, the Lieutenant Colonel with the Swiss Guard. He wants me to bring you to see him immediately. You have no objections?"

"Why me?" Paul felt his heart skip a beat.

"It's about the officer who was murdered yesterday. The Lieutenant Colonel wants to talk to you about three Americans who were near the man when he died. Two men and a woman. The Vatican Gendarmes handed them over to the Swiss Guard. They are in custody now."

Paul was stunned. Americans. Two men and a woman? He thought of a sentence he repeated often with first year students back at Cornell: *In the esoteric mind, coincidence is another name for karma.*

4

Rome, Italy

Karl stared out through the frosted windows of the black Mercedes sedan. Doctor Fleischer sat beside him in the back seat. The ancient white-haired driver had insisted on loading their bags into the car and spoke only to tell them how proud he was to be chosen to drive them to the airport. The man had been part of Italy's most infamous Masonic Lodge in "the good old days." Silvestro Nardo sat beside the driver. Mike, his mother, Miss Meyer and Herr Ackermann followed in another car.

"I must make a phone call," Karl announced. He pulled out a cell phone.

The giant doctor did not move a muscle. He continued to gaze out the window, ignoring Karl Heisman completely.

Karl sighed. "We need to inform Dave Dunigan of this unfortunate occurrence."

Fleischer spun quickly and aimed his dark eyes at Karl. His deep voice was angry and contemptuous. "We should have put that pathetic creature out of his misery last night when we had the chance."

"You know we could not have done that," Karl said. "It was agreed upon long ago. That is not Ahriman's destiny."

Nardo turned to face the men in the back seat. His eyes fixed on Karl. "You know I questioned that agreement at the first meeting." He sucked air quickly through gritted teeth. "One bullet between the eyes and Ahriman would have been out of our way for good last night."

"It is not that simple," Karl said calmly. "There is a necessary balance in these matters. Surely, I should not have to inform such knowledgeable men. We all have our roles to play." He met Nardo's eyes and then looked at Fleischer. "Need I remind you both that I was not in charge of security in Rome? This most unfortunate escape was not my doing."

Fleischer leaned into Karl and turned a meaty hand into a fist. "Don't you dare try to blame—"

"Gentlemen, please," Nardo said from the front seat. "This is no time to stray off course."

"Our distinguished colleague is correct," Karl said. He punched numbers into his cell phone as the doctor returned his gaze outside. The black sedan slowly made its way to the Leonardo da Vinci airport on the outskirts of Rome.

Over seven thousand kilometers away, Dave Dunigan was meeting with a local politician named Harvey Gossman, in a large office at the Manitoba Legislative Building. Gossman was short and fat and quick with a handshake and a smile. It was well past midnight and except for a small custodial and security staff, the building was empty. Dunigan had met with Gossman a few times already and was not convinced of his ability to complete his end of the bargain.

"I trust you understand our need for privacy," Dave Dunigan said.

"You have mentioned it several times now," Harvey Gossman replied. "I trust you understand my position, as well. What you ask of me is very difficult. You require access for a large group of visitors to a private office in a government building. I have worked hard on this requirement of yours and—"

"And you will be well paid for your efforts. I understand you have already spent the deposit on certain . . . habits. Is this not correct?" Dunigan knew of Gossman's addiction to gambling and expensive hookers.

The pot-bellied politician shifted in his chair and looked at the thick carpet under his desk. "I have had to rearrange shifts for more than a few people, including external and internal security, in order to secure the room you need. People are asking questions and my reputation is on the line here."

Dave Dunigan looked at his watch. "I need to know that access is a certainty. Do you need more money? Is that the problem?"

"I might need to compensate one more guard and then there is my secretary . . ."

"I see. If I double the payment, can you guarantee us access? I'll pay you one hundred thousand dollars—US."

Harvey Gossman's eyes widened, and then moved from the carpet to Dunigan and back to the carpet. "I think that will suffice," he said. "It's not about me, you understand. It's just that I need to make sure everything will be in order for—"

"Fine," Dave Dunigan interrupted. He tossed a wrapped stack of bills onto the desk. "Half now and the rest when we leave the office. We'll be here in a couple of days." His cell phone beeped.

Dunigan left the room and answered his phone in the hallway. The call was from Karl Heisman. Although he was upset to learn of Paul Sung's escape, Dunigan tried to sound calm and professional. "This is not good news," he said. "But karma is our friend."

"I like your attitude." Karl's voice was calm, always confident. "Ahriman's destiny is entwined with ours. Not everyone understands the depths of this karmic connection."

Dunigan changed the topic. "The reactor in China is ours, Karl. The world will never be the same. All is set for the day after tomorrow."

"The balance will be restored," Karl said. There was a moment of silence. "But I'd like to move our plans ahead by one day."

"What? Why move it up a day?" Dave Dunigan felt his throat constrict; he hoped his voice did not sound weak. Weakness was unacceptable.

"The traitors in Dornach are meeting soon." Karl sighed. "Betrayal will not be tolerated and karma dictates that we act in a timely fashion. Is everything ready there?"

"Yes, but—"

"Can you arrange to move it up one day?"

"Perhaps, but—"

"Do it."

"It will take more money."

"Use the same account. Money is no problem."

Dave Dunigan was silent for a moment. "I'll see what I can do." He heard Karl sigh into the phone.

"The traitors from the Vorstand will learn about karma. And it must happen soon."

Dunigan quickly put his mind to work on this new problem. "I'll see to it, Karl. The boy is fine?"

"Yes," Karl said. "The glorious time is at hand."

Dave Dunigan stepped back into the office. Harvey Gossman quickly covered the cash with file folders on his desk. He had been counting the money. Surprise and guilt were written all over his chubby face.

"There is a change," Dave Dunigan said. "We will need access one day earlier than previously planned."

"What? That means tomorrow! I cannot—"

"Two hundred thousand dollars," Dave Dunigan said slowly. He pulled another stack of bills from his jacket and tossed it onto the desk. "You will have the balance by this time tomorrow. He leaned across the desk. "Do we have an agreement?"

Perspiration covered Harvey Gossman's forehead. He held the new stack of bills for a moment and then shoveled all the money into a drawer and took a nervous breath. "Yes."

5

Rome, Italy

The top floor of the building was the inconspicuous and temporary office of the Pontifical Swiss Guard. The space was sparsely decorated and under-furnished, with only a desk, a few wooden chairs, a crucifix and a photo of the Pope on one wall. An armed guard watched them from just inside the door. Mark, Kate and Chris stood silently by the window, staring out over the piazza.

The view was fantastic. Under different circumstances, Mark would have taken the time to enjoy the sweeping panorama of St. Peter's Square and the magnificent old basilica below. In the middle of the square, he could see the ancient obelisk jutting into the clear blue morning sky.

Major Kappel had died beside that famous landmark, but Mark could still hear his voice, as if he were standing beside him now, proudly talking about Rome:

"It's a sundial, did you know? The obelisk was made in Egypt and brought by barge to Rome in A.D. 37. Then, in 1586 it was moved to the piazza—the square—and it is now one of the last of the great obelisks still standing in the world."

After the major's murder the previous day, Mark, Kate and Chris had quickly made their way through the crowd and back to the house, where they gathered their things and checked into a small hotel. They did not know whom to trust. After discussing various options for most of the night, they had been considering Mark's idea of phoning Paul Sung's Rome contact again when there was a knock at the door.

Four armed officers explained what would happen. "You will please come with us." It was not a question.

The officers were polite but professional. During the short trip to the Pontifical Swiss Guard office, the Americans learned there were at least two organizations involved in security at the Vatican. Apparently, there had been plenty of debate in recent years between the Pontifical Swiss Guard and the Vatican Gendarmerie, about the extent of each group's role in guarding the Pope at home and abroad. Both organizations had been jockeying for a better position for quite some time. In this case, it was decided the Swiss Guard would deal with the murder of Major Kappel. They would interview the Americans seen leaving the crime scene.

Mark turned from the window to see a very old bald man walk into the office. The man introduced himself as Lieutenant Colonel Christen.

Mark knew the name and the voice. "I spoke with you on the phone the other day," he said. "I got your number from a friend of yours here in Rome, remember?"

"Yes, that's right." The old man sat at his desk and studied the Americans. "And here we are. One might say this is quite a coincidence." He raised a bushy white eyebrow, as if waiting for a response.

The decorated military uniform he wore was impressive, but could not add youth to the old man inside; Mark guessed him to be in his eighties, maybe older. He walked with a limp and rows of wrinkles covered a weathered face. Remarkably, his blue eyes were crystal clear.

Kate and Chris had agreed to let Mark do the talking—Chris readily and Kate reluctantly.

The old man took a deep breath and sighed. "Major Kappel was an excellent officer. He stood for justice and he had integrity." The voice was surprisingly strong and although they knew he must be Swiss—a prerequisite for anyone joining the Swiss Guard—the accent was distinctively British.

Mark studied the man before responding. "I know I speak for all of us, Lieutenant Colonel Christen, when I say how sorry I am that Major Kappel is dead. While we only knew him briefly, there is no doubt he was a man of integrity. If there is anything we can do to help with the—"

"You left him dead at the crime scene," the old man interrupted. He stared at Mark. His eyes then flitted to Kate and over to Chris.

For a moment, Mark was lost for words. "It's complicated," he finally said. "I would like to explain."

Lieutenant Colonel Christen stared blankly at the top of his oak desk and sighed before speaking. "I knew his father. He had no other family—his mother died when he was a child. No siblings, nothing. His father died in the line of duty, as well."

"He mentioned that to us," Mark said.

The old officer eyed them suspiciously. "He told you about his father? He must have trusted you."

"As we trusted him." Mark reached under his coat and pulled Major Kappel's handgun from the belt below the small of his back, and slowly slid it across the desk to Lieutenant Colonel Christen. "This belonged to his father."

The old man picked up the SIG P210 and caressed its wooden handle. There was a hint of softness in his eyes as he held the gun. "Yes, this is what we carried in the old days." He looked at Mark. "And you managed to take this from Major Kappel by the obelisk?"

"It was purely instinctive," Mark said. "I knew he had been murdered and I had no weapon. I needed to assume the assailant was nearby and about to kill again."

The old man rolled the weapon in his hands. For a few seconds, the expression on his face told Mark he was a million miles away, perhaps reliving a moment from his past.

There was a knock on the door. A guard entered, followed by an elderly man in a suit and a disheveled-looking smaller man Mark doubted he would ever see again.

"Paul!" Mark stood and stared in disbelief. Kate and Chris jumped from their chairs, eyes wide. Mark was on him in a second, pumping his hand and grinning.

"Coincidence is just another name for karma, right?" Kate said.

"In the esoteric mind," Paul replied. He winked and stood by the window, admiring the view for a moment before sitting.

"It really is good to see you, Paul," Mark said. "His eyes scanned the professor. "But you look awful."

"And I feel worse," Paul said. "We have some catching up to do. Time is of the essence."

More chairs arrived and introductions were made. As soon as Paul mentioned seeing Mike only hours ago, Chris demanded more information.

"Is he OK? Did they hurt him? Where are they now?"

Paul rubbed a hand across his face. "Short answers: Yes. No. Probably flying over the Atlantic Ocean. I have some questions for you, as well."

Lieutenant Colonel Christen reminded them all that this was officially a murder investigation and his inquiries would need to take precedence. They agreed. He asked questions of Paul and the others, taking notes as they spoke, seeking more clarification from time to time.

By noon, it was evident that although Lieutenant Colonel Christen was old, his mind was sharp. After hours of what could only be considered a mild interrogation, Mark felt as if he had just spent time with a wise old grandfather, rather than an officer of a foreign police force. They told him—and each other—everything.

Kate glared at Paul. "They think you're Ahriman? The evil spirit? Un-fucking-believable!"

"I've been called worse," Paul said. He managed a smile.

Lieutenant Colonel Christen frowned at Kate's expletive but was interested in the Anthroposophists' ideas about Michael and their belief that the boy was a recent incarnation of Christ or Steiner.

"When his Holiness Pope Benedict re-introduced the Prayer to Saint Michael the Archangel, many people at the Vatican were upset," the old man said.

"And of course," Paul added, "the Papal edict would be deeply disturbing to at least some members of the Anthroposophical Society."

"Indeed," the old man said. "We have suspected for some time that a fringe group of Anthroposophists has been meeting secretly to discuss such things. And we also think that group has a contact in the Vatican Bank. That was part of Major Kappel's investigation."

"So why did nobody stop them?" Kate asked.

Lieutenant Colonel Christen smiled a grandfatherly smile. "There is no law against people meeting to discuss things. Until a law is broken—"

"Law?" Kate raised both hands in frustration. "They killed people in New York and took my nephew from Oregon! And what about Major Kappel?" She pointed out the window to the obelisk in St. Peter's Square. "He was murdered right there, yesterday!"

The old man sighed. "Yes. It is tragic and we will continue with our investigation." He looked around the room at each of his guests. "Please don't think we treat these matters lightly. For your information, the woman who killed Major Kappel was found dead in a hotel room less than thirty minutes after the major's murder. An apparent suicide." He paused. "These are difficult times."

Kate sat back in her chair and folded her arms.

"I understand your frustration," the old man said. "I too am deeply disturbed—loss of life is upsetting and sad but quick reactions without appropriate deliberation can only exacerbate difficult situations." His eyes narrowed. "Politics and religion are rarely the best of friends."

A plate of sandwiches and bottles of juice arrived. Mark felt comfortable sharing food and information with this man; although his position was second in command of the Pontifical Swiss Guard, he did not play power games with the Americans. There was a real sense of trust between them. When the Lieutenant Colonel excused himself to confer with someone on the telephone, Mark was not surprised to see a smile finally appear on the old man's face after he hung up.

"Gentlemen," he said, "and lady." He glanced at Kate. "You will be taken to the airport." He looked at Paul. "As you unfortunately arrived in our country under less than normal circumstances, you will depart with no need for documentation. All we ask is that you all leave Italy now." He paused. "As you have expressed an interest in traveling to Canada, I have arranged for a flight to Winnipeg that leaves in a few hours. Unless you would care to stay and be interrogated again by my colleagues from another police agency?"

Mark stood. "This has been informative and helpful," he said.

Chris agreed. "And thank you for understanding our situation."

Lieutenant Colonel Christen stood and extended a hand to Chris. "I cannot profess to truly understand everything about your dilemma. I trust you know there are limits to the help I am able to offer. Unfortunately, at this point in time, other security agencies do not seem interested. Interpol, for example, has been dismissing our concerns outright for quite some time. They think this is simply a religious struggle between different denominations and such potentially volatile issues are not something they want to be involved with. It distresses me a great deal to learn that, once again, this Doctor Fleischer has found a way to escape. My own situation becomes . . . difficult and political from time to time." He frowned. "I will pray for your son and your wife." He sighed and looked at each of them in turn. "I wish you all God's speed."

They shook hands and as Mark was leaving the office, the old man called him back. "Detective," he said, "I think you should have this." He gave him Major Kappel's gun—the old wooden-handled SIG P210. "Based on what I have learned today, I am sure this is what Major Kappel and his father would have wanted."

Mark was speechless. "But I cannot—"

"I see the pain of injustice in your eyes. You will take it," the old man said.

"Thank you."

As if reading his mind, the Lieutenant Colonel added: "I will make some phone calls so you should have no problems boarding the plane with the weapon or carrying it into Canada." He smiled. "Go now and look after your friends. I do not need to tell you about the power and cunning of your adversary."

"I understand."

"My prayers are with you, detective."

Mark caught up with the others and a few minutes later a black stretch limousine carried them and their luggage to the Leonardo da Vinci airport.

Paul thanked Alfonso Costa for his help and told him to visit New York again when "life gets back to normal." As they boarded the elegant Gulfstream V—courtesy of the Vatican—Paul tried to remember just what "normal" might actually feel like.

But first things first: What would they find in Winnipeg?

6

En Route to Canada

Aboard the lavish jet, Paul was relieved to discover a tiny shower in the little washroom. Hot water and plenty of soap were just what he needed. He was delighted when the flight attendant offered him a set of clean clothes. Surprisingly, everything fit—shirt, tie, dress pants and even a fine Italian tweed jacket. He would need to thank Lieutenant Colonel Christen for this thoughtful gesture.

They were the only passengers on the aircraft. Feeling somewhat rejuvenated after the shower, he accepted a glass of Italian red wine from the flight attendant as he watched the Italian coastline fade into the distance below. The alcohol helped to calm his nerves, but Paul's mind was still busy trying to unravel the incredible events of the past few days. He made his way to where Chris was sitting with his sister beside a small table near the front of the aircraft.

Mark sat alone farther down the aisle, in a swivel armchair. He picked up one of the jet's satellite phones from a desk at his side. It was mid-afternoon in New York but he quickly discovered that his boss was not at the office; apparently he was taking a few days off.

Although he had the phone number, Mark had never called his boss at home and the thought of disturbing him did not sit well. It was a known fact that the chief did not take his work home and was known to ignore his cell phone after hours. Mark needed to tell the chief that Major Kappel was dead. He needed to explain that the Swiss Guard had helped him and that the major had been a trustworthy ally. He felt compelled to let his boss know that the Vatican was paying for his flight to Canada and that Paul Sung was alive. They were on the trail of the surgical killer. He relaxed into the soft chair and dialed Chief Bischel at home in Ithaca.

"Hello?" The voice was female and sounded tired. The phone connection was not good.

"Mrs. Bischel?"

"Yes."

"I'm sorry to disturb you but I need to speak with Chief Bischel. It is urgent."

"He's not here." Pause. "I was taking a nap." The woman was clearly annoyed.

The line was full of crackle and static but Paul continued. "I apologize. Do you know where I can reach him?"

"He's at the Christian Community retreat with the others."

Mark felt confused. "Sorry—what's that?"

"He's at the Christian Community retreat with Bruce Bander, Ron Martins and someone from New Jersey, I think. And the Canadians."

Bander and Martins were the Homeland Security agents Mark had met in the chief's office. He needed answers. "Where is this retreat?" he asked. The phone line crackled badly.

"Canada—Winnipeg," she said, sounding annoyed. "You should know that." More static in the phone and then: "I can't hear you very well. This line is terrible, Karl. Are you calling from an airplane again?"

Mark slammed down the phone and felt his heart pounding hard.

Karl?

He replayed the conversation in his mind and then dissected the last few days—especially his conversations with Chief Bischel. His boss had been very curious about Major Kappel. Mark had fed him a steady diet of important information and now Major Kappel was dead. Mark's mind spun back to the safe house. Two officers murdered and Paul's abduction. It had seemed like an ambush. Mark would never forget that day. What had the receptionist said when he arrived to meet with the chief?

The chief just arrived with the two agents . . .

Where had they been? At the safe house . . . killing cops? Impossible. Or was it? Mark felt sick as more questions swirled in his mind.

He sat, feeling stunned, gazing out the aircraft window at the vast, dark Atlantic Ocean below. Chief Bischel had only been stationed at Ithaca for the past year. Could he be involved in the murders and this secret criminal organization? It was hard to believe. Guilt and fear and a thousand unanswered questions raced through Mark's mind. The flight attendant passed, looked at him and asked if he was feeling all right.

"I'm fine," he lied. "Do you happen to have a cold Becks?"

She smiled and returned with the familiar green bottle, ice cold. He waved away the frosted glass and made his way up to where Chris, Kate and Paul were huddled over the laptop, and looking at a map of Winnipeg.

Mark's face was white. He stared at Paul. "What do you know about something called the Christian Community?"

Paul frowned. "Why do you ask?"

Kate looked curiously at Mark. "You OK?"

Mark ignored both questions. The unmistakable tone of panic grew in his voice. He could feel it. "What is the Christian Community?"

"It's a movement for religious renewal," Paul said. "It's based largely on Steiner's Anthroposophy. A German theologian initiated the Christian Community with Steiner's help in 1922."

"What's wrong, Mark?" Chris asked.

Mark sat beside them and ran fingers through his hair. He emptied half his beer in one long gulp. "I just learned that my boss—the Chief of Police in Ithaca, New York—is involved in the Christian Community."

"So what," Kate said. "It doesn't mean anything."

"Yes, it means something," Mark said. "I've been giving my boss updates of all our activity, including everything about Major Kappel—and now I learn that Chief Bischel has left New York with two men who I thought were with Homeland Security and guess where they are right now?"

"His surname is Bischel?" Paul asked.

"Yes," Mark said. "So?"

"He could be related to the late Franz Bischel, a leading figure in the Christian Community in Germany. Bischel was also a prominent Nazi with a keen interest in racial ethnography. He died recently."

Mark finished his beer and spoke slowly, as if in a dream. "Someone once told me the chief's father used to be some bigwig religious figure in Germany. I just assumed it was old-fashioned Christianity."

"You gotta be kidding," Kate said. "One of the cult terrorists just happens to be the top cop in the same university town as the anthro expert, Professor Paul Sung? Nobody thinks that is one hell of a coinci—?" She caught herself and looked at Paul.

"Exactly," Paul said, "it is no coincidence." He looked at Mark. "How long has Bischel been the Chief of Police in Ithaca?"

"Under a year," Mark said.

Paul rubbed a hand across his brow. "Interesting. These people certainly have connections. My guess is he was stationed there to monitor my department at Cornell. They were probably concerned about Greg Matheson's research and Bob Richardson and, of course, me. My book—especially the unpublished chapter—must have caused them grave concern, and their paranoia meant killing those who might have even a hint of knowledge of their plans." He looked up. "Paranoia is not uncommon in esoteric groups."

"No offense, Professor," Kate said, "but why did they not simply kill you, too?"

"Remember, they think I am the incarnation of Ahriman. Killing me would be bad karma. It has to do with balance. In other words, I suspect that Karl is slightly afraid of me—for now."

"God damn," Mark said. "It makes sense. I had no leads on the murders—none. Bischel must have made sure of that. He was helping Fleischer all along—covering tracks, blocking the investigation."

"You're probably right," Paul said. "But I am sure that has nothing to do with the Christian Community, per se. They would certainly not condone his actions."

"I should have seen it," Mark said. He shook his head and gazed through the tiny window into the clear blue sky. "I should have doubted those two characters in the chief's office. Something was wrong. Damn. I should have known."

Kate was beside him. She put a hand on his shoulder and gently rubbed. "You couldn't have known," she said softly. She massaged his shoulders with both hands.

Mark tensed and then relaxed as Kate gently squeezed his shoulders. Her hands felt good, strong and confident. Still, the murder scenes played loops in his mind. Rooms full of misery.

Kate's hands continued to work their magic and slowly . . . slowly, the gruesome images faded. He suddenly wanted very much to push this entire ordeal away. Just forget it. Take some time off from the job. Stop obsessing, if that's what he was doing again. He wanted to turn around and hold Kate in his arms, but instead he took a deep breath, looked over his shoulder and managed a smile.

She returned his smile and the sight of her perfect lips, high cheeks and soft blue eyes tore the last of the murder scenes from his mind. She finally pulled her eyes away and a brief moment of awkward silence was replaced by the professor's voice:

"The Christian Community includes priests and plenty of religious services, but the religion itself is far from anything resembling conventional Christianity. There is a very distinct occult foundation."

Kate sat beside Mark. "You said your boss and his pals went somewhere?" she asked. "Where are they?"

"Let me guess," said Paul. "They are in Winnipeg."

7

En Route to Canada

The sleek aircraft sliced through the sky as its passengers gathered together and tried to make sense of all that had transpired in the past few days. Kate and Chris were adamant that their priority should be to find Mike. Mark, however, was also concerned with the bigger picture. Paul was fascinated and disturbed at the unfolding events. He wanted desperately to find pieces to fit the puzzle.

"They are planning an act of terror," Mark said. "We need to stop them."

Paul looked at the laptop Chris had opened beside him. A map of Winnipeg appeared and information about the city popped up as Paul sent the cursor crawling across the screen. Winnipeg is the seventh largest Canadian city with a diversified economy and a large indigenous population. Hot summers and very cold winters, a decent number of museums and galleries. Nothing of note to attract a group of fanatical Anthroposophists. Winnipeg did not even have a Waldorf school.

Paul's mind spun back to the occult world of Nardo and Fleischer. What was so important in Winnipeg? He sipped from his second glass of wine and spoke his mind: "They have probably spent years planning. Unfortunately, I am sure Lieutenant Colonel Christen is correct. We cannot expect any of the authorities to help—unless we have evidence."

"When you were with Karl's gang," Mark said to Paul, "did they say anything about Winnipeg?"

Paul rubbed a hand across the back of his neck. "I've been trying to replay that ordeal in my mind. To be honest, I spent most of the time simply hoping they would not kill me. I don't remember all the details."

"What about when Mike came downstairs to help with your escape?" Kate asked. "Did he say anything to you about what they might be planning?"

"He knew they were going to Winnipeg," Paul said. He stared through the window at the clear blue sky. "He also told me there were forty-eight people involved in Karl's gang. Actually, I think Silvestro Nardo also spoke to me of a Group of Forty-Eight—as if he believed he and Doctor Fleischer were destined to be part of that group. Fleischer said something about it being part of the true leadership of the Goetheanum." Paul stared outside again and then tapped some keys on the laptop. He searched various online sources for a few minutes until a smile slowly appeared on his face. He had found a website to answer at least one question.

"Well, now," he said. "Steiner often spoke in riddles." He stared at the screen. "In the last public lecture before his death, he spoke about a group of four times twelve human beings from the leadership of the Goetheanum and how this group is needed for the Michael Stream to flourish in the future."

Chris was the first to respond. "Four times twelve human beings—forty-eight people. And what about that other lecture Major Kappel found—the really weird one about atomic energy?" He looked at Paul. "It was from your notes."

"I know the one," Paul said. His mind was busy. He turned to Chris. "You said you met a Canadian at the Goetheanum."

Chris nodded. "He was such a strange guy. Racist and weird."

"What did he say?" asked Paul. "Exactly—what did he say?"

"I'll never forget," Kate said. "He told us the *chinks* would never know what hit them. Then he realized we were not in his group. He appeared shocked at his mistake and he bolted."

Chris tapped Kate's shoulder. "He also said he was from . . . I can't remember, but it was not Winnipeg."

"It was some letters, like an acronym or something," Kate said. "A.C.E.L maybe?"

Paul tapped those letters followed by the word *Canada* into the search engine and they all leaned over to see the results. "Nothing jumps out," he said. He tried a different combination of the same letters with similar results. He tried a third combination: AECL.

Kate was first to react. "What the hell?" The first result from the search engine showed *Atomic Energy of Canada Limited*.

8

En Route to Canada

Paul pulled the laptop closer. "Did the fellow tell you his name?"

Chris looked at his sister. "It was Dave something, wasn't it, Kate?"

"I think so. Dave Davidson . . . Duncan . . . something like that."

"Let's try to find out," Paul said, typing and clicking with new energy.

Websites and online newspaper articles appeared and disappeared in a flash as Paul's fingers danced over the keyboard. He grunted and sighed as he worked. The others sat back and looked at each other with raised eyebrows, unable to concentrate on the screen because of Paul's speed.

"I saw the professor do this in New York," Mark said. "Too fast to follow."

Paul glanced up but continued to work. "Sorry," he said. "Give me a few minutes."

The flight attendant arrived with plates of poached halibut, rice and salad. As Kate, Chris and Mark began on their meals, Paul continued to work. For the moment, his hunger could wait. Finally, he pushed the laptop aside and dug into his fish. "Could the name be Dave Dunigan?"

"That's it," Kate said. "Dave Dunigan."

"There's the connection," Paul said. "Amazing. And terrifying. He's a scientist with Atomic Energy of Canada and works mainly out of Chalk River, Ontario. Lots of seniority. He's been back and forth to China many times in the past few years because of some AECL reactor sales there. And . . . it seems that many years ago he addressed a few Michaelmas conferences in Dornach."

"So what does it mean?" Mark asked.

"It means," Paul said, "that at least one First Class member of the School of Spiritual Science might be in a position to cause a major nuclear event." He looked at the screen. "Until recently, AECL was a crown corporation—a corporation established by the federal government in Canada. After lots of lobbying, the Canadian government recently privatized some of the company—the part that deals with selling and servicing reactors."

"So, you're saying a private company would sabotage its own reactors?" Mark asked.

"If some people on the inside of that company believe it is their karmic duty to do so—yes. That is what I am suggesting." Paul continued tapping at the laptop. "Dave Dunigan is on the Board of AECL and is also directly involved in the technical part of the operation. He makes decisions and is able to see them through. He has it covered from both ends."

Mark frowned. "But China must have its own safety inspectors. They would not simply purchase and allow a faulty reactor into their country."

"You might be surprised," Paul said. "It seems the new heavy water CANDU reactors are very advanced pieces of equipment. Dave Dunigan has been training people in China for years and they already have purchase agreements for more reactors. The Chinese would have no reason to suspect him of anything other than helping them to understand and use the technology. He would probably have unlimited access to the reactor."

Paul tapped more keys on the laptop. "This Dave Dunigan's a real genius. Started as a teenage whiz-kid, PhD in nuclear engineering at age twenty-two, another one in nuclear physics and . . . only worked a couple of years in a university and then he went private for a while. Also a telecommunications expert—wireless technology, microwaves. He's been all over the world as a trouble-shooter. Very well connected—and has a brilliant mind."

"Obviously a sick mind," Kate said. "You really think they want to blow up a reactor in China? Could they actually pull it off?"

Paul finished his salad and stretched his legs. He looked and sounded and felt exhausted. "Hard to believe, I know, but it is conceivable—think of what happened to Mike and me and how they feel about Steiner's backward yellow race in China . . . and listen to this." He pushed a few laptop keys and read aloud: "In late November 2008, there was a fifth anniversary ceremony celebrating the completion of the Qinshan Phase III CANDU nuclear power plant located southwest of Shanghai." He paused. "Dave Dunigan has spent lots of time there. It says here he was at the celebration."

Paul looked up from the laptop. "Anyone know the largest city in China?"

Chris answered. "It's got to be Beijing."

"That is what most people think," Paul said. "The largest city in China is Shanghai with a population of more than twenty million." He sighed. "I suspect they will make it look like an accident but that will not help the people in Shanghai."

"Holy shit," Kate said. She pushed herself back in her seat and closed her eyes. "How many people would die?"

"Hard to know," Paul said. "It would depend on the extent of the explosion and subsequent radiation leakage. And wind direction. A major meltdown would be catastrophic."

"How can they believe that killing innocent people will help humanity?" Chris asked.

"You forget," Paul said, "this group does not see what you call innocent people as anything other than skin and bones—especially those people not meant to be important parts of the future race. Karl and his gang are concerned with the life of the soul. Death of the body is not the end of the soul. This has nothing to do with guilt or innocence of individuals. They believe they are doing the souls of their victims a favor by freeing them from those particular bodies."

"They are insane," Kate said. "Fucking crazy."

The flight attendant arrived and asked them to prepare for landing. They buckled up and stared outside as the jet engines slowed on descent. As the jet broke through the clouds, they saw the city stretch across the prairie landscape below.

"What I really do not understand," Paul said to nobody in particular, "is why we are all converging on Winnipeg. If the target is in China, why would they need to be in a relatively small city in Canada?"

Paul pulled his eyes from the window, and was about to close them when something caught his eye. He snatched a brochure from the pouch in the back of the seat in front of him. His eyes grew wide with excitement as he stared at a map of North America.

He tapped Chris's shoulder. "Look!" He pointed to the brochure map. "Look!"

Chris raised an eyebrow. "I'm looking . . . but what am I supposed to see?"

"Winnipeg," Paul said. "It is in the middle of North America."

"Interesting," Chris said. "But what does it have to do with anything?"

"It's important," Paul said. He opened the laptop and pulled up a map of North America; lines of latitude and longitude appeared on the screen. "It's amazing," he continued, "that the city of Winnipeg lies at the very center of

North America. Steiner believed the spiritual future would belong to the West, the white race in the West."

"Probably too much dark skin down in Central and South America," Kate huffed.

"You could be right," Paul said. "Karl and his gang would see it that way. This secret Group of Forty-Eight believes it is destined to give birth to the spiritual future of white humanity. So it needs to happen from Winnipeg."

"Sorry," Chris said. "You lost me there."

Paul could feel his heart pounding hard. "Steiner spoke about the earth as a living being. Just as the impulse to create human life stems from the center of physical Man and Woman—penis, vagina and womb—the esoteric forces needed to create a New Age for humanity must originate from the centre—the womb—of the most western of continents." Paul's eyes were pensive but excited. "This esoteric act of unthinkable terror—and a new beginning for humanity—must be given birth from the center of the White West—the centre of North America."

Kate and Mark listened closely to Paul's explanation. The aircraft engines hummed and changed gears. The runway was fast approaching.

Chris tore his eyes from the window and looked at Paul. "And Winnipeg," he said softly, "lies at the centre of North America."

Paul managed a weak smile. "Exactly. We are all converging on the womb of the West while anticipating the cataclysmic birth of a New Age."

Chris returned his gaze to the city below. "And my wife is using our son as a pawn in this insane plan." He looked at Paul. "Please tell me we'll find Mike down there."

"No guarantees," Paul said. He looked outside as the sun was going down and the aircraft touched the runway. "But I suspect some of our questions will soon be answered."

9

Winnipeg, Manitoba

Mike sat on the bed and stared at the chrome clock on his hotel room wall. He was calculating time differences between Oregon, Dornach and Rome and Winnipeg. How long it would take for jet lag to disappear? Last year he had planned on being a pilot when he grew up but after the past few days, he decided a job with less travel might be better.

He ran to the window and looked out over downtown Winnipeg. The gray prairie sky was quickly turning dark and lights sparkled in the surrounding buildings.

It reminded him a little of Portland—clean, green space here and there and a few tall buildings. Mike used to enjoy visiting his aunt in Portland. He gazed through the window and could see people out walking in the streets below. Some of the old buildings in Switzerland and Italy were interesting but Winnipeg reminded him more of home and home is where he wanted to be.

They had checked into the fancy Five Oaks Hotel earlier that day and now Mike had his own little sleeping area in a suite on the top floor of the building. Herr Ackermann and Doctor Fleischer had the other part of the suite and his mom and Miss Meyer were just down the hall in another room.

For the past few hours people kept arriving, and there was lots of hand shaking and the occasional hug between old friends. Mike's mother told him that lots of important people would be there for a reunion and he might even recognize some of them from that special late-night ceremony back at the Goetheanum. Mike learned that their group had reserved the entire top floor of the hotel.

"So there will be forty-eight people all together, mom?"

"Yes dear, that's right. Plus a few others." She paused. "Like me."

"That must cost a lot of money, huh?"

"It's not important."

"And what are they all doing here in Winnipeg? And why are *we* here, mom?"

"So many questions," she said. She tried to smile but Mike could see that her eyes were not smiling.

He thought of telling his mom about how he had helped that nice man, Paul, escape and how he had almost got caught by that creepy Doctor Fleischer. He thought of telling her that more than anything else in the world, he wished she would leave these people and take him home to Oregon—take him home to dad and maybe he could change schools and never see Miss Meyer again.

And then his teacher came along and told him he was so lucky to be able to visit these wonderful places, and she pointed out the window and said that tomorrow they would all be able to visit "that beautiful old domed building over there."

For dinner that night, they all sat around four large tables in a conference room in the hotel. Trays of food were carried in by men and woman dressed in white clothes. Mike heard people talking about a biodynamic farm and how nutritious and delicious the food was that night.

During dinner it was as if people were trying not to stare at him but it was impossible for Mike not to notice them staring. Some of them smiled when he met their eyes with his, while others simply looked away quickly. They seemed nervous.

Before bed that night, Mike heard Herr Ackermann and Doctor Fleischer talking in the other part of the suite. They were out of sight but loud. Doctor Fleischer was going on and on about Paul's escape in Rome and it sounded like Herr Ackermann was tired of the conversation.

"I don't know about the plate. How many times do I need to tell you?"

"Who took the garlic bread downstairs?" Doctor Fleischer asked. His voice was always loud, deep, and threatening.

Mike wondered why they were speaking English when German was their first language. Did they want him to understand?

"Maybe it was Silvestro's wife," Herr Ackermann said. "Ich habe keine Ahnung—I have no idea."

"She swore it was not her. Somebody took the plate of bread to him and somebody helped him to escape."

Mike heard Herr Ackermann start to speak again as Doctor Fleischer stepped around the corner and stared at him in his bed. Mike pretended to be asleep.

10

Winnipeg, Manitoba

Serena tried to relax and let things unfold naturally, but she was unable to chase away the knots in her stomach. She lay facing Sophia in a large, rounded Jacuzzi tub. Masses of bubbles covered all but their heads; the scent of lavender was everywhere. The Winnipeg Five Oaks Hotel penthouse suites came with decorated skylights over whirlpool tubs.

"The glorious day is about to unfold, Serena," Sophia said, smiling. "It is truly a blessing."

Serena rested her head against the padded edge of the tub and stared through the glass ceiling into the dark night sky. "I don't feel well," she said. "I don't—"

"You're fine," Sophia said. She splashed Serena playfully. "I'm sure you're just excited to be part this event."

"But am I part of this, Sophia? Neither of us is even in the Group of Forty-Eight." She frowned and tears formed in her eyes. Days of mounting frustration needed an outlet. "I've only ever felt like extra baggage on this trip. I have no idea what is really going on. Even when I meditate on one of the mantras, something still doesn't feel right."

"That's enough!" Sophia's smile disappeared. She sat upright in the tub and rubbed soap over her shoulders. "This is our destiny, Serena, and we cannot question such things." The smile returned and she rubbed a foot against Serena's naked thighs underwater. "Are you saying you have not enjoyed spending time with me?"

Serena met her gaze. "Of course I have enjoyed your company. It's just that—"

"Just nothing." Sophia glided her wet body around the rim of the tub until she sat beside Serena under the bubbles. Then she reached out to push a button that sent pulsing underwater jet streams into the bath, soothing and relaxing their naked bodies.

They kissed and Serena felt warm, wet hands on her breasts.

"Just relax," Sophia said.

Serena tried to relax but then pulled away and avoided eye contact. "When did you first take an interest in me?"

"What do you mean, Serena?"

"I mean, I don't really know when this all began." She frowned.

"Don't be silly," Sophia said. "It is never good to question karma." She rubbed a hand over Serena's shoulders. "Tomorrow has been destined for such a long time. We are blessed to be playing a role in—"

"I don't understand!" Serena glared at Sophia.

The smile left Sophia's face again. Her eyes were suddenly cold. "All right," she said. "It is simple, Serena. I saved you. You confided in me that you once had a secret girlfriend in college and you missed the touch of a woman. You were unhappy in your materialist marriage. He did not understand your new spiritual life. You need guidance and I am here for you."

Serena tried to make sense of her tangled thoughts. The jet streams stopped and neither of them spoke. She finally looked up and said, "I . . . don't know if . . ."

"This is our karma," Sophia continued. "This is soul work. Period."

Serena tried to recall when Sophia had changed from being her son's teacher to her lover. She needed answers: "And what about Mike? I mean, if Mike were not with me, would you still—"

"Stop!" Serena grabbed Sophia's wrist and held tight. "Do not question our collective destiny—ever!"

Serena tried to pull her hand away. "You're hurting me, Sophia." She pulled hard and her hand finally came free. "I don't want it to be like this. I just need to know—" She stopped midsentence and suddenly felt very much like crying.

"Shhh . . . let our souls bloom in love for all existence. Tomorrow is a special day." Sophia stroked Serena's forehead and hair. She pointed to an oil painting on the wall of their beautiful hotel. "The penthouse of the Five Oaks Hotel is where we are meant to be, Serena. Relax and enjoy the moment."

Serena leaned back, looked up to the skylight again, and saw a full moon slip out from behind dark clouds. As she fought back tears she felt Sophia's lips on her neck. She thought first of Mike and then, despite her best effort to push him from her mind, she thought of her husband.

11

Winnipeg, Manitoba

Winnipeg International Airport was not busy as Paul, Chris, Kate and Mark walked through the foyer to a waiting stretch limousine. Surprisingly, a driver had greeted them, carried their luggage to the car, and told them his orders were to see they were checked in to one of the city's best hotels. It seemed the archdiocese of Winnipeg had made all the arrangements. Paul imagined Lieutenant Colonel Christen working the phones after they had left Rome.

As the black limousine slid through the quiet streets, Paul tried again to fit pieces of the puzzle together.

Karl is somewhere in Winnipeg? Where, exactly, is he and what will he do next?

"We must contact the authorities," Chris said. He looked at Paul. "If you are right, we must stop this—we need to let someone know about this terrorist group in Winnipeg."

"He's right," Kate said. "Why not go to the police right now? I mean, this is serious—if these people are truly attempting to sabotage a nuclear reactor in China . . ."

"We have no proof," Mark said. "Cops need evidence—trust me."

"Forget about the local police, then. What about calling the FBI?" Chris said. "Or the Canadian version of the FBI?"

"That would be the Royal Canadian Mounted Police—the RCMP," Mark said.

"OK," Chris continued, "we need to let them deal with these whackos. They're used to this type of work."

"Same problem," Mark said. "The FBI or RCMP won't act on wild conspiracy theories. Lieutenant Colonel Christen has more clout than us and remember what he told us about trying to involve Interpol? There was no interest."

"But that was not about nuclear threats," Chris said. "This is different."

"Even if we involve the police," Paul said, "they won't know where to look. We can assume the Group of Forty-Eight is somewhere in Winnipeg, attempting to accomplish their task but we don't know how or when they plan on doing it or where they are now. I agree with Mark. I think we need some evidence. I also think we need some sleep—I know I do."

"What if they act tonight?" Kate asked.

"They've been planning this for years," Mark said. "I doubt they would feel compelled to act as soon as they arrive in Winnipeg. Besides, we are all exhausted. I think we should all try to get some sleep."

The concierge at the hotel insisted that payment had already been made. "I'm sure you will like your rooms. They are one floor down from the penthouse with wonderful views of the city."

They passed potted palms and columns of colored tile in the elegant lobby before riding an elevator up to their rooms on the twenty-first floor of Winnipeg's Five Oaks Hotel.

The Last Day

1

Winnipeg, Manitoba

Mike awoke feeling tired. He had not slept well knowing Doctor Fleischer was in the adjoining room of the suite. He quickly dressed in the white cotton pants and light green tunic Miss Meyer had laid out for him the previous night. He would have preferred jeans and a t-shirt but this was supposed to be a "special day" when they would visit the "special building," and apparently he needed to wear "special clothes." Mike hoped *special day* also meant he would finally be going home.

Karl had waited his entire life for this day and the excitement had kept him awake most of the night. His time was now and he needed to appear calm and confident in front of his colleagues. He was their leader, their guide and spiritual mentor. The future of humanity was on his shoulders.

The spacious conference room served once again as a restaurant for the Group of Forty-Eight. After breakfast, Karl gave a short speech and followed it with a prayer.

"Friends," he began, "as our foolish colleagues engage in trivial meetings at our spiritual headquarters in Switzerland, it is the Group of Forty-Eight—the true leaders of Spiritual Science—who will accomplish great things today."

He pulled out his grandfather's old silver pocket-watch. Then he closed his eyes and thought of his grandfather at Rudolf Steiner's side at lecture after lecture, following the great Initiate throughout Europe, willing to open his heart and soul with trust and respect. His grandfather had passed on important spiritual knowledge to his son, who had in turn blessed Karl with tremendous responsibility.

Karl Heisman would not fail. He straightened his back and spoke with clarity and conviction. "In exactly one hour in Dornach, some of our traitorous colleagues will meet secretly in an attempt to ban the Group of Forty-Eight from the Society. They will attempt to alter the course of destiny by publicly distancing the Society from what they call Rudolf Steiner's controversial beliefs."

Karl tried to control the anger that grew from the pit of his stomach. "The fools will not succeed, my friends. They will not blacken the name of Rudolf Steiner or the Vorstand or the Goetheanum. The true leaders—those of us who are destined to fathom such things—understand that these are matters of the soul. Those souls we free today will, in the future, rejoice in knowing that the true Disciples of Spirit Knowledge have taken the Mik-eye-ell Stream into our collective souls. Join me in contemplating the last words from the last public address of our spiritual leader as spoken at Michaelmas in September of 1924:

> Ye, the disciples of Spirit-Knowledge,
> Take Mik-eye-ell's Wisdom beckoning,
> Take the Word of Love and the Will of Worlds
> Into your souls aspiring, actively!

There was a moment of silence before they all followed Karl down the hall to the bank of elevators. A few minutes later, Mike and forty-seven others filed through the hotel lobby, out the front doors and into a series of black stretch limousines.

2

Winnipeg, Manitoba

Mark, Kate and Chris sat at a booth in a tiny café across the street from the Five Oaks Hotel. They told each other they had slept well but each of them knew that a good sleep was only a memory.

Despite the dire situation, Mark could not help but continue to stare at Kate. She wore a burgundy tracksuit and looked young, fit and very attractive. She was talking about Mike, wondering how he would be holding up and hoping that Paul would be able to shed some light on his whereabouts.

"Where is Paul, anyway?" she asked.

"He wanted to make a phone call before breakfast," Mark said. "He'll be here in a few minutes." Mark had seen Paul briefly in the hotel lobby. The professor had still looked tired.

It was a cool, gray day in Winnipeg, threatening rain. Men in suits and well-dressed women scurried along the city streets, oblivious to the fact that a group of occultists was gathered somewhere in their city that day, hoping to change the course of history.

"Here he comes," Mark said. He watched Paul make his way across the street and join them in the booth.

Chris opened his laptop and slid it across the table. "It's all yours, Professor. This place has Wi-Fi and you're the wizard. Where the hell are they?"

"I phoned a colleague in Switzerland," Paul said. "An Anthroposophist in Dornach. I might have mentioned Benjamin to you earlier—he's a progressive member of the Vorstand. As you know, this is the time of the Michaelmas Conference at the Goetheanum."

"And . . . ?" Kate asked.

"We know there has been a serious division in the Vorstand for a few years now. Obviously, not all First Class Holders are at the Michaelmas Conference in Switzerland now."

"No kidding," Kate said. "The criminally insane ones are somewhere in Winnipeg."

Breakfast arrived and Mark made no excuses for digging into an extra helping of bacon with his fried eggs. "Better than the breakfast snacks in Switzerland," he said. He looked at Kate. She ate fruit salad and toast with honey.

Paul sipped his coffee. "Benjamin told me there will be an extremely important meeting today. It seems that many members of the First Class have been waiting a long time for such a meeting. It's not supposed to be public knowledge but under the circumstances, I was given the information. They will deal with two topics. As you know, there's much more to Anthroposophy than reincarnation and racial hierarchies. Steiner encouraged followers to develop new faculties of spiritual perception. He spoke often of cosmic love and social harmony." He looked at Chris. "This is a common theme in cults and is what attracts most people—like your wife I would think."

"Maybe," Chris said. "But her love and social skills with me went downhill as she became more involved with Anthroposophy. It's as if I don't know her anymore."

"Like other gurus," Paul said, "Steiner was indifferent to personal or erotic love. A cosmic mission can make such things seem unimportant."

"So what else did you learn?" Mark asked.

Paul continued: "A group of progressive Anthroposophists from the Vorstand believe that in order for the Society to move toward social harmony while working with the spirit in today's world, they will need to deal with Steiner's outdated racial theories."

"That would be a welcome development," Chris said.

"And very difficult for Karl and his ilk," Paul added. "Apparently, this is the day the progressive group at the Goetheanum will attempt to draft an open letter to members worldwide distancing the Anthroposophical Society from Steiner's racist teachings. It is an important, yet controversial step in the evolution of Anthroposophy."

"And what's the other topic at this big meeting?" Kate asked.

Paul finished his coffee. "The other item on their agenda today deals with dissention in the Society."

"Which means giving the boot to Karl and his gang?" Mark asked.

"Probably," Paul said, "but until recently, it seems that most members of the Vorstand were not too concerned about Karl's fringe group. They are starting to believe that Karl's gang is dangerous."

"No shit," Kate said. "About bloody time they clued in."

As he accepted more coffee from the waitress, Mark ran the problem through his mind. You want to catch the bad guys—try to think like those bad guys. Mark had used this technique many times throughout his career. *Think like the bad guys.* He looked through the window into the cool Winnipeg morning. Gusts of wind whipped up, forcing people on the street to hold hats and reposition umbrellas. Mark watched fat raindrops hit the window by their booth, carving jagged little water patterns as they slid down the glass. He sat silently lost in thought, gazing outside.

"Hey Mark—anyone home?" Kate tapped his arm.

Mark turned to face his companions. "If Karl's gang knows about this special meeting today, I wouldn't be surprised if they hatched a plan to wipe out their competition back in Switzerland."

"You think they'd kill their colleagues?" Chris asked.

Kate said, "They killed Dott, remember?"

"They have no moral dilemmas in killing people," Mark said. He thought again of the Richardson family and the symbolism that accompanied the trail of death.

Paul blinked and took a deep breath. Something Mark had just said reso- nated with him. He looked at the detective and suddenly felt grateful to know the man—Mark's was a mind he could understand and appreciate. And trust.

"Sometimes," Paul said, "we don't look for the obvious. That which the esoteric mind sees is usually not actually hidden at all." He looked at Mark. "Do you know the word *occult* only really means *hidden knowledge*? Know- ledge is never really hidden—it's just that it is rarely sought."

"You've lost me again," Chris said.

Paul frowned. "We need to know when they are planning their act of terror. The timing of the event will be as symbolic as the place. I was up much of the night at a computer looking for an Anthroposophical event from the past that would symbolically relate to the time of their planned terrorist act. But occultists often believe they are on the cutting edge of tomorrow. Karl's group is all about the future. They don't necessarily need to align their actions with dates from the past—they could use the present to affect the future." He looked at Mark. "I think you are right."

Kate shook her head. "I still don't understand—"

"I do," Mark said. "Karl and his gang are planning to murder their competition—the more progressive leaders back in Switzerland—as they begin their meeting today. At the same time they will somehow launch their terrorist action in China." He paused. "They will not see acts of terror but acts of karma."

"Son of a bitch," Kate said.

Paul asked to borrow Mark's cell phone. "I was told the special meeting of the Vorstand will be at 6:00 p.m. today at the Goetheanum."

He took the phone, punched in a long distance number and waited a few seconds before speaking: "Benjamin, it's Paul Sung again. What we spoke about earlier is very real. I am now convinced that you and your colleagues are in danger."

Paul waited for the response. When it came, the usually good-natured Anthroposophist sounded distraught. "This is hard to believe, Paul," he said. "Do you know what you are saying?"

"Yes, Benjamin, I do know. I told you earlier about the murders and about my own abduction. You can easily discern fact from fiction if you choose to do so."

"I trust you, Paul," Benjamin said. "It's just that—"

"I know," Paul interrupted. "But we must act now." Paul thought for a moment and decided to continue speaking his mind: "Benjamin, your movement has been in denial far too long. You can no longer avoid dealing with the racism that lies at the foundation of your belief system. You must not eschew your responsibility if you are truly wanting social renewal."

Silence.

"Be careful," Paul added. "Time is not on our side, my friend."

Benjamin's voice sounded low and distant. "I will phone you when I have news," he said. "It was not supposed to be like this, Paul." Pause. "I am sorry."

Paul handed the phone back to Mark.

"Does he believe you" Mark asked. "After all, you're Ahriman, remember?"

"No," Paul said, "I am Ahriman only in the demented minds of Karl and his gang."

Chris looked at his watch. "It's 10:15 now and they'll be meeting tonight. That gives us most of the day to find them."

Mark shook his head. "You're forgetting the time difference. 6:00 p.m. in Switzerland is . . . 11:00 a.m. here in Winnipeg. If the theory is correct, we have less than forty-five minutes to find and stop them."

"Shit!" Kate yelled. An old couple in the next booth turned and scowled. "They're gonna blow up a nuke in China and kill their pals in Switzerland in forty-five minutes . . . from here in Winnipeg? How? And why do they need Mike?"

"They've been planning this for years," Paul said. "I don't have all the answers." He looked at the laptop.

Kate pounded a fist on the table. "They could be anywhere in this city."

"Not anywhere," Paul said. He was back to dancing his fingers at light speed over the keyboard. "Let's see if we can find them."

Mark was trained to use logic in solving crimes. What was he missing? What had he learned in the past few days that could help them now? He remembered a conversation he had with Paul a few days earlier. He looked at the professor. "Didn't Steiner say Freemasonry would be significant in the future? What about the Freemason angle from your book? That's what got them paranoid in the first place, remember—the unpublished chapter about Freemasonry and Krishnamurti. They have their new messiah in Mike but where does Freemasonry enter the equation—perhaps a Masonic Lodge?"

"That's right," Chris said. "Their world headquarters in Switzerland is named after Goethe—a Freemason, right? Maybe there is a Masonic Lodge here in Winnipeg."

"Let's find out," Paul said. He punched keywords into Google. A satellite image of Winnipeg appeared on the screen.

"We have forty-three minutes," Kate said.

Mark watched the professor open more windows on the laptop. The man worked at incredible speed.

"There are a couple of small Masonic Lodges in Winnipeg," Paul said. His fingers clicked various thumbnail photos to life. He zoomed in and out of the satellite image of the city, clicking faster and faster, speed-reading captions on each page. Mark, Chris and Kate watched over his shoulder, trying to keep up.

"Can I ask what exactly we are looking for?" Chris asked.

"We know why they chose the centre of North America," Paul said, "but there must be a significant building for them in this city. It will need to be symbolic."

More buildings and churches and landmarks filled the little screen as Paul continued to click from place to place, window to window, studying each image quickly, before moving on to the next one.

Mark tore his eyes from the screen for a moment as strong gusts of wind and sheets of rain rattled the windows. Three people entered the restaurant, seeking shelter from the storm. It was mid-morning but the sky was black.

"The Masonic halls in town are nothing special," Paul said. "Let's have a look at the city from up higher . . ."

Mark stood behind Paul, staring over his shoulder at the satellite image of Winnipeg. He tried to follow, tried to keep up with Paul's incessant tapping on the keys. He was not entirely sure what he was looking for in the maze of buildings and streets that rolled across the laptop screen. Suddenly, something caught Mark's eye—it was small and slightly blurred at first in the low resolution, and it seemed out of place but somehow familiar.

"Stop!" he said. Mark leaned closer to the laptop. "Why is that there?"

Paul frowned as his fingers paused on the keyboard. "What do you see?"

Mark stared at a corner of the screen. "I gotta be honest, Paul," he said. "I was not able to get much from trying to read your book but I did manage to look at all the pictures." He aimed a finger. "I am sure I saw something like this on one of the pages."

"Well now," Paul said. He gazed to where Mark was pointing.

"You see what I see?" Mark asked.

Paul nodded and grinned. "Yes." He tapped a key and zoomed in closer. "Why is a stone sphinx on a big building in Winnipeg?"

Paul used the keyboard to change the camera angle, giving them a better view of the area.

A massive, old domed building filled the screen. It was surrounded by green space and took up a large part of the city center. Paul sat back and shook his head, his eyes still glued to the little screen. He appeared to be in shock.

Mark also stared at the photograph. "What is it?"

Paul spoke slowly: "Ancient Egyptians would place a sphinx at the entrance to temples in order to guard the mysteries inside. Freemason architects have been using the sphinx for years." Paul sat up straight and tapped more keys.

"The building is huge," Mark said. He tried to read some of the articles beside the image as Paul brought up more windows of photos and text.

Paul leaned forward, gawking at an article he had just opened from the latest window. He raised his eyebrows. "Incredible!" He looked at each of them in turn. His eyes were wide—excited. "They were *all* Masons. From 1872 until 1968—*all of them!*"

"Who were all Masons?" Mark asked.

"The premiers of the province of Manitoba," Paul said, beaming. "Almost one hundred years of Freemasonry controlled the center of North America. That is how they built and maintained the building all this time!"

"For Christ's sake," Kate said. "This is all fascinating, but we have forty minutes to find them." She looked at the laptop. "What does this have to do with anything?"

Paul's eyes were still wide. "I am sure this is where we will find the Group of Forty-Eight."

Mark stared at the massive building on the screen. "What is it?" he asked.

"The Manitoba Legislative Building," Paul said. "This is where the provincial government works. And if I'm not mistaken, it could also be the most significant Masonic Lodge in the world. It's incredible!"

Mark felt stunned. It seemed impossible but Paul would certainly not invent such a story. Mark knew the professor was exhausted after what he had gone through during the past few days. And Paul had just told them he had been up late researching via the Internet most of the night. Was his mind simply slipping from fatigue or . . . ?

Mark watched Paul get to his feet and walk to the entrance of the restaurant. He then opened the door and quickly walked out into the storm.

"What the hell?" Kate said.

"I trust him," Mark said. "Let's go."

The waitress eyed them suspiciously but agreed to keep the laptop safe until their return. Mark handed her the breakfast money and a big tip and asked her to call a cab.

"It might take a while," the waitress said. "With the storm, lots of people will be looking for cabs."

They were huddled under a narrow awning in an attempt to avoid the downpour. Mark stared hard at the professor. The wind muffled his voice. "The province of Manitoba has had almost a century of premiers who all happened to be Masons and a huge government building is a secret Masonic

Lodge? And this is where our terrorists are right now? You realize how crazy that sounds, right?"

Paul kept his eyes on the street. "It's true. You think this is all just one big coincidence?"

Kate looked at her watch and then at Paul. "We've only got thirty-five minutes to stop them. Where is the fucking taxi?"

A steady stream of cars drove by, but no cabs. They waited a few more seconds and then, incredibly, Paul began to run.

"I'm not sure about this," Chris said. "I doubt he's in good shape. I hope it's not far."

They quickly caught up with Paul and ran together for a block, and then another, until he stopped, completely out of breath. They were all soaked by sheets of cold, blowing rain.

Mark put a hand on Paul's shoulder. "How far are we from the building?"

"According to the Google map, it's only about seven blocks from here." Paul continued gasping for air.

Curious locals stared from cars at the strange tourists sprinting through a storm, making their way down Portage Avenue on their way to the Manitoba Legislative Building.

Strong wind pushed over a garbage can as a nearby sandwich board crashed to the sidewalk. Rain pounded the street and Kate had to yell in order to be heard. "We're running out of time. Let's go!"

Mark ran beside Paul, glancing at him occasionally and feeling surprised at the older man's stamina. The past few days must have been hell for Paul. Mark could only hope the professor's heart was as strong as his brain.

3

Winnipeg, Manitoba

Mike watched the storm from the comfort of the limousine. When they arrived at their destination and he stepped out of the car, despite the wind and rain, he felt compelled to stand and stare at the building. Although it reminded him of the Goetheanum, it was definitely more impressive. As the Group of Forty-Eight approached the six huge pillars at the front of the building, Mike noticed part of a giant stone sphinx on the corner of the roof.

He had studied ancient Egypt in school and this place reminded him of pictures from those lessons. He looked up and saw stone statues and busts on the outside of the building. He remembered how Miss Meyer had taken extra time explaining the symbology to him.

A security guard approached and was waved away by a short, pudgy man in a suit who had just exited the huge front doors at the top of the steps.

"Would you like a short tour of the interior?" The pudgy man introduced himself as Harvey Gossman. Rain pelted his expensive-looking suit. He seemed nervous. Mike could barely hear him above the noise of the storm.

Herr Ackermann leaned into Mike. "He's a local politician. A man of some importance here in Winnipeg."

Mike stood on the steps, surrounded by the Group, all of them protected from the downpour by big black umbrellas.

Dave Dunigan made his way to the front and stood beside Karl, Doctor Fleischer and Silvestro Nardo. He glared at Harvey Gossman. "We do not require a tour. We will proceed."

"Of course, of course," the man said. He chuckled nervously and motioned for them to follow him up the steps and into the building. "Let's get out of the rain, shall we?"

Once inside, they left their umbrellas in black wire baskets and followed Harvey Gossman across the shiny marble floor to the base of a spectacular staircase.

Mike looked all around as they walked. The interior of the massive build-ing was magnificent. Stone columns and archways were everywhere; ancient busts jutted from giant stone slabs in the walls. Medusa, Athena and the heads of lions and stone ox skulls decorated the great hall. Mike remem-bered some of them from pictures at school.

As he walked up the steps, Mike stared at the statues of two life-size black bison that appeared to be guarding each side of the grand staircase—as if ready to attack unwanted intruders. A few men in suits were coming down the stairs and cast curious looks as the Group of Forty-Eight marched up together.

"Awfully large tour," one man said.

Harvey Gossman nodded and smiled and hurried them along a marble-tiled hallway until they stood outside a set of beautiful cherry wood double doors. A thick, black cord stretched across the closed doors, a clear warning not to enter.

An elderly security guard arrived, spoke into a walkie-talkie, frowned at the large group and whispered something to Harvey Gossman. The visitors stood silently watching and waiting.

Mike felt uncomfortable with these people—this Group of Forty-Eight. They were all strange—with their serious faces and old-fashioned clothes. Where were his mother and Miss Meyer?

Nobody seemed to notice when he slowly walked away from the Group. Mike passed over a geometric pattern inlaid into a beautiful, stone-tiled rotunda. He arrived at a circular stone balustrade, made from what looked like three-foot-tall marble pillars, connected by a thick, circular cement rail at the top. Surprisingly, the rail surrounded a perfectly round hole cut into the floor. He guessed the hole to be about twelve or thirteen feet in diame-ter. Mike leaned over the rail and peered through the opening to see an eight-pointed black star built into the glistening marble floor below.

He slid a hand along the smooth cold rail and walked slowly around the edge of the hole. Curiously, the black star below always seemed to be near him—no matter where he stood around the outside of the ring. Mike then gazed up at the interior of the dome above. The concave ceiling looked old and fancy—he saw shades of pale blue, painted with intricate gold-leaf geometric designs.

"Beautiful, isn't it?" Herr Ackermann's voice startled him.

"Yes," Mike said. He stared down at the black star. "Are we almost fin-ished here? Can I go home soon?"

Herr Ackermann smiled. His forehead was shiny with sweat. "All in good time, Mik-eye-ell," he said. "It's a wonderful day. A special day."

Herr Ackermann guided Mike back to join the others.

Mike heard Harvey Gossman talking with the elderly security guard. "Are the cameras off?" the politician asked.

"Out of commission." The older man pointed to cameras attached to the walls and ceiling. "They will be out for an hour. No problem."

Harvey Gossman appeared concerned. "And the Lieutenant Governor is out?"

"Yes."

"Are you absolutely certain?"

"He has taken an early lunch," the guard said with a slight Scottish accent. "I invented a pest control company needing to check for rodents. He rarely spends time in this office, anyway."

Mike wondered why they would need to make up a story about rodents. He hoped there were no rats there. He hated rats. He stepped back when Doctor Fleischer approached the little security guard. He suddenly felt sorry for the guard.

"Is there a problem?" Doctor Fleischer asked. "I do not like problems."

The big doctor with the horrible voice seemed to catch the security guard by surprise. He stepped back. "There is no problem," he said. He looked to his right and left, and then unhooked the cord. Mike followed the others into the room.

Harvey Gossman wished this day would end now. He and the guard tried to follow the Group inside until Doctor Fleischer held up both arms and blocked their way.

"We need privacy," Fleischer said.

The guard appeared agitated and spoke quickly. "But you cannot be in there unsupervised. I realize we have made an exception for you to be here today, but please—this is not simply a tourist attraction. This is the Lieutenant Governor's Private Reception Suite. It deserves respect."

"Do not speak to me of respect!" Doctor Fleischer towered above the little guard.

The man stepped back. "Now see here," he said.

Harvey Gossman put a hand on the guard's arm. "Let's not get in the way now," he said. "We'll just let them go about their business."

The guard pulled his arm away. "Mr. Gossman, please tell me—just who are these people?"

"No problem," Gossman said. He felt his knees turn to rubber. "It's all been taken care of. You have already accepted a token of their gratitude. Shall I take the five thousand dollars back?"

The guard frowned. "No, but I could lose my job. You never said anything about them being in this room alone."

"Ten thousand then," the politician said. He glanced around the hall. "I'll give you an additional five thousand tomorrow." He forced another nervous smile. "It's a group of distinguished visitors. They just need some privacy for a few minutes of important work. No problem."

"But this *is* a problem," the security guard said. "Nobody is allowed in that room—especially unsupervised!"

"I do not like problems," Doctor Fleischer said again. He glared at both men. "What do you know of our work?"

Harvey Gossman wiped his sweaty face with a sleeve. How he wished these people would simply leave! "Mr. Dunigan told me you have a very special reason to need this room and—"

"What do you know of our need for this room?"

Dave Dunigan stepped back into the hallway. "It is almost time to begin," he said, looking at his watch.

Harvey Gossman stepped forward. "Mr. Dunigan, you'll only be a few minutes, isn't that right?"

Dave Dunigan ignored the question and looked at the doctor. "We need to begin," he said.

"Now see here, Mr. Dunigan," Harvey Gossman said. "You told me you won't need much time. Isn't that right?"

Dave Dunigan looked at Harvey Gossman and the guard. "You can leave us now."

Doctor Fleischer gazed at the back of the politician as he turned and followed the security guard down the hall, the latter complaining about, "this unusual and unprecedented occurrence."

The doctor watched them for a moment longer, and then he looked back at Dave Dunigan in the doorway. "Prepare the Group. I'll be with you shortly," he said. He turned and followed Harvey Gossman and the elderly guard.

Inside the office, Mike watched the Group separate into two rows, forming perfect semicircles against wood-paneled walls. It was as if they had rehearsed the scene a thousand times. Silvestro Nardo closed the heavy blue curtains behind an antique desk at the back of the room. Each member of the Group produced a long beeswax candle and a tall thin man in an old suit walked ceremoniously up and down the lines, striking wooden matches and lighting wicks. He was muttering German words that Mike could not understand. Doctor Fleischer entered the room and stood beside Silvestro Nardo.

Karl had never felt so alive! He took Mike by the hand and sat him on an antique chair behind the desk. A final candle came to life in front of the boy. Forty-eight candles now created eerie shadows on somber faces and dark walls. Karl could feel his important destiny unfolding as he looked at his old silver pocket-watch. It was 10:41 a.m.—5:41 p.m. in Switzerland and almost time for the secret meeting of traitors at the Goetheanum. Two significant events were about to occur. It was time for a glorious lesson in karma. It was time to set history on its proper spiritual course.

> Death to the Vorstand traitors!
> Death to the races best left behind!
> Long live the race of the future . . .
> The Superior White Race!

Karl smiled. All eyes were on Mike.

4

Winnipeg, Manitoba

Mark ran beside Paul, holding his arm occasionally, afraid the older man might fall. Hard rain bounced off the pavement and drenched their shoes and pants. People gazed at them in disbelief from cars and buses. They were ill-equipped, soaking wet and sprinting along the lonely Winnipeg sidewalks during a torrential rainstorm.

Mark suspected that Professor Paul Sung was not used to this much exercise and wondered how much longer he could run. "Almost there," Mark said, pointing down Memorial Boulevard and holding Paul's arm. They could see the dome of the building in the distance. "It's only a few more blocks."

Mark wiped rain from his forehead and eyes and felt his cell phone suddenly vibrate in a pocket. He stopped running and the others took a break, as well. Mark pressed the phone to his ear and then handed it to Paul. "Your friend, Benjamin, in Switzerland."

The professor listened carefully before handing the phone back to Mark. "We were right," Paul yelled above the noise of the rain. "The police were called up to the Goetheanum. Someone was preparing to poison members of the Vorstand. Benjamin and his colleagues are safe."

"Finally, some good news," Mark said. He glanced up the street. "Let's go!"

"Wait a second," Chris said. "Has anyone thought of what to do if we find them there?" Chris had to yell in order to be heard over the rain.

"I might be able to talk to Karl," Paul said.

"Ya right!" Kate said. "Like he'll listen to you? In case you forgot, they think you're the friggin' anti-Christ."

"Ahriman is not the anti-Christ," Paul said. "I need to speak with Karl. Perhaps I can reason with him."

"Let's go," Mark said again. "First, we'll see if they are there." He kept an eye on Paul as they jogged along the boulevard, their destination showing itself occasionally between office buildings and trees. Finally, at 10:42 they stood in front of the Manitoba Legislative Building.

"Incredible!" Paul stared in awe. "I never would have imagined that such a place could exist—especially in the middle of North America." He followed the others up the steps, his eyes all over the façade of the magnificent building. "And in the middle of a city! How could I not have known about this place?"

Gusts of wind and rain hammered them hard. Paul stopped to pass a hand over one of the massive stone columns at the entrance. "Six columns," he said. "Classic temple architecture." His words were carried away by the wind.

Mark opened the big front door and looked back. The professor seemed lost in thought, his eyes wandering over the façade. "Paul, we need to get inside—come on!"

They stepped through the huge, arched doorway and walked into a spacious foyer. Their clothes were soaked and Mark knew they looked out of place. A few men in suits peered at them curiously and Mark also noticed a female security guard watching from a distance. She spoke into a walkie-talkie.

Paul left tracks of water on the marble floor as he walked quickly to the base of the grand staircase. His eyes were all over the interior of the magnificent hall. He could not control the excitement in his voice: "This is the first chamber!" His eyes darted everywhere—stopping briefly on the statues and busts and intricate carvings in stone. He glanced from one black stone bison to the other as he ran up the stairs, stopping briefly to look down at Mark, Kate and Chris.

"Thirteen," Paul said, his voice echoing throughout the hall. "Thirteen steps in each of the three sections of stairs." He pointed to the pair of life-size stone bison. "Icons—to ward off evil. They would have been horned bulls in ancient Egypt but these are more appropriate here." He bounced up the remaining stairs as if he had not just run over a mile to get there.

Mark walked to the base of the stone steps. He wondered if Paul was losing his mind. "Where are they, Paul?" he asked.

"Yes!" Paul ignored the question as his voice echoed off the walls. "The second chamber is exactly where it should be—it's stunning!" He grinned. "They must be up here!"

Mark started up the stone stairs. Kate and Chris quickly followed.

"Hey!" a voice boomed from below.

Mark turned to see a smartly dressed young man staring at them from the base of the stairs. "I'm Corporal Johns with the Royal Canadian Mounted Police."

"We're just visiting," Mark said.

Kate stood beside him and whispered: "We should tell him what's going on. We can use some help."

"Come down here—now," the young man said.

"He'll think we're nuts," Mark said to Kate. "We need evidence, remember?"

Mark walked back down the stairs and stood beside the young officer. Mark's clothes were soaked, and after the run, he knew he looked and smelled out of place.

"Sorry," Mark said. "We're from out of town. Our friend is a university professor and is very interested in the architecture."

Corporal Johns looked at Mark and then up at the others on the stairs. "All of you—down here now!"

"We don't want to cause a problem," Mark said.

"Then why are you carrying a weapon?" the corporal asked. He glared at Mark. "Our detector picked it up as you entered the building."

"We have fourteen minutes!" Kate's voice echoed.

The young corporal produced a handgun and stared hard at Mark. "Put both hands in the air and let me take your gun." He looked up the stairs. "The rest of you, come down here right now. I will not ask again."

They obeyed. Kate swore under her breath.

Mark raised his hands and tried to sound calm as he spoke. "I know this will sound crazy but we have reason to believe there is a group of terrorists in this building and—"

"You're right," the corporal said. "Sounds crazy." He pulled Major Kappel's old gun from Mark's jacket pocket and held it gingerly in one hand. "What the hell is this?"

"It's a long story," Mark said.

Surprisingly, the corporal smiled. "It was a rhetorical question. I know what this is. It's an old SIG P210—made in Switzerland." He gripped the gun by its wooden handle and locked eyes with Mark. "Guns are a hobby." He paused. "Let me see some ID."

Mark slowly pulled out his wallet. "I'm a cop." He flipped his badge.

"A detective from New York. What are you doing here?"

"Please," Chris interrupted. "My son's life is in danger. He's with them now."

The corporal looked at Mark. "You say there is a group in here?"

"Yes."

Corporal Johns spoke into a lapel microphone. He also wore an earpiece. "Was there a tour group in here this morning?" Waiting . . . "I had no group on my list. Who'd they book through?" He appeared to be confused.

Mark thought: *They are here.*

Corporal Johns spoke again into the tiny microphone. "You're telling me they arranged the tour through a member of the legislature—a politician?" Pause. "Where are they now?" The young man waited for the answer. "Both cameras cannot be down at the same time. It's impossible." His face was suddenly tense. "Who's on duty upstairs?" Waiting . . . "I'll head up there now."

"Ten minutes!" Kate was glaring at the young corporal. She tossed her tracksuit jacket to the floor and held out both hands. She wore a blue tank top, burgundy sweat pants and white running shoes—all soaking wet. "I'm unarmed," she said. She pointed to Chris. "Same with him and you have his weapon." She aimed a finger at Mark. "And you know he's a cop, so please— let's just go and try to stop something terrible from happening. We need to save some lives—my nephew is in danger."

Kate turned towards the grand staircase again and looked at Paul. "Where are they, Professor?"

Paul followed her to the base of the stairs. "There are three chambers," he said. "This chamber is the area of protection. I saw the second chamber, the altar, upstairs—it's a rotunda, complete with renaissance architecture. The third chamber will be upstairs as well, and that is where we will find the Group of Forty-Eight."

Paul and Kate ran up the stairs. Kate looked over her shoulder. "We've got about eight minutes! Let's move!"

"Hey! Maybe you did not hear what I said." Corporal Johns held out his gun. "Get back down here now!"

"Listen!" Mark yelled. "I'm telling you there is a group of people in a room up there planning to carry out a very lethal act of terror."

The young corporal frowned. "Highly unlikely," he said. "But if so, I'll check it out and call for back-up."

Mark put a hand on the young officer's shoulder. "There is no time. Call for back-up if you like, but please let us go now."

Corporal Johns seemed perplexed. "Put yourself in my place, detective. Your story is incredible."

"It's the truth. You have my word," Mark said. He knew what he needed to do. He sprinted up the stairs. Chris followed.

Corporal Johns hesitated a few seconds, and then was right behind them.

5

Winnipeg, Manitoba

Paul stood on the rotunda, peering down over the circular balustrade to the inlaid black star in the floor below. Kate, Chris and Mark joined him and gazed around the room. "This is the altar," the professor said. "The second chamber." He pointed to the floor below. "And that is known as the Pool of the Black Star. This place is truly remarkable."

"You said there is a third chamber," Chris said. "Where is it?" He sounded scared. "We have seven minutes!"

"It will not be a large room," Paul said. "It's twenty by twenty cubits and must be nearby."

Kate was fuming. "What the hell is a cubit? We're running out of time!"

"It's an old Egyptian measurement—also used in Roman and medieval times." Paul bent his arm at the elbow. "It's the distance between a man's forearm and the tip of his middle finger—or about fifteen inches. In other words, the room we seek is not large."

Corporal Johns joined them by the balustrade and started to speak but was interrupted by a high-pitched scream from down the hall. They ran.

A middle-aged cleaning woman staggered from a public washroom, a hand over her mouth and she was trembling badly. Her eyes were wide and terrified. She tried to speak, and then she pointed behind her and collapsed to her knees on the marble floor.

Kate checked the woman's pulse while the others ran into the washroom.

Mark was the first to see it. The stall door was swinging back and forth and there, sitting fully clothed on the toilet, was an elderly security guard. His head was bent back at an impossible angle and although he was dead, his eyes were wide open and still full of fear. His neck had been partially severed. Blood flowed down the front of his uniform and dripped off the toilet seat onto the floor.

The others stood behind Mark, looking in horror at the disgusting scene. Paul turned and vomited in a sink. Chris pulled his eyes away from the body and ran back to the hallway. The young corporal moved to the next toilet stall and pushed at the closed door. It would not move. He knocked and there was no response.

He pointed his gun at the door. "Police—open the door!"

No response.

Mark ran and stood beside him. He motioned for the corporal to step back. "Cover me," he said.

The young man complied, steadying his weapon with both hands. Mark raised a leg and kicked hard. The flimsy stall door flew off its hinges and landed beside the body of a pudgy little man in a gray suit, propped up on the toilet seat.

"My God," said Corporal Johns. "It's Harvey Gossman." He looked at Mark. "He's a cabinet minister."

The man's head was tilted to one side and blood oozed from a deep gash in his neck. Mark looked up and saw a gooey reddish mess balancing on the top of the cubicle. The little man's lifeless head was missing one ear and his pants were gone.

"God damn," Mark said. "Doctor Fleischer is definitely here."

6

Winnipeg, Manitoba

Mark turned to see the corporal speaking into his lapel microphone. The young man then stood by a sink and splashed cold water on his face.

Mark felt his stomach turn. Revulsion quickly changed to anger. He turned to Corporal Johns. "I know who did this and I need to find him now."

"This is my responsibility," Corporal Johns said. "It's my job. I'm a cop."

"So am I," Mark said. "And I'm telling you he'll kill you. He managed to get at least a knife by your security system and he will have no trouble killing again."

The young officer's face was tense. "You want your weapon I suppose," he said.

Footsteps echoed everywhere. Kate appeared. "Mark—we know where they are. There's no time. Come on!"

The corporal pulled Major Kappel's old gun from his belt and left it by the sink. He managed a weak smile. "Take it—despite my better judgment. I'll wait here for back-up."

Mark grabbed the gun and followed Kate down the hall. A medic was covering the sobbing cleaning woman with a gray blanket. They found Chris and Paul standing outside the closed cherry wood double doors, not far from the rotunda.

Chris was pulling and pushing at the doorknobs. The doors remained shut.

"They are in here," Paul said. "The entire building is built around this room. This is the third chamber."

Mark looked back down the corridor. Two officers ran past them towards Corporal Johns and the bodies in the bathroom. Mark threw himself against the doors, to no avail. "How can you be so sure they are in there?"

"This place is not just a Masonic Lodge," Paul said. "This entire building is *the central symbol of International Freemasonry*. It represents the uniting of the underworld with the heavens. The occultist knows that the truth is always hidden in plain sight."

Kate hammered on the doors. "For fuck's sake—times up—we need to get in there!"

Mark could feel adrenalin pulsing through his veins. "Someone here must have a key."

Paul seemed distracted, distant, pensive. "We don't need a key. I think *they* will open the doors," he said. "I think Ahriman must be present at this moment in time."

Mark glared at Paul. "They knew we would come here?"

"Yes," Paul said. "In fact, I suspect Karl has been waiting for me." He looked at each of them in turn. "You will need to understand something before we enter. It's very important."

Mark glanced at Kate and Chris. They seemed confused. So was he. He looked again at Paul. "What are you talking about?"

Paul gazed around the interior of the building. "I know it is hard to understand, but I now know where we are. It is remarkable."

"Go on," Mark said.

Paul took a deep breath and let it out slowly through pursed lips. "It all fits," he said. "We are in a magnificent replica of King Solomon's Temple."

Chris gasped. "What?"

"It all fits," Paul said again, gazing in awe at the interior of the building.

Mark heard sirens fast approaching. "SWAT team," he said. "They can handle this."

Paul shook his head. "No. You don't understand. A show of force will result in many deaths. I must try to reach them in their world—the spirit world."

"You're not going in there alone," Mark said.

"Then listen to me." Paul pointed to the doors again. "To us this is simply a reception suite in the Manitoba Legislative Building, but for Freemasons—and the Group of Forty-Eight—this room is the very heart of the temple—the Sanctum Sanctorum—the Holy of Holies. In King Solomon's time it is said to have contained the Ark of the Covenant. But there will be no box containing God's presence on earth—the Ten Commandments—in there now. The room, however, holds the same symbolic power—*tremendous power*." He looked at Chris. "Your son."

Kate looked at her watch. "One minute!"

"If you decide to enter," Paul said, "you must be very careful and let me speak with Karl Heisman."

Mark looked at Kate and Chris. They nodded. "Agreed," Mark said.

Paul took a deep breath and pounded on the doors. "Karl Heisman!" His voice was surprisingly loud and strong. "You know who I am!"

The doors slowly opened and they stepped into the room.

7

Winnipeg, Manitoba

Nothing could have prepared Mark for what he saw in the room. Men and women lined the walls two deep in a semicircle, each holding a lighted candle. The men wore vintage suits and ties and the handful of women were also dressed in period attire. It was like staring at a scene from one hundred years ago—the time of Rudolf Steiner. The people fit the room. Everything about the place was remarkably antique.

Mark stared in silence and breathed in the strong scent of melting beeswax. Shadows danced over a lush blue and gold-trimmed carpet and across black walnut walls. Ornate mirrors were positioned to reflect the candlelight towards the center of the room where Karl stood, staring out at Paul.

"Greetings Ahriman," Karl said. "Your timing is impeccable."

"Karma leaves nothing to chance," Paul said. His voice sounded calm, confident.

Karl smiled. "Indeed. You will now witness the glorious spiritual impulse of a New Age."

Karl turned and walked to the back of the room, as if he had rehearsed his scene a thousand times. He joined three men who stood like statues in front of an antique desk.

Mark recognized the men immediately. "God damn you," he said.

"Detective Mark Julian. How are you?" Chief Bischel stood between the two men Mark had known as agents Bander and Martins back in Ithaca.

Mark felt his pulse exploding. Only one word escaped: "Why?"

"If you need to ask the question," Bischel said, "the answer will make no sense."

Bander grinned. "Maybe you were never meant to understand, detective," he said.

Mark resisted the urge to attack, to beat his boss to a pulp for betraying him—for betraying the others. "You killed them, didn't you?" He stared at

Chief Bischel. "You killed Officers Derrick and Cooper at the safe house. You waited for me to leave and you shot them." He felt his muscles tense as he spoke. "And you were involved in the other murders. The deaths of innocent people."

Bischel stood perfectly still. He wore an old-fashioned three-piece suit—just like his colleagues. "There is no death," he said. "Only eternal life for those who understand the depths of the soul."

Chris stepped forward. "Where is my son? What have you done—"

"Dad?" A tiny voice came from the behind the desk, hidden from view by the three men.

"Mike!" Chris burst into the room but was blocked by Chief Bischel. Bander and Martins wrestled Chris to the floor. Bander pinned him there, face down, hands behind his back. "Move again and you will die," Bander said.

Kate made a move towards her brother. Mark grabbed her arm. "Don't do it, Kate. They'll kill him."

"Dad!" Mike jumped but a strong hand pressed him back into the chair.

Mark stood in the doorway, gazing around the room at the Group of Forty-Eight. He could clearly see Mike now, frightened and sitting at the desk.

"We're here to help you, Mike," Mark said. "I'm a policeman."

"Here to help?" Karl mocked. "Unlikely."

Mike's eyes widened when they found Paul. Instant recognition. Paul slowly shook his head—signaling for Mike to stay quiet. *Do not let them know you helped me to escape in Rome.* As if understanding the voiceless suggestion, Mike turned away.

Kate looked at her nephew. "It's all right, Mike. We're going to take you home."

There was a moment of silence and then Paul spoke. "Remarkable," he said. "Truly remarkable."

Silvestro Nardo smiled. "So, Karl, your clairvoyant revelation is impressive. Ahriman has arrived. Now we can begin."

"Let the boy come with us," Mark said. He quickly took in the strange scene, his mind churning methodically, searching for possible solutions to this situation. Mike looked terrified.

"The boy stays," a deep, guttural voice said from beside the desk. The man was a giant.

Mark stared into the dark, cold eyes behind the black-rimmed glasses. Finally, he thought. *This is the surgical killer.* "You must be Doctor Fleischer."

"That is correct."

Mark's pulse was racing. Instinct told him to attack—rip the man apart for his horrific crimes. But his training and experience restrained him. Talk to the man—diffuse the situation: "How can you call yourself a doctor?"

"I am a doctor for the soul of humanity." Fleischer stood by Mike and pulled a large knife from his khaki overcoat. The long blade glistened in the candlelight behind Mike's blond curls as Fleischer's huge fingers slowly wrapped around the knife's ornate handle.

Kate was less diplomatic in her approach. "You're dead, you bastard! You hurt him and I'll end your life right now!"

Mark put a hand on her shoulder as she stepped forward. She stopped but he could feel her muscles tensing. He heard surprised murmurs and gasps from some of the Anthroposophists.

Herr Ackermann spoke up from the front row. His face was soaked with sweat. Ackermann looked at Kate and forced an awkward smile. "No, no," he said. "You do not understand, young lady. Doctor Fleischer is an Initiate. He is immune to the material world. His soul cannot cross the threshold unless he so chooses. You would not be able to kill his material body. Quite impossible."

"You're fucking nuts," Kate said.

Paul knew he would need to proceed with caution. He cleared his throat and addressed the Group. "You need to realize that unless you surrender now, your spiritual paths will take a most unfortunate turn for the worse. You must—"

"Do not try your Ahrimanic tricks here!" Karl stepped out from beside the desk.

Paul studied the man. Karl's lifelong mission was culminating here and now. He appeared to be excited but stressed, and perhaps even frightened. Paul would need to try to connect—to put himself in Karl's position and somehow find common ground. But how does one speak rationally with an irrational madman?

"Karl," he began, "if you cross the threshold today, or if you are captured, there will be no guarantees for the future success of your mission. The deaths of innocent people will accomplish nothing but infuriate your adversaries. Imagine the repercussions—"

Karl hammered the desk. "For centuries you have deceived humanity and now the balance will shift. Today, the Will of the true leadership of the

Anthroposophical Society will work with the Christ Impulse!" He waved a hand in recognition of the Anthroposophists in the room. "These brave souls understand the true School of Spiritual Science. As I speak, the traitors at the Goetheanum are paying for their treachery!"

"No," said Paul. "The woman you hired to replace the old cook—Dott—has been arrested in Dornach. It seems she was attempting to poison your colleagues during dinner, as they were about to meet to discuss important issues regarding the future of the Society."

Karl appeared momentarily confused. Then his eyes became flooded with anger. "You lie!"

Paul spoke clearly, calmly. "Karma does not lie—it cannot deceive and cannot be altered. There are those who believe it is time for the Society to distance itself from Steiner's racist beliefs. There is a willingness, Karl, to work only with those spiritual impulses that will guide humanity to a healthy future. Karma unfolds as we speak."

Karl's face was damp with sweat. "Lies! The traitors meet and die. It is their karma!"

"You are correct," Paul said. "They are meeting now but they are not dying. Your murderous plans have failed and those progressive members of the Vorstand are alive and well. Change will happen, Karl—with or without you."

"No!"

Murmurs and gasps erupted from a few members of the Group.

Doctor Fleischer glared at Paul. "Deception has always been your game. I will end your life with my bare hands when the time comes."

Karl was visibly upset as he spoke: "We cannot trust these empty words. This is Ahriman." He glanced around the room. "Friends . . . we must follow our destiny."

Karl pulled a small white cell phone from his pocket. He pushed three keys and then laid the phone gently on the desk.

"*The Archangel Mik-eye-ell and Human Evolution*," he said, looking at Paul. "Sound familiar, Ahriman? It is time." Karl suddenly appeared exhausted as his eyes moved downward. "Mik-eye-ell," he said softly, "it is time for you to complete your mission."

Mike looked up at Karl, his eyes brimming with tears. "And then we can go home?" he asked.

"Yes," Karl said. "Then we go home."

8

Winnipeg, Manitoba

Mike picked up the phone.

"Of course," Paul said. He recalled the prophetic words of Rudolf Steiner:

> A man standing here, let us say, will be able by pressing a button concealed in his pocket, to explode some object at a great distance . . .

Paul stared at the cell phone in Mike's little hand and then moved his gaze to Karl. "This is how you will detonate the device in China."

Dave Dunigan gasped. He stood beside Karl and frowned at Paul. "How can you know about this?"

"It does not matter," Karl said. "Ahriman cannot alter destiny."

Dave Dunigan seemed furious as he addressed Karl. "Does he know about the other targets?"

Others? Paul's mind raced through what he knew about this Canadian scientist. Could he have sabotaged more than one reactor?

"You know the procedure, Mik-eye-ell," Karl said. He looked at his pocket-watch. "I have entered the numbers needed to dial out of Canada. Your destiny now unfolds." He smiled and looked at Paul. "Thirteen digits in all." His eyes returned to Mike. "I already told you how to use letters instead of numbers. Spell the name. You embody the spirit of the name. Please begin now."

Mike looked at the phone and pressed a button on the keypad, and then another and another. He looked up. "I want to go home," he said.

Paul's mind was buzzing . . . country code, area code and a seven digit local number. Thirteen in all using letters on a phone pad. Paul stared back at Karl. "Steiner," he said quietly. "The thirteen digit phone number spells

Rudolf Steiner." Paul leaned to Mark and whispered: "China is not their only target."

"Where else?" Mark asked.

"Dunigan was in Israel twice last year at a research reactor—one that is used to supply their nuclear weapons program." Paul felt his heart pounding as he tried to remember his recent study of the Canadian scientist. "He also has connections in South Africa. He worked at a reactor near Cape Town."

"You're saying," Mark began, "they can blow up reactors in three countries with one phone call?"

"If anyone could manage such a thing, it's Dunigan. He is the expert. They are preparing for Steiner's prophetic race war of all against all. They believe that Asians, Blacks and Jews need to be culled . . ."

Paul raised his voice and addressed Karl's colleagues. He would need to be careful. "Listen to me. Karl has taken Steiner's words and twisted them to fit his fanatical views. Rudolf Steiner never supported acts of terror."

"Enough!" Karl was fuming. "This is not about life and death in the physical world. You know nothing about the criteria applying to the spiritual world!"

Karl leaned across the desk, his wild eyes fixed on Paul. His breathing was heavy as he quoted his master loudly and from memory:

> ". . . if you analyze the matter and look at the individuals who have been dispatched to their death in this way—what you call murder, Professor—you realize that they must have been selected on purpose, though not on the basis of criteria applying to the physical world but rather on the basis of criteria applying to the spiritual world."

Paul shook his head and stared at the angry Anthroposophist. "The War of All Against All is not part of your personal destiny."

Karl looked down at the boy. "Continue with your task, Mik-eye-ell."

Mike looked again at the cell phone and tapped a key . . .

Suddenly, Doctor Fleischer reached for the phone. "Let me do it." His other hand pressed the knife to Mike's neck. "I never trusted this boy."

Karl raised a hand. "No! We cannot interfere with Mik-eye-ell's destiny!"

"You do it, then Karl," Nardo said. He sounded nervous. His eyes darted between Paul and Mike. "Take the phone and do it yourself. Ahriman and the boy—something is wrong. You do it before it's too late!"

"Patience, my friends," Karl said. His eyes were on Paul. He spoke again, as if he were possessed:

> "But it was for the sake of bringing down the spiritual impulse that Christ became flesh in a human body. And the characteristic of the mission of white humanity in general is to carry down the spirit, to impregnate the flesh with the spirit. Man has his white skin that the spirit may work in the skin when it descends to the physical plane."

There was a commotion in the hall outside the office. Corporal Johns leaned through the doorway and whispered to Paul: "The SWAT team is waiting. We're monitoring this conversation, Professor. We've got a couple of psychologists out here who think you have a useful rapport with Karl. They say he's insane but he might subconsciously want to hear you out—as if he needs or respects you. They say it's a love-hate dynamic."

Paul wondered what the psychologists knew about occultism. A disturbed esoteric mind with years of training needs more than psychology. He looked back at Karl and then saw Mark step up and whisper something to Corporal Johns.

"I'll see what I can do," the corporal said. He then looked at Paul. "Can you continue to keep Karl engaged—stall him . . . and the phone call?"

"I'll try," Paul said. "If I can connect with a few of them . . ."

"Divide and conquer?" Mark asked.

"Maybe," Paul replied.

Corporal Johns stepped through the doorway quickly and ran down the hall. Paul moved his eyes over to Karl. "You are interfering with destiny, Karl. This is not your personal mission. You and your colleagues can be part of a positive change within the Vorstand in dealing with outdated racial beliefs. I can assure you all that China is no threat to Anthroposophy and neither is Israel or South Africa."

"Damn you!" Dave Dunigan boomed. "How can you know about these things?" His face was contorted, as if he were in terrible pain. "Damn you!"

Karl leaned across the desk and scowled at Paul. "Ahriman is clever but his time is over! He is a materialist! A Chinese Jew! An atheist! But the Stream of Mik-eye-ell soars above his empty lies!" Karl continued to quote his master:

"Jewry as such has long since outlived its time; it has no more jus-
tification within the modern life of peoples, and the fact that it
continues to exist is a mistake of world history whose consequences are unavoidable. We do not mean the forms of the Jewish
religion alone, but above all the spirit of Jewry, the Jewish way of
thinking."

Karl continued:

". . . only those human beings are atheists in whose organism
something is organically disturbed . . . atheism is a disease."

Paul saw Mike looking at him; it was as if the boy knew that he needed to
stall. Mike was intelligent—Paul remembered that much from Rome. Mike
stopped pushing buttons and held the cell phone in both hands.

Paul cleared his throat and spoke loudly as he addressed the Group of
Forty-Eight. This was Professor Paul Sung, as if speaking to his university
students with unprecedented conviction:

"Listen to me now before it is too late. You all must realize that Anthroposophy does, in fact, incorporate a spiritualized version of racial hierarchy.
The idea of racial and ethnic karma, indeed a central part of Anthroposophy's
cosmology, is built around these notions. Thus, in your defensiveness and
denial, you have lost sight of simple truths about your chosen worldview.
Your colleagues in Dornach are trying to deal with these issues at this very
minute. The literal definition of Anthroposophy is 'wisdom of the human
being.' This is your opportunity to connect with that wisdom tradition and
be part of humanity's progressive evolution."

"More lies!" Karl's eyes darted longingly over the faces of his peers. "My
grandfather spent years with Rudolf Steiner. He then passed on deeply
spiritual lessons to my father, who in turn blessed me with the task before us
now. It is my—it is our—karma to accomplish great things. It is our destiny!"
His eyes were pleading with his colleagues. He glared again at Paul and
continued to quote his master:

"Certain nations are predestined to carry out a particular mission.
The nations which today are the vehicles of Western civilization
were chosen to lead the fifth age to its zenith."

Karl beamed at Paul. "I am—we are—chosen to be those leaders!"

Paul stepped forward but stopped when Doctor Fleischer pushed the knife against the skin on Mike's neck. The giant shook his head and smiled.

The image of Fleischer, his knife and Mike gave Paul an idea. What had Mark said—divide and conquer? Paul addressed the Group: "Look at your new messiah. Is this how you would treat him? Would an authentic Initiate hold a knife to the throat of such a prominent incarnation?"

"Lies—all lies!" Karl said.

But there was no questioning the look of concern on the faces of several members of the Group.

9

Winnipeg, Manitoba

Mark heard a helicopter buzzing overhead. Sirens wailed outside as shouts and footsteps echoed in the hallway. He looked around the room. It seemed surreal—the silent group of stone-faced Anthroposophists, each holding a candle, their eyes glued on Mike.

Karl was babbling again—more Steiner quotes from memory:

> " . . . one can only understand history and all of social life, includ-ing today's social life, if one pays attention to people's racial charac-teristics. And one can only understand all that is spiritual in the correct sense if one first examines how this spiritual element oper-ates within people precisely through the color of their skin."

Karl hammered the desk again and continued:

> "A center of cosmic influence is situated in the interior of Africa. At this center are active all those terrestrial forces emanating from the soil which can influence man especially during his early child-hood . . . The black or Negro race is substantially determined by these childhood characteristics."

As Karl spoke, Mark watched the members of the Group of Forty-Eight. Most of them seemed trance-like, standing like statues and listening to Karl recite messages from their master. But some of them were looking at Mike, their faces showing signs of concern. Mark studied the situation, and as an idea formed in his mind, he slowly concealed himself behind Kate and Paul.

In rapid flashes, Mark saw Fleischer's victims: the Richardson family in Ithaca—their bloody corpses burned into his memory forever. He saw the young officers at Cornell, blood pouring from gashed necks. Then the young policemen shot at the safe house near Ithaca. He saw Greg Matheson, the gaping neck wound, the larynx on the ceiling and the ear . . .

Karl continued to quote his guru, his low, monotone voice never wavering, never hesitating:

> "If all the souls had progressed, the backward races would either
> have decreased very much in population, or the bodies would be
> occupied by newly incoming souls at a low stage of development."

Mark stood silently still behind Kate and Paul. "Mike is trying to give us time," he whispered to both of them. "He is stalling." He glanced back through the doorway, looking for Corporal Johns. There was no sign of the young man. *Damn!*

With eyes forward, Mark slowly felt for Major Kappel's old hand-gun. He carefully pulled it from under his belt, felt the cool touch of the wood handle against his palm. The gun was well concealed as he raised it behind Kate and Paul.

Fleischer grabbed Mike's hair and pulled his head back. "Push the buttons, boy!" Fleischer was furious, as if he would snap at any second.

Mike trembled in the chair. He looked terrified.

Kate stepped forward, but Paul grabbed her arm and held tight. "Careful," he said quietly. "They are beyond reason."

Mark leaned into Paul and whispered: "There is no more time. I need to do this now."

Paul slowly turned his head and met Mark's eyes with his. "I have done what I can. Good luck, my friend."

Tears welled in Mike's eyes and he pushed another key on the phone.

Karl wiped sweat from his forehead. His eyes were wide and crazy, his voice loud:

> "But these things do not enter the world without the most vio-
> lent struggles. White humanity is still on the way to take the
> spirit more and more deeply into its own being. Yellow humanity
> is on the way to conserve that age in which the spirit is held away
> from the body, is sought purely outside the human physical or-
> ganization. This makes it inevitable that the transition from the
> fifth culture epoch to the sixth will bring about a violent struggle
> of the white and yellow races in the most varied domains. What

precedes these struggles will occupy world-history up to the deci-
sive events of the great contests between the white world—"
Karl pounded the desk— "and . . . the . . . colored world!"

Karl's eyes were fixed on Paul. "Ahriman! You cannot stop what is meant
to be!" The madman then spoke loudly, yelling the words as if his life were
at stake:

"The White Race is the Race of the Future!"

The Group of Forty-Eight chanted in unison: "The White Race is the
Race of the Future!"
Mark watched Mike hesitate, his fingers hovering above the cell phone.
Mark knew he would need to act soon.
From behind them, Mark whispered to Kate and Paul: "Do . . . not . . .
move."

Herr Ackermann could not control his mixed emotions. He had come to like
the boy over the past few days and was deeply troubled at seeing a knife
against his throat. True, Doctor Fleischer was a respected Initiate but why
should he threaten Mik-eye-ell in this manner? The young boy was also a
reincarnated Initiate—and one of extreme importance. Was this really part of
their collective destiny?
Herr Ackermann reviewed the predicament. What of his own role in these
matters? Was this simply a deception of Ahriman? Maybe not. Surely, Rudolf
Steiner would not stand idly by as one Initiate held a knife to the throat of
another. No, Herr Ackermann would need to speak up. This was his karma.
He cleared his throat. "Doctor Fleischer," he said weakly, "is there any
need for the knife? Destiny will unfold according to . . ."
Fleischer turned and scowled at Ackermann. "You cannot understand the
depths of my soul . . ."

This was the moment Mark needed. Fleischer was distracted. Mark tuned
out the doctor's words and raised the old gun. *Concentrate.* Years of target
practice and rapid-fire pistol events had prepared him for this moment. Or
had they . . . ? Fleischer was glaring at Ackermann, dismissing him with
contempt. Mark took a deep breath, held it, and moved quickly from behind
Kate and Paul. He aimed and pulled the trigger.

The sudden explosion forced Paul and Kate to jump back instinctively. There were surprised gasps from many in the Group. The knife fell from Doctor Fleischer's hand and stuck in the antique desk. His black glasses fell to the carpet. A curious, shocked expression formed on the doctor's face and he let go of Mike's hair. His dark eyes stared back at Mark and then opened—remarkably wide.

A perfectly round, small hole in the middle of his massive forehead leaked a stream of blood that dripped off the tip of his big nose and onto the desk. His huge body wavered for a moment and then toppled to the floor with a crash.

Karl quickly pulled Fleischer's knife from the desk and pushed it against Mike's neck. He crouched behind the boy and seemed oblivious to the sudden death of his colleague.

The other Anthroposophists, however, were stunned. Many of them screamed and stared wide-eyed at the body on the floor. *Doctor Fleischer is an Initiate! He cannot cross the threshold like this—it cannot be his Will! Impossible!*

Mark pointed the gun at Karl but Mike was in the way.

The SWAT team started to move in through the doorway.

"I'll kill him!" Karl pulled on Mike's hair and pressed the blade hard against the little neck.

Mike cried. The SWAT team stopped moving, weapons ready.

Silvestro Nardo stared at the doctor's body in disbelief. Rage erupted in a terrible scream and he ran at Mark. Kate was on him in a second. She punched him twice in the face, exploding his nose in a mess of blood and sending him hard to the floor. He did not move.

Most of the Group of Forty-Eight had their eyes on Karl while others stared in shock at the lifeless body of the Great Doctor Fleischer—their fallen warrior. Blood flowed from the hole in his forehead. Three people ran for the door. Others followed.

Herr Ackermann appeared to be stunned. His eyes flew from Mike to Karl to the dead giant on the floor. Then he looked at Silvestro Nardo's crumpled body, the expensive suit covered in blood, his disfigured nose still bleeding. Ackermann gazed again at Mike, trembled for a moment, and then walked towards the door, stepping over the unconscious Nardo. He sobbed and held his hands high, ready to surrender his body and soul to the enemy.

"Ackermann!" Karl was furious. He shielded himself behind Mike and whispered in his ear. "I know you only have two more letters to push, Mike-eye-ell. You are destined to do it now."

Mike hesitated. He was still crying. "I just want to go home," he said between gasps.

Mark moved to his right, aiming and looking for a better angle. "Leave the boy, Karl," he said. "It's over now."

"Nobody moves!" Karl pressed the knife closer to Mike's neck. He blinked sweat from his eyes and glared at Paul. He was out of control—well beyond reason.

Dave Dunigan stood beside Karl, his eyes glued to the cell phone. "I'll do it, Karl," he said, his voice shaking. "Give me the damn phone!"

Karl glanced up at his colleague. "No! Great truths concerning the evolution of humanity are placed before us. At this sacred place at this blessed time, detonation is the destiny of Mik-eye-ell."

Mark heard a commotion on the floor by the entrance. He saw that two members of the SWAT team had managed to free Chris from his captors. Chris then stood beside his sister. Bander, Martins and Bischel were quickly cuffed and taken from the room.

Chris made a move towards Karl. "Let my son go! Can't you see this is over?"

Karl shook his head and clung to Mike. "Stay away or this life ends now!"

Chris stepped back, his eyes on his son. He tried to sound convincing. "It'll be all right, Mike. I promise."

"Dad . . . I want to go home." Tears streamed down Mike's cheeks.

Karl spoke again to Mike. "Finish your mission now. Then you will go home."

Mark watched as Anthroposophists scrambled for the door. Dozens of police officers escorted them down the hall. Except for the unconscious Silvestro Nardo on the floor, Karl Heisman and Dave Dunigan were the only Anthroposophists remaining in the room. Wisps of smoke from extinguished candles swirled near Karl. He seemed dazed, unaware of what was happening to his colleagues.

Dave Dunigan wiped the sweat from his forehead with a sleeve and loosened his tie. "The kid will not finish the phone call, Karl. Cut his throat and do it yourself!"

"Patience," Karl said. "I have waited a lifetime for this moment."

"Enough!" Dunigan yelled. It happened quickly—unexpectedly. Dunigan snatched the phone from Mike and punched in the last two digits. He then grinned and tossed the phone onto the desk.

Mark watched in horror, unable to do anything. It was over. "My God," he said. "What have you done?" But he knew the answer. Dunigan had just unleashed a nuclear nightmare. Mark felt sick as the gravity of the moment quickly sunk in.

"I have fulfilled my destiny!" Dunigan boomed. A demented smile crept across his face. "It was my karma after all! A New Age has begun!"

"No!" Karl glared at his colleague, his face red with rage. "No, it had to be done by Mik-eye-ell!"

Nobody moved or spoke until the eerie silence ended when the little white cell phone buzzed and vibrated on the desk. Karl stared, a curious expression sweeping across his face. The phone buzzed again. Karl picked it up and pressed it to his ear. His mouth opened but he said nothing. Tears filled both eyes. He handed the phone to his colleague.

Dave Dunigan listened intently to the voice on the phone. His face was frozen, eyes straight ahead, staring at nothing. Expressionless. He blinked once, took a deep breath and spoke slowly: "That is simply not possible. I do not make mistakes." He listened again and then closed his eyes and dropped the phone.

Mark studied the two men. Dunigan seemed confused or angry or was that fear in his eyes? Karl appeared to be in shock. As a new thought entered his mind, Mark felt his pulse suddenly racing. *Maybe . . .*

He turned to the doorway and as if on cue, Corporal Johns stepped into the room. The young man handed something to Mark—a small black metallic box with a tiny antenna.

"Had a hell of time finding this thing," Corporal Johns said. "They're illegal you know. But I think it worked."

"What is it?" Paul asked.

Mark grabbed the box. He immediately felt a tremendous sense of relief. "It's a cell phone jammer." He looked at Karl Heisman and Dave Dunigan and held up the box for them to see. "Your call never went through. It's over now."

Dunigan's face collapsed. "No!" He glared at Karl. "You took too long! Damn you and that damn boy! He reached into a jacket pocket, pulled out a small handgun and aimed at Karl. "You failed us!"

Six members of the SWAT team filled Dave Dunigan's body with an explosion of bullets. He twitched, dropped the weapon and fell to the floor. One of the officers grabbed the fallen gun as his colleagues aimed their weapons at Karl.

Mike screamed as Karl yanked him from the chair by his hair. Karl's other hand pressed the knife against Mike's neck.

"Everybody out!" Karl was still shielded behind the small body. "Or I will end his life now. You have five seconds. One . . . two . . . three . . ."

The senior officer barked an order and the SWAT team quickly filed out of the room.

Chris looked at Mike and then at Karl. "Please," he said. "Please don't—"

"Four!"

"We need to leave," Paul said. "He'll do it." He grabbed Chris by the shoulder and pulled him through the open door.

Mark felt the gun in his hand. He wanted to shoot the bastard and save the boy. He looked again at Karl. The man was unhinged—insane. But Mark knew that if he made a move now, Mike would die. There might be another opportunity. He put a hand on Kate's arm. She cursed once and they left the room together.

10

Winnipeg, Manitoba

Chris should not have felt surprised to see that a large crowd had ga-thered near the front entrance to the Manitoba Legislative Building. But he was surprised. It seemed surreal. Television trucks and reporters jostled for position as local police officers lined the plaza with what seemed like miles of yellow tape. The rain had almost stopped but black clouds threatened another downpour.

Chris stood with Kate, Mark and Paul on the first few steps leading up to the front doors. Corporal Johns joined them. "A hostage negotiator is on the way," he said.

"That will not help here," Mark said.

"I agree," Paul said. "Karl is too far gone."

A woman screamed and pushed frantically through the crowd. An officer held her from passing through the tape.

Chris recognized the voice and saw his wife—sobbing and trying to free herself from the grip of the policeman.

"Do you know this woman?" Corporal Johns asked.

"It's my wife," Chris said. "Mike's mother."

"Can she help?"

"No," said Kate, glaring at Serena.

Chris took a deep breath. "She might have information."

Corporal Johns nodded and the officer let Serena pass under the tape. She was crying non-stop. An officer handed her a tissue and she tried to compose herself.

Chris was surprised by a fleeting feeling of sympathy. Then came anger. His eyes ripped into his wife like cold daggers. "How the hell could you let this happen?"

"I'm sorry . . . I'm so sorry." Serena shut her eyes tight but could not stop the endless streams of tears that escaped and poured down her cheeks. She spoke in short gasps. "It was not supposed to . . . they told me it would be different . . . I saw this on television from the hotel. I'm sorry." She sobbed again, crossed her arms, clenching her raincoat with trembling fists. She stepped towards Chris, looking for forgiveness or consolation.

Kate glared at Serena. "You stupid fucking—"

"Kate, stop," Chris said. He stepped back from his wife. He was in no mood for a hug. "Mike needs help. Tell us what Karl might do."

Serena ran some fingers through her messy hair. "I don't know, Chris. He might kill Mike. I'm so sorry . . . oh God—what have I done?"

An officer arrived with Sophia Meyer. "Says she's family," the cop said. He walked back to his post.

Sophia stood beside Serena, staring coldly at Chris. She glanced at Kate and Mark. Then she saw Paul and her expression turned to pure rage.

"Ahriman! We never should have let you leave Rome!"

Sophia snatched a knife from her coat pocket and lunged at Paul. He jumped but the blade dug into his right shoulder as he fell.

"Stop!" Corporal Johns drew his weapon and aimed at the crazy woman.

Mark reached for Sophia, but she managed to jump away and hurl herself at Paul. She pulled the knife from his shoulder.

Mark grabbed Major Kappel's gun from a pocket.

Corporal Johns approached Sophia. "Put the knife down. Now!"

Sophia glanced at Mark and Corporal Johns as she held the knife over Paul.

"Drop it now!" Corporal Johns stepped towards her, gun in hand.

Kate approached quietly from the other side. Suddenly, she attacked. Her foot connected with Sophia's face, throwing her from Paul.

Sophia got to her feet, spitting blood. She held the knife out, threatening Kate, a twisted smile appearing on her face as she quoted her guru: "Karma holds sway in our willing . . ."

Kate did not hesitate. Her right foot flew up, smashing Sophia's hand. The knife landed harmlessly on a step as Kate approached her defenseless prey again. Using a mix of martial arts, she landed three consecutive blows to the head that sent Sophia sprawling across the stone steps leading up to the magnificent building. Sophia Meyer did not move.

Mark looked at the bloodied woman and then at Kate. "God damn," he said quietly.

A police officer approached Kate cautiously, as medics arrived with a stretcher for the unconscious woman on the steps.

Corporal Johns waved the constable away. "It's all right." He looked at Kate. "But please let us do our jobs here."

"Mike is inside," Kate said. Her voice trembled slightly as she looked from Mark to Chris. A medic was treating Paul's shoulder, trying to get him into an ambulance.

Chris stood with his wife while watching his sister. He felt useless. *Now what?*

Kate turned to him. "Stay here—please, Chris." She then ran to the stairs, picked up Sophia's knife, sprinted past the massive stone columns and disappeared through the front doors.

Corporal Johns yelled at her to stop and then looked at Mark. He shook his head. "Don't do it," he pleaded.

Mark glanced at the old Swiss gun in his hand and then looked at the corporal. "Sorry," he said and quickly followed Kate into the building.

11

Winnipeg, Manitoba

The place felt empty. Mark slowly made his way to the base of the grand staircase. There was no sign of Karl and Mike. Or Kate. Despite what he had learned of her ability to look after herself, he could not help but feel concerned for Kate's safety.

Mark gripped Major Kappel's old handgun and crept slowly up the stairs, peering around the huge hall as he walked.

He stopped after the first flight of thirteen steps, crouched and looked around. After the next set of steps he heard the shuffling of feet coming up the stairs. Corporal Johns had joined him.

"You are making my life miserable," the young corporal said. "You should have let us handle this."

"Maybe," Mark said, "but you don't know these people."

"Professor Sung spoke with me briefly," Corporal Johns said, "so I have some background info. My superior has given me ten minutes to resolve this unfortunate situation before the negotiator and SWAT team will enter the building."

They made their way to the top of the staircase and stood by a statue beside the open cherry wood doors leading into the so-called Holy of Holies. Mark readied his weapon and spun into the office, gun hand extended and scanning the room for signs of life.

"They're not here," Mark said. He glanced at Fleischer's massive body on the floor by the desk. His eyes were closed, his face covered in blood.

Silvestro Nardo lay where Kate had floored him. He was a mess. His expensive suit was ripped and blood oozed onto his shirt and tie from a broken nose. More blood dripped from a gash on his cheek.

Mark knelt and checked for vitals. "He's alive. But he needs help." He frisked Nardo for weapons.

"It'll have to wait," Corporal Johns said. "I'm not risking a medic's life with this crazy cult leader on the loose." He bent down beside Mark, slipped handcuffs onto Nardo's wrist and attached him to the desk. He glanced at Mark. "In case he wakes up."

Mark noticed the corporal's ring—gold with a prominent symbol etched between a series of tiny inlaid stones. "Square and compass," Mark said. "I'll be damned. You're a Mason?"

"That's right, as were my father and my grandfather. They both worked here. A family tradition, you might say."

Mark looked around the room. "So you know about the symbolism in this building?"

"Truth be told, detective, my spiritual life involves protecting this building—and her secrets."

Mark felt stunned. The last few days had been one surprise after another. "What do you know of Karl—where would he be now?"

"These people are not Freemasons, detective. They have no business here."

Mark stood by the door, looking down the hall to the grand staircase. "But they seem to know about the building. Do you have an idea of where Karl might be?"

"Karl's mission has crumbled," Corporal Johns said. He took a deep breath and let it out slowly. "But he might have made a back-up plan. Long ago, temples were used as places to offer gifts to the Gods. Karl might try to offer himself as a sacrifice in order to secure an eternal home for his own soul. He could believe in the power of this place to aid his next incarnation."

"And Mike? Will he sacrifice the boy?"

The corporal's silence was answer enough.

"Where would he take Mike?"

The young man thought for a moment and then answered: "This way."

Mark followed Corporal Johns along the empty hallway and stopped at the spacious area the professor had called the second chamber—*the altar*.

They found Kate crouching beside the stone balustrade, peering between the little pillars to the floor below. Mark remembered seeing the eight pointed black star at the centre of the bottom floor. The professor had called it *The Pool of the Black Star*.

Kate turned and saw them approaching across the marble rotunda. She motioned for them to get down and be quiet.

Mark heard quiet mumbling, soft echoes bouncing off the walls and domed ceiling. He crept over to join Kate by the stone rail. The corporal followed. Carefully, they leaned over to look down through the circular opening.

Mark felt his heart pounding hard. The scene below would be etched forever into the emulsion sheet of his mind. Karl stood with his back to them, arms stretched outward. He did not seem to know he was being watched from above. His head was bowed and his eyes were fixed downward. One hand held Doctor Fleischer's knife. A small body lay over the centre of the black star. The boy stared up past Karl and locked eyes with Mark. There was no mistaking the look on his face. Mike was terrified.

12

Winnipeg, Manitoba

Mike's eyes darted from Mark to Kate. She held a finger to her lips, silently telling him to say nothing . . . *don't make a sound.*

Mark watched as Karl slowly paced the perimeter of the star, constantly staring down at Mike. Karl was mumbling a combination of German and English and what sounded like Latin:

"*Ex deo nascimur . . . In Christo morimur . . . Per spiritum sanctum revivisci-mus . . .*"

Mark could make out a few of the English words:

"*Luciferic Impulse . . . Guardian of the Threshold . . .*"

Mark spoke quietly to Corporal Johns: "What is he doing?"

"The eight-pointed star," whispered the corporal, "is a Gnostic symbol of fertility—the octagram of creation or regeneration. It is the place of sacrifice and rebirth."

Kate whispered to Mark: "I tucked that crazy bitch's knife into my pants. If I throw it and miss, I'm afraid he will kill Mike." She paused. "Use the gun. You're the sharpshooter. Hit him in the back."

The thought of shooting a man in the back was abhorrent but Mark knew it made sense. He pulled Major Kappel's old gun from beneath his belt.

"It's a very old weapon," Corporal Johns whispered. "Would you prefer mine?"

Mark looked at his gun. "This one is fine." He thought again of the hole in Fleischer's forehead and gripped the wooden handle, steadying the gun between two small pillars in the balustrade.

Karl continued his trance-like march around the black star. Then he stopped walking and stood directly under Mark. He knelt over Mike, raised the knife high and spoke about ". . . *strength that will come from the spirit world until rebirth . . .*"

Mark moved his head from side to side, trying for a better angle. *If I miss by half an inch, I'll put a bullet into the boy*. He held his breath, and aimed . . .

The deafening *crack* of a gunshot exploded behind them. They all spun instinctively but saw nothing.

Mark looked at Corporal Johns. "Your guys?"

The corporal glanced at his watch and shook his head. "No way."

Kate yelled and hopped to her feet. "Shit!"

As if suddenly appearing from a bad dream, Silvestro Nardo was limping towards them, broken handcuffs dangling from one hand. His other hand held a gun. It was aimed at Mark.

"Drop it!" Nardo said. "Slide the gun to me."

Mark had no choice. *Where did Nardo get the weapon?* He waited a second and then pushed the old gun across the marble floor.

Nardo picked it up with his free hand and admired the wooden handle. "Very nice," he said. "Compliments of our friends at the Pontifical Swiss Guard, I suppose." He playfully weighed the two guns in his hands. His face was a bloody mess—the broken nose was twisted badly.

Corporal Johns reacted. He reached to unbutton his holster but Nardo saw him, aimed, grinned and fired both guns. The corporal's body jolted backwards and then fell to the floor. One hand touched his chest and then went limp. His eyes closed.

Kate started towards the corporal.

"You stay there," Nardo said. He aimed both guns at Kate now.

She stopped and glared. "You bastard!"

An amplified voice boomed up from the downstairs lobby: "Corporal Johns—the SWAT team is coming up now!"

Nardo looked down the hall. "I will kill them all!" he yelled. "You stay away or I kill them all!"

"We need to talk," the voice returned. "What do you want?"

"Eternal life!" Nardo yelled. He grinned and looked at Mark. "They will not understand such things." He yelled down the hall again: "Stay away or they all die!"

Nardo stuffed Major Kappel's old gun into a pocket. He smiled and held the other gun high like a trophy. "My old friend, Doctor Fleischer, always carries his father's German Luger from the glorious days of the Third Reich. I found it tucked into his vest. A bullet from the luger easily broke your shackles." He dangled the broken cuffs and then pointed at the young corporal's body on the floor. "And as you see, the German Luger can also kill."

Nardo wiped blood from his face. He glared at Kate. "Puttana! You hurt me!" He aimed the gun at Kate. "Now I hurt you."

As the gun fired, Kate jumped. The bullet grazed past her shoulder. Incredibly . . . horribly . . . she stumbled and fell over the balustrade.

"No!" Mark reached over the edge. He missed.

Kate thrust her hand through the inside and grabbed the bottom of a small pillar in the balustrade as she fell. Her long slim body jerked and then dangled high above the bottom floor.

From below, Karl spun and stared at the strange sight of the dangling woman above his head. His frown turned into a demented smile. When she fell, she would be crippled or dead—another soul to offer in return for his salvation . . .

Mark crouched to the rotunda floor, reaching Kate's hand as she lost her grip on the pillar. "Kate!" He stretched an arm between the columns and managed to grab her hand.

Kate's weight pulled him hard against the stone pillars. *How long can I hold her?*

He peered over the edge. Their eyes met for an instant, and then he noticed blood spots seeping into the waistband of her track pants. The knife she had tucked there earlier must have cut her as she fell.

"Silvestro!" Karl's voice boomed from the floor below. "Is that you?"

The old Italian walked to the balustrade and peered over the edge. "Karl!"

Karl grinned. "Destiny continues to baffle mere mortals."

"Indeed." Silvestro Nardo looked down at Kate, dangling above the black star by one arm. "Well now," he said. He wiped blood from his nose and smiled. "What have we here?"

Kate looked up. "Fuck you," she said.

13

Winnipeg, Manitoba

Mark closed his eyes. Suddenly, the strain and pull from below was more intense. He felt Kate's weight shift and twist, and as if in a nightmare, he felt her hand begin to slip from his grasp.

What is she doing . . . ? Stop moving!

Silvestro Nardo peered over the edge again at the dangling Kate. He then grinned and moved his foot closer to Mark's arm as it stretched out, hand extended through the pillars of the balustrade, aching and straining—refusing to let go of Kate.

She was slipping . . .

Mark opened his eyes and watched . . . as if in slow motion . . . while one of Nardo's expensive Italian shoes rose off the floor and hovered over his arm, ready to come down hard and sever the connection he had with Kate. Nardo then put his foot back on the floor and pulled Major Kappel's old weapon from his pocket. He now held a gun in each hand and aimed them both at Mark.

The madman grinned. "Which one shall I use—the SIG P210 or the Luger? Swiss Guard or the Third Reich?" Nardo playfully put the barrels of each gun to Mark's head. Then he raised his foot again and held it over Mark's arm. "Or perhaps I will simply crush your arm with my foot and we can both watch the bitch fall and die?"

Mark had never felt more angry or exhausted or helpless in his life. He knew Nardo was right. Kate would die—as would he. Sweat burned his eyes as he held Kate with the last of his strength.

Mark felt Kate shifting again, jerking her body and his arm as she dangled below him. The muscles in his arm were on fire. How much longer could he hold her . . . ? He peered over the edge. Her beautiful blue eyes were telling him something but exhaustion ripped at his arm and at his mind. He looked beneath Kate to see Mike, his little body still lying across the black star, an expression of sheer terror on his face.

Why is Kate moving?

Mark looked up at Nardo—he saw cold, dark eyes staring down at him. The old man was enjoying this waiting game, savoring the intensity of the pre-murder moment. Mark took a deep breath and looked up past Nardo to the inside of the dome. A sliver of sunlight beamed through a stained-glass skylight and surprisingly, Mark felt a moment of peace.

Is this what it's like—the moment before death?

His mind suddenly shifted to the feeling of Kate's hand in his and he imagined what might have been. His grip was slowly slipping as she continued to twist in his grasp. Silvestro Nardo's foot would come down hard and they both would die . . .

Mark saw Nardo lean over the stone rail to look at Kate and suddenly, incredibly, something small and black flew up from the opening below, like a bat—inches from Mark's extended arm.

Mark then heard three strange sounds, almost simultaneously: first came a warning cry from Karl below, followed by the *thud* of impact above, and then a strange gurgling noise. Mark was shocked to see Nardo staring down at him again, but with a stunned expression on his face. The black handle of a knife protruded from the front of Nardo's neck, just under his chin. Blood gushed from the wound as his mouth opened and closed. More blood spilled from his lips and dripped onto the shiny marble floor.

Mark suddenly realized why Kate had been twisting and turning. With her free hand, she had managed to pull the knife from her waistband, and had somehow found the strength to hurl it up accurately, and with tremendous force.

Both guns fell from Nardo's hands and disappeared through the opening in the floor. The luger hit the marble tile below and smashed into a dozen pieces. Major Kappel's gun bounced once and came to rest near the black star.

Silvestro Nardo collapsed by the balustrade and lay beside Mark, eyes slowly narrowing, mouth leaking blood, opening and closing like a fish out of water. Finally, his eyes closed and he moved no more.

Mark shoved his free hand through the pillars. "Reach up with your other hand," he said. "I might be able to pull you over the rail but you'll need both hands. Reach for me, Kate!"

She swung her hand up but missed his by a few inches. She twisted her body and tried again with the same result—but she was closer. "Hold me, Mark!" she said, swinging herself up again. She grimaced and twisted and reached . . . and finally Mark felt her hand in his.

"Stop!" Karl was staring up at them, his hand still gripping Doctor Fleischer's deadly knife. Karl's back was to Mike, who remained stretched out over the black star. "Or I will end the boy's life!"

Mark could hear the insanity in Karl's voice. He sounded exhausted, deranged.

"Mik-eye-ell's present incarnation," yelled Karl, "will serve him well during subsequent lifetimes. Since ancient days, occult wisdom teaches that crossing the threshold while over the Pool of the Black Star in the temple . . . blesses the soul in the spirit world!"

Mike lay on the cold marble floor, gazing past Karl and up to his aunt. He looked into her blue eyes and suddenly, surprisingly, he stopped trembling. This last week seemed like a strange dream now, or more like a nightmare. He had never asked for any of this and it seemed terribly unfair—all these strange people deciding where he should go, what he should do and eat and say and think. He was tired and only wanted to go home and be with his dad. He also wanted his mom back—without Miss Meyer.

Mike glanced at the back of Karl Heisman's brown leather jacket. He did not like that jacket and he liked the man wearing it even less. Slowly, he bent his legs and sat hugging his knees. The sun suddenly poured in again from the oval skylights in the dome above. Mike noticed the gun that had fallen through the hole a minute ago. Not the broken one but the gun with the wooden handle. It was on the floor, just beyond the farthest point of the black star. Quietly, carefully, calmly . . . Mike stood and walked to Major Kappel's old weapon.

Karl was staring up at Mark and Kate. "Your souls are not advanced," he said. "You do not understand matters of karma and destiny. You do not understand!"

"I understand," Mike said. He saw Karl turn to face him and was glad to notice Mark use the distraction to pull Kate up over the rail. His aunt was safe.

Mike gripped the gun with both hands and aimed it at Karl. "I understand," he said again.

Karl's dark eyes bore into Mike for a moment and then he noticed the old weapon. Karl then raised both eyebrows and appeared to be confused, shocked. He shook his head slowly, held out the knife and a tired smile appeared on his face. "Of course," he said. He took a deep breath and charged at Mike.

For the first time in a long while, Mike knew what he needed to do. A strange sick feeling formed in his stomach, but only for a second and then for some strange reason, he felt calm. Mike knew he needed to focus on this one moment in time. He suddenly remembered seeing someone shoot a gun on television—before TV had been banned in his house. He stood perfectly still, extended the weapon in both hands, and squeezed the trigger. The recoil jerked his arms back hard and it hurt, but he aimed and fired again . . . and again.

From that place on the black star, at the very centre of the magnificent temple, the echo from the blasts was deafening. But Mike did not mind the noise. Somehow, the explosions from the gun were almost like music to his ears.

Karl stopped, stood straight and still, dropped the knife and put both hands to his chest. Then he pulled them away and smiled. They were covered in blood. He wavered for a moment, as if contemplating his destiny, and then he fell.

Epilogue

Mike stared at Karl's body and then dropped the gun and ran to the base of the grand staircase. Within seconds he was in the arms of his aunt. Kate hugged him hard.

The lobby was swarming with members of the SWAT team. Dozens of cops poured in through the front doors. Chris and Serena followed and quickly found their son.

Chris pulled Mike from Kate and hugged him—again and again. Serena stood beside them, sobbing uncontrollably.

Mike cried and trembled in his father's arms. "I had to shoot him, dad," he said. "Karl was going to kill me. I had to shoot him." He could not stop crying.

"I know, Mike. It's all right now. I love you."

Mike looked into his dad's blue eyes. It felt good to be in his arms, to feel the warmth of his father's body against his. Finally. For some reason, though, he felt sick and very weak. It was as if he had just woken up from a long, strange, and terrible nightmare. Mike clung to his dad and looked at his mom. Tears flowed from her eyes too, but she managed a smile.

"It's OK Mom," Mike said. He wiped at his tears. "It'll be all right now."

Kate stood beside her brother and noticed her own tears flowing, as well. She tried not to think of the therapy Mike would need in the weeks and months ahead. For the first time in many years, she did not try to stop her emotions from escaping.

Kate turned and found Mark kneeling beside two medics near the rotunda. They were working on a man lying on the floor, propped up on an elbow. As she approached, she was shocked to see it was young Corporal Johns. He appeared slightly stunned but certainly not dead. His shirt was off and a gray vest lay beside him.

Mark looked up at Kate as she arrived. "Seems Canadian cops wear the latest bullet-resistant vests when they work in government buildings. He has bruised ribs but no bullet holes."

Kate wiped at her tears and smiled at the corporal. "I'm glad you're OK." She then grabbed a gauze pad and some tape from an open first aid kit and proceeded to patch the cut on her hip. A medic tried to help but she pushed him away. Her eyes then moved around the interior of the building. "Is this place really a Masonic Lodge?" she asked. "Or King Solomon's Temple?"

"Perhaps," the young corporal said. "But only for those who need to know about such things." He smiled. "This sacred place is careful about sharing her secrets." He coughed and winced and put a hand to his chest. Two officers arrived to check on their colleague.

Mark walked with Kate across the rotunda to the stone balustrade. Without thinking, he put his arm around her shoulder and squeezed. It felt good and she did not resist.

"You're not going to beat me up, are you?" He grinned.

"Not now," she said. "My arms feel like rubber and I'm too damn tired." She leaned into him and they kissed. Mark felt the tension of the past week slowly begin to fade.

Paul Sung made his way through the crowd of police and forensic specialists and walked up the grand staircase. His arm hung in a sling. He stopped after the first set of thirteen steps and marveled again at the magnificence of the Great Hall. Then he continued up the final steps, walked across the rotunda and stood with Mark and Kate by the stone balustrade.

"Did you know the young Canadian corporal is a Mason?" he asked.

"Yes, we know," Mark said.

"Quite a coincidence," Kate said, smiling. "Would you agree, Professor?"

Paul returned her smile. "No. It's just old-fashioned karma." He passed a hand over the smooth hard rail of the balustrade and then looked up to the interior of the dome. "There must be a thousand secrets in this Temple."

Kate followed his gaze and sighed. "Probably more."

"Ever thought about becoming a Mason?" Mark asked. "You could learn all about those secrets."

"To become a Mason, you must profess belief in a god or supreme being," Paul said. "They would have serious concerns with me being an atheist."

"It's never too late to change your evil ways," Mark said. He smiled.

Paul laughed. "I'm afraid Ahriman has no choice in his destiny. But Corporal Johns has invited me to stay with him for a few days in Winnipeg. Although he will not share the deepest secrets of this place, he has graciously offered to answer at least some of my questions. That's probably more than a dark spirit like me deserves."

"So now the professor becomes the student," Mark said. "Imagine that."

"I suppose one can never be too old to learn," Paul said. He smiled at Kate and Mark. "Seek and ye shall find." He peered over the edge of the balustrade.

Forensic cameras clicked and policemen stood and stared. Paul was not at all surprised to see that Karl Heisman had crossed the threshold into the spirit world while lying at the exact center of the Pool of the Black Star.

The End

Author's Note

To the best of my knowledge, all Rudolf Steiner quotes in the novel are accurate translations. The two magnificent buildings in the story do exist. Although the characters sprung from my imagination, the bulk of their dilemmas have roots in history.

I sincerely hope any discomfort (or curiosity) some readers might feel with this novel will serve to ignite their own research and foster critical thinking and healthy discussion. Albert Einstein once wrote: "The important thing is to not stop questioning." I agree.

Tony Norse, September, 2010